Revolutionary Britannia?

Reflections on the threat of revolution in Britain 1789–1848

Edward Royle

MANCHESTER UNIVERSITY PRESS
Manchester and New York

distributed exclusively in the USA by St. Martin's Press

Published by Manchester University Press
Oxford Road, Manchester M13 9NR, UK
and Room 400, 175 Fifth Avenue, New York, NY 10010, USA
http://www.manchesteruniversitypress.co.uk

Distributed exclusively in the USA by
St. Martin's Press, Inc., 175 Fifth Avenue, New York,
NY 10010, USA

Distributed exclusively in Canada by
UBC Press, University of British Columbia, 2029 West Mall,
Vancouver, BC, Canada V6T 1Z2

British Library Cataloguing-in-Publication Data
A catalogue record for this book is available from the British Library

Library of Congress Cataloging-in-Publication Data applied for

ISBN 0 7190 4802 8 *hardback*
      0 7190 4803 6 *paperback*

First published 2000

09 08 07 06 05 04 03 02 01 00   10 9 8 7 6 5 4 3 2 1

Typeset in Palatino with Frutiger
by Servis Filmsetting Ltd, Manchester, UK
Printed in Great Britain
by Biddles Ltd, Guildford and King's Lynn

Contents

Contents

Acknowledgements

A wide-ranging work of this kind could not have been written without the previous research of dozens of other scholars whose hours of painstaking labour in the archives, especially in the voluminous files at the Public Record Office, have been put into the public domain in the monographs and articles cited in the notes. I have merely added my own research and interpretation but could not have proceeded without their help, which I gratefully acknowledge. Wherever possible I have checked the references for lengthy quotations found in such secondary works and have cited the original references as well as the secondary locations. I wish to acknowledge the Crown Copyright of records in the Public Record Office, and the following for permission to quote from manuscripts in their care: the British Library Board (London Corresponding Society, Place Papers and Letter Book of the Convention); the County Archivist, Tyne and Wear Archives (Joseph Cowen Papers); the County Archivist, West Yorkshire Archives Service, Wakefield (Elland Clerical Society records); the Trustees of the Rt Hon. Olive, Countess Fitzwilliam's Chattels Settlement and the Head of Leisure Services, Sheffield City Council (Wentworth Woodhouse Muniments, Sheffield Archives); the Fitzwilliam (Milton) Estates and the County Archivist, Northamptonshire CRO (Fitzwilliam Papers); Lord Halifax and the Director of the Borthwick Institute, York (Hickleton Papers); the International Institute of Social History, Amsterdam (Harney Papers); the Trustees of the National Library of Scotland (Melville Papers); Lord Sidmouth and the County Archivist, Devon CRO (Sidmouth Papers); and the Principal Archivist, Manchester Local Studies Unit, Manchester Central Library (J. B. Smith Papers).

Acknowledgements

While every reasonable effort has been made to attribute quotations and trace holders of copyright, if any infringement of copyright has taken place, I apologise and ask anyone claiming copyright to write to me. I should also like to record my thanks to the staff at the above archive offices and at the city libraries in Leeds, Manchester and York, the British Newspaper Library at Colindale, and the University Library, York.

Edward Royle
University of York

Abbreviations

BIHR	Borthwick Institute of Historical Research, University of York
BL, Add. MSS	British Library, Additional Manuscripts
BPU	Birmingham Political Union
CRO	County Record Office
FO	Foreign Office papers
HO	Home Office papers
LCS	London Corresponding Society
LWMA	London Working Men's Association
NCA	National Charter Association
NUWC	National Union of the Working Classes
OED	*The Oxford English Dictionary*, second edition (Oxford, Clarendon Press, 1989)
PC	Privy Council papers
PMG	*Poor Man's Guardian*
PP	Parliamentary Papers
PRO	Public Record Office, Kew
TS	Treasury Solicitor's papers
WWM	Wentworth Woodhouse Muniments

Introduction

The detachment of Britain from the mainstream of political development on the continent of Europe has a long history. In the age of revolutions between 1789 and 1848, in Britain there was no revolution – at
least, not in the sense that the word had acquired by the early nineteenth century. The concept preferred by contemporaries was 'reform'
or even 'amendment', comfortable words suggesting minor and sensible adjustments to changed times, however radical the changes
might actually be.[1] Even before 1850 there was a confidence among
contemporaries that Britain (or England) was somehow different from
Europe. Revolutions were how 'foreigners' conducted their political
affairs. In Britain things were managed better.

This complacency became deep-rooted in historical writing
because the reason that Britain (meaning England) was different was
due to the earlier revolution of 1688 and the Whig constitution
derived from it. Successful negotiation through the difficulties of
1831–32, and the sensible extension to the franchise enacted in 1832,
simply confirmed a confidence in the stability of the British political
system which could be accepted by politicians and historians of all
parties. Britain was self-consciously different and, by implication,
superior.

Yet it was not always so. In the eighteenth century Britain was
seen as a revolutionary state with an 'ungovernable people'.[2] The
English and Scots had defeated their king in battle and executed him
in 1649. They had deposed another king in 1688 and their kith and kin
in the American colonies had dispensed with the services of a third in
1776, establishing the first modern republic in the western world.
These events were alive in recent memory in 1789 when the absolutist
monarchy collapsed in France. There was nothing to suggest then that

Britain would be immune from the French contagion which swept across Europe, destroying old political systems in its path.

The aim of this book is to invite the reader to take this perspective seriously and to suspend that hindsight by which we know Britain to have been different. Two interesting questions follow. What is the evidence for the contemporary belief that Britain came near to revolution? How did Britain avoid revolution? When the French historian, Elie Halévy, raised the second of these questions in 1913 he was unusual in seeing a potential for revolution in Britain as something needing prevention.[3] Most British historians of the earlier twentieth century thought there was little to explain away. They attributed unrest to economic conditions – high prices and unemployment: when conditions improved, the causes of discontent went away. Only troublemakers, an untypical and unpatriotic minority, sought to turn such economic unrest into revolutionary protest. The mainstream of the British radical tradition was peaceful and non-revolutionary. In *The French Revolution in English History* (1918), P. A. Brown identified the importance of what he called 'The survival of the Revolutionary Tradition in Politics', but then marginalised it as follows:

> The strain of violence which runs through the constitutional agitation of the Chartists can be traced backwards for a considerable period. Some traces of Physical Force can be found at the time of the Revolution. But, though inflammatory speeches and even plans of violence can be found to match the evidence of this kind at a later date, they were not characteristic of the English school between 1790 and 1800. The fire-eating orators, Henry Hunt, before the Reform Bill, O'Connor and others between 1830 and 1850, were not in the old tradition of English political reformers. Its truer heirs were Place and Lovett, leaders who differed in most points except the belief that full political education was the only road to reform.[4]

He was followed in this interpretation by generations of scholars who, like him, read William Lovett's *Chartism* (1840) and *Life and Struggles* (1876), and delved into the riches of the Francis Place Papers in the library of the British Museum. This influential collection of manuscripts, press cuttings and commentaries shaped the way much radical and labour history was interpreted throughout much of the twentieth century, establishing Place's own approach to political action as the norm from which others misguidedly deviated.

2

However, the most recent biographers of Hunt and O'Connor, though they would agree that their subjects did indeed offer a different way from 'the old tradition', have identified them not as revolutionaries but as occupying a position mid-way between Place and the violent revolutionaries, advocating peaceful, mass action to force political change on reluctant governments and pushing to the margins of history both the extreme revolutionaries and people such as Place and Lovett.[5]

Brown's work, undertaken before the First World War, in which he was killed, was written contemporaneously with *The Chartist Movement* (1918) by Mark Hovell, who was another wasted victim of the war. In this book Hovell saw Chartism as primarily the product of 'hunger politics'. The masses, incapable of political action, were responding to economic and social grievances. The political dimension, if it existed at all, was supplied by a minority of what Disraeli called 'trading agitators'.[6] This view also shaped the work of sympathetic liberals like J. L. and B. Hammond, whose *The Skilled Labourer, 1760–1832* (1919), remains a moving tribute to the victims of early industrial society. In turn, their work influenced F. O. Darvall in his important study of Luddism published in 1934. His conclusion was well-reasoned and became orthodoxy:

> There was no cause, and no banner, for the discontented and disorderly manufacturing population in Regency England. Each of the disorderly districts had its own cause, and its own banners. It was for particular limited objects – their old conditions – and not for the general causes of the time, repeal of the Orders in Council, peace or parliamentary reform, that the riotous mobs in 1812 were willing to fight. Until some general cause should arise with a powerful enough appeal to rally all these different elements in the nation's life, and to make them forget their particular selfish objects, there was, despite all the discontent and the restlessness of the workers, and despite the weakness of the forces of order, no serious danger of revolution.[7]

This approach to popular movements as manifestations of economic discontent has sometimes degenerated into a crudely economic interpretation of history in which hunger is made to explain everything. When the economic historian, W. W. Rostow, in 1948 constructed a 'social tension chart' out of stages in the trade cycle and the price of bread, he appeared to offer the unwary an instant explanation for most upsurges of discontent and agitation between 1790 and 1850. Students who have not read the original remain unaware of Rostow's opening caveat: 'It is perhaps unnecessary to emphasise the essentially approximate and *descriptive* nature of these calculations', and instead they take them to be *explanations*. Rostow's theory provides no more than

> a useful summary of a considerable body of evidence, and the results conform fairly well to qualitative political and social data. Intervals of 'high social tension' bred known symptoms of unrest, which, in many cases, expressed themselves in important legislation or in the activities of the Luddites, the Chartists, and other groups.[8]

A different form of economic argument, equally simplistic when misapplied, is Marx's 'historical materialism' – that is, the view that historical development takes the form of class struggle which is generated by and in reaction to underlying economic structures.[9]

Both forms of economic determinism were challenged in 1963 by Edward Thompson's *The Making of the English Working Class* which, rejecting the cruder forms of historical materialism, took the insights of the younger Marx to develop a genuinely dialectical view of the relationship between economic and cultural causes, between structural influences and the free human agency of active participants in history – the view that men make their own history. Thompson's book put politics back into the picture and invited the reader to see them not as an alternative to economics but as their complement. This called for a rethinking of the nature of popular politics and of the relationship between the alleged minority of political troublemakers and the majority of supposedly unreasoning hungry protesters.[10] Though Thompson did not abandon the 'England is different' thesis, he detected a different English tradition, drawing on the seventeenth century and the idea of the liberties of 'the freeborn Englishman', which was capable of sustaining revolutionary activity.[11]

One of the first scholarly examinations of popular radicalism in the 1790s was G. S. Veitch's *The Genesis of Parliamentary Reform*, first published in 1913. He argued persuasively that

> [Pitt's] policy of repression was supported by the majority of the nation, and supported so emphatically as to render it unnecessary. It was as if a nation of self-appointed policemen had turned

out in force to keep guard over a handful of suspected pickpock-
ets. Both Pitt and the nation were, in fact, over-anxious. Their
fears were wasted, and they spent much rhetorical and legisla-
tive powder upon foemen who had neither the desire nor the
strength to fight. But it is both just and easy to make excuses for
the man, as for the nation, that erred in an hour of conflict when
mankind was struggling with one of the darkest problems in its
history, and when, in the words of Grattan, it seemed as if the
fortunes of the world were in the scale, and the intellectual order
in danger of kicking the beam.[12]

This interpretation remained current until challenged by Thompson
in 1963, but in 1977 it was upheld by Malcolm Thomis and Peter Holt
in *Threats of Revolution in Britain, 1789–1848*. Like Veitch they exam-
ined carefully the Home Office, Treasury Solicitor's and other files,
concluding that the anxiety of the authorities was understandable but
misplaced. The threats of revolution, and actual risings, were real
enough, but they were the work of a small and untypical minority
whose plans and exploits were exaggerated by magistrates' spies
whose evidence was by its very nature highly suspect. Thomis had
earlier (1970) also supported the older view of Darvall, that Luddism
was an industrial movement of protest in defence of an older way of
life, literally reactionary though none the less bitter and violent for
that.[13]

The debate since 1963 has been shaped largely by Thompson's
book and reactions to it. Thompson responded in a lengthy Postscript
to the 1968 paperback edition of his work. In reviewing his critics, he
was right to observe that a key controversy concerned his 'suggestion
that there is a continuous underground tradition, linking the Jacobins
of the 1790s to the movements of 1816–1820', with its implication that
Luddism was in part a political movement and within this tradition.[14]
He was also right to avow 'that I was too reticent about this underground', for even in 1968, subsequent research had shown – and has
continued to show – evidence for the existence and importance of this
tradition. This present book draws on such research and these inter-
pretations. Not all agree with one another or with all that Thompson
wrote, but the general drift of the argument has moved in his direction. Roger Wells has probably gone furthest in his claims, but he has
been supported by the findings of Ann Hone and Iorwerth Prothero
on London, and Marianne Elliott on the Irish dimension to British

radical protest.[15] Further light on the nature of radicalism, which adds to the plausibility of Thompson's account, has been shed by Albert Goodwin's work on the popular societies of the 1790s and Iain McCalman's study of the Spenceans from the 1790s to the 1820s.[16] Even a considered sceptic like John Dinwiddy came to accept that a Lancashire spy with the improbably apt name of Bent could be believed on occasions,[17] and most scholars would now settle for the measured conclusion of H. T. Dickinson that, 'it is no longer possible to accept that the Luddite disturbances of 1811–12, any more than the naval mutinies of 1797 or the Black Lamp agitation of 1801–2, were solely and simply the product of economic distress and sought only the amelioration of material conditions.'[18] This political reinterpretation of economic protest has also been applied to Chartism, principally by Dorothy Thompson and a stream of younger scholars influenced by the work of both Thompsons.[19]

If it is now widely accepted that politics should be reinstated within the protest movements of early industrial Britain, there is still little agreement about their nature and extent. In his survey of Chartism (1971), J. T. Ward continued to emphasise the social and economic dimension to Chartist unrest,[20] while Dorothy Thompson, who maintains the centrality of the political dimension, stresses the constitutional nature of those politics. From their very different perspectives neither historian has regarded the revolutionary threat as serious in the 1840s. If they are correct, then had this always been so? If it had, why was this? And if it had not, then what had changed and why, between the 1790s and the 1840s?

All history is a matter of interpretation: it is what historians believe the past to mean. This is not to say that historians can invent the past, but the ambiguities of the evidence and the language in which the evidence is expressed will always lead to disputed conclusions. I have therefore inserted into the argument throughout the book extracts from primary sources to give a sense of what the evidence is and I ask the reader to assume that those responsible for policy at the Home Office were not stupid and that the evidence presented to them was neither wholly fabricated nor distorted beyond credibility. This enables me to put positively in Chapters 1–3 the argument for the existence of serious incidents of revolutionary activity at various critical points in the history of Britain between 1790 and 1850, leaving Chapter 4 for some thoughts on why, after all, there was no revolution.

To keep the work within limits, I have had to make some arbitrary decisions about subject matter, so I shall not examine every 'disturbance' in the period. Some riots have by general consent been interpreted as concerned mainly with the price of food, or seats at the theatre, or the way the army and navy got their recruits. The history of these events and their cultural implications has been well told elsewhere.[21] If they can also be shown to have a political dimension which was potentially revolutionary, that would strengthen my point. Neither am I concerned with the history of all attempts at radical political reform. Again, that has been the subject of many books.[22] Though constructed as a narrative, Chapters 1–3 will refer only to a selection of those events which were widely believed, or were alleged at the time, to constitute a real threat to the established political order.

One of the most important developments in recent historical writing has been a growing awareness of the language used to describe events.[23] Far from words having a prescribed meaning, they assume shifting identities to fit the contexts within which they are used. Words such as 'Jacobin', 'patriot', 'revolutionary' and 'constitutional', employed in contemporary propaganda, embodied values and ideologies that constituted an important element in *shaping* the events they purported to *describe*. They were used to manipulate events. For example, those opponents of revolution who applied the word Jacobin to British reformers were seeking to identify them with a certain style of French politics associated with extremism and violence, a charge denied by many so-called Jacobins but which came to be widely believed. The word revolution in its conservative sense meant a return to the former proper state of affairs, so that the restoration of Charles II in 1660, no less than the replacement of James II by William and Mary in 1688, could be described as a revolution.[24] Radicals seeking to defend and restore the ancient constitution could identify with this conservative use of the word to emphasise their British credentials at the same time as conservatives could use the radical meaning associated with the French experience after 1789 to assert the alien nature of the reformers. In an age when 'the right to bear arms' was regarded by some as 'constitutional', and the demand for a radical but peaceful reform of existing institutions could be seen as 'revolutionary', no contemporary usage can be taken at face value and there are many surprises awaiting the unwary.

Virtuous words were claimed by each side and denied to the

other. Conservatives and radicals alike identified themselves as patriots, lovers of their country, and defenders of the true constitutional liberties of the people. The concept of 'the people' was itself a matter of fierce debate, depending on the political angle being argued. They were the electors – the political nation; or they were those who sought to become electors by virtue of their similarity to those who were; or they were those who were excluded from the political nation.[25] Language was thus used to organise how different parties wished their 'reality' to be represented, to include and to exclude, to praise and condemn, according to the political object of the speaker or writer. However, in stressing the importance of language in historical interpretation, I do not propose to adopt the extreme 'postmodernist' position of denying to the past any existence separate from the language in which it is expressed.[26]

A further difficulty with language comes with changing styles of delivery. Much of the period studied in this book falls within what is conventionally regarded as the age of romanticism, when melodramatic forms were current on the platform as well as in the pulpit and on the stage. The problem, as summed up by G. Kitson Clark in 1955, is,

> the relation of what is mere literary form to what is a not unreasonable appreciation of the real situation. On the one hand many orators are using language in which appeals to dread alternatives, just vengeance, or liberty or death, are almost a literary convention, but on the other hand the misery of sections of the working class in England and the peasantry in Ireland was so great and the obduracy with which redress seemed to be refused was so impregnable that without that stimulus men might understandably come to believe that violence was the ordinary resort.[27]

In other words, the language of revolutionary oratory may have been empty rhetoric conditioned by the dramatic conventions of the day and understood for what it was by both speaker and audience; or it may have expressed in the rhetoric of the day a reality of revolutionary anger which was heard by the audience as a call to action. It was sometimes hard for magistrates' spies to tell the difference. Sometimes one wonders if the speakers or audiences themselves knew. It is very hard for the historian to unravel the layers of possible meaning within the words of the historical evidence.

In Chapters 1–3, I recognise that contrasting categories of historical explanation – economic or political, peaceful or violent, constitutional or revolutionary – do not exist in the 'reality' of the past but merely as representations of different arguments in the past. While acknowledging these problems of the status and meaning of language, I have chosen to interpret the language of revolution in the light of the context within which the evidence is found. My conclusion is that much of the revolutionary rhetoric should be taken as both expressing and creating a situation in which violent action was intended to accomplish – or was perceived as aiming to accomplish – political changes which more peaceful means had failed to achieve. For an event to be discussed as revolutionary, therefore, I have taken it as sufficient that some significant group chose to regard it as revolutionary, whatever that might mean. In Chapter 4, I then consider in further detail the implications of this ambiguity of language for the nature of revolutionary movements and the opposition to them.

If it can be established in Chapters 1–3 that these threats of revolution, rebellions, uprising or 'ebullitions' – to use a contemporary term, with all its significant medical connotations – were serious, then the question posed in Chapter 4 becomes historically far more interesting than if there had been little to explain: that is, why did revolution not take place? In 1969, George Rudé's answer for the early 1830s was that 'nobody of importance wanted one' and, with reference to 1848, the question was 'hardly worth asking'.[28] Nevertheless, since Ian Christie's 1984 Ford lectures the question has continued to be asked with increasing frequency, particularly of the period 1790–1820.[29]

When mildly accused by one reviewer of ignoring 'the flag-saluting, foreigner-hating, peer-respecting side of the plebeian mind', Edward Thompson accepted the criticism as fair.[30] Since then there has been a resurgence of interest in the nature and strength of popular conservatism. The credibility of its ideology was restored in 1977 by H. T. Dickinson, *Liberty and Property*, followed by A. D. Harvey, *Britain in the Early Nineteenth Century* (1978), Jonathan Clark's general survey of the 'long' eighteenth century, *English Society, 1688–1832* (1985), and a series of studies on the development of the British 'nation' in relation to its Protestant identity, notably Linda Colley's *Britons* (1992).[31] The cumulative effect of this new interest in conservatism has been to make the case for the revolutionary threat far more plausible, for the conservatives' success lay in their opposition to something worth opposing.

The reality of revolutionary contagion in Europe in 1789 and 1848 was brought home once more by events in central Europe in 1989 when apparently strong if not stable political regimes crumbled overnight before the forces of popular revolution. With this experience of revolution in our own time we can more easily shake the kaleidoscope of history to seek different and more diverse patterns in the past than might be suggested by the assumption that stability was the norm, against which men and women strove to create forces for change. Maybe in Europe for the generation or two after 1789, revolution should be seen as the norm and what has to be explained is the stability created in the larger of two smallish islands off the northern coast of France.

The conclusion offered by Christie was that the strength of the British state and society prevented the *desire* for revolution; mine is that this strength undermined any realistic *hope* of successful revolution. The equilibrium about which the British people felt so complacent by 1850 was a delicate balance, achieved with difficulty over the two generations since 1789. During this period forces operating on one side of the fulcrum pressed hard for radical political change and were prepared on occasion to use force to achieve it, while on the other side equal force was applied to resist them. The result was a compromise. That there was no revolution should therefore be seen not as a negative consequence of the superiority of the British system and natural good sense of the British people over their continental neighbours, but as the positive achievement of a governing class willing to concede in detail while maintaining the essentials of power by all the means at its disposal: legal, political, economic, ideological and – in the last resort – military.

Notes

1   D. Beales, 'The idea of reform in British politics, 1829–1850', in T. C. W. Blanning and P. Wende (eds), *Reform in Great Britain and Germany, 1750–1850*, Proceedings of the British Academy, 100 (Oxford, Oxford University Press, 1999), pp. 159–74.
2   J. Brewer and J. Styles, *An Ungovernable People: The English and their law in the seventeenth and eighteenth centuries* (London, Hutchinson, 1983).

Introduction

3   E. Halévy, *England in 1815* [1913], translated by E. I. Watkin and D. A. Barker, (London, Benn, 1961), pp. 424–8.

4   P. A. Brown, *The French Revolution in English History* (London, Crosby, Lockwood and Son, 1918), pp. ix, 206.

5   J. C. Belchem, *'Orator' Hunt: Henry Hunt and English Working-Class Radicalism* (Oxford, Clarendon Press, 1985); J. Epstein, *The Lion of Freedom: Feargus O'Connor and the Chartist Movement, 1832–1842* (London, Croom Helm, 1982).

6   *Hansard's Parliamentary Debates*, House of Commons, 12 July 1839, col. 247.

7   F. O. Darvall, *Popular Disturbances and Public Order in Regency England, being an account of the Luddite and other disorders in England during the years 1811–1817 and of the attitude and activity of the authorities* (London, Oxford University Press, 1934), pp. 317–18.

8   W. W. Rostow, *British Economy of the Nineteenth Century* (Oxford, Clarendon Press, 1948), pp. 123–4; my italics in the first quotation.

9   See, for example, J. Kuzcinski, *The Rise of the Working Class*, translated by C. T. A. Ray (London, Weidenfeld & Nicolson, 1967), pp. 140–60.

10   E. P. Thompson, *The Making of the English Working Class* (London, Gollancz, 1963). In later notes the Penguin Books edition (Harmondsworth, 1968) has been used.

11   D. Eastwood, 'E. P. Thompson, Britain, and the French Revolution', *History Workshop Journal*, 390 (Spring 1995), pp. 79–88.

12   G. S. Veitch, *The Genesis of Parliamentary Reform* (London, Constable, 1913), p. 342.

13   M. I. Thomis and P. Holt, *Threats of Revolution, 1789–1848* (London, Macmillan, 1977); M. Thomis, *The Luddites: Machine-breaking in Regency England* (Newton Abbot, David & Charles, 1970).

14   Thompson, *The Making*, p. 923. He was not the first to advance this view: see A. W. Smith, 'Irish rebels and English radicals, 1798–1820', *Past & Present*, 7 (April 1955), pp. 78–85.

15   R. Wells, *Insurrection: The British Experience, 1795–1803* (Gloucester, Sutton, 1986); J. A. Hone, *For the Cause of Truth: Radicalism in London, 1796–1821* (Oxford, Oxford University Press, 1982); I. Prothero, *Artisans and Politics in Early Nineteenth-Century London: John Gast and his Times* (Folkestone, Dawson, 1979), republished (London, Methuen, 1981); M. Elliott, *Partners in Revolution. The United Irishmen and France* (London and New Haven, Yale University Press, 1982).

16   A. Goodwin, *The Friends of Liberty: The English Democratic Movement in the Age of the French Revolution* (London, Hutchinson, 1979); I. McCalman, *Radical Underworld: Prophets, Revolutionaries and Pornographers in London, 1795–1840* (Cambridge, Cambridge University Press, 1988).

17   J. R. Dinwiddy, 'Luddism and politics in the northern counties', *Social History*, 4:1 (January 1979), pp. 33–63, reprinted in *Radicalism and Reform in Britain, 1780–1850* (London, Hambledon Press, 1992), pp. 371–401. Subsequent page references are to the latter.

18   H. T. Dickinson, *British Radicalism and the French Revolution, 1789–1815* (Oxford, Blackwell, 1985), p. 61.

19   D. Thompson, *The Chartists* (London, Temple Smith, 1984); D. J. V. Jones, *Chartism and the Chartists* (London, Allen Lane, 1975); D. Thompson and J. Epstein (eds), *The Chartist Experience* (London, Macmillan, 1982).

20 J. T. Ward, *Chartism* (London, Batsford, 1971).
21 See J. Stevenson, *Popular Disturbances in England, 1700–1870* (London, Longman, 1979) and later editions; K. J. Logue, *Popular Disturbances in Scotland, 1780–1815* (Edinburgh, John Donald, 1979); J. Bohstedt, *Riots and Community Politics in England and Wales, 1790–1810* (Cambridge, MA, Harvard University Press, 1983).
22 D. G. Wright, *Popular Radicalism: The Working-class Experience, 1780–1880* (London, Longman, 1988); C. Behagg, *Labour and Reform: Working-class Movements, 1815–1915* (London, Hodder & Stoughton, 1991); J. Belchem, *Popular Radicalism in Nineteenth-Century Britain* (Basingstoke, Macmillan, 1996); R. McWilliam, *Popular Politics in Nineteenth-Century England* (London, Routledge, 1998).
23 J. Vernon, *Politics and the People: A Study in English Political Culture, c. 1815–1867* (Cambridge, Cambridge University Press, 1993), pp. 295–330; J. Epstein, *Radical Expression: Political Language, Ritual, and Symbol in England, 1790–1850* (New York and Oxford, Oxford University Press, 1994), pp. 3–28; J. Vernon (ed.), *Re-reading the Constitution: New Narratives in the Political History of England's Long Nineteenth Century* (Cambridge, Cambridge University Press, 1996), pp. 1–122.
24 See the discussion of 'Revolution' in R. Williams, *Keywords* [1976], reissued (London, Fontana Press, 1983); also *The Oxford English Dictionary*, second edition, (Oxford, Clarendon Press, 1989) (hereafter *OED*).
25 J. Fulcher, 'The English people and their constitution after Waterloo: parliamentary reform, 1815–1817', pp. 66–70, 75–6 in Vernon, *Re-reading the Constitution*, pp. 52–82.
26 For the debate on 'postmodernism', see the exchanges in the journal *Social History*, 17–21 (1992–96) and for a subsequent review of the issues which approximates to my own position, see R. Price, 'Postmodernism as theory and history' in J. Belchem and N. Kirk (eds), *Languages of Labour* (Aldershot, Ashgate, 1997), pp. 11–43.
27 G. Kitson Clark, 'The romantic element, 1830 to 1850', in J. H. Plumb (ed.), *Studies in Social History* (London, Longman, 1955), pp. 234–5.
28 G. Rudé, 'Why was there no revolution in England in 1830 or 1848?', in M. Kossok (ed.), *Studien über die Revolution* (Berlin, 1969), reprinted in H. J. Kaye (ed.), *The Face of the Crowd* (Atlantic Highlands, Humanities Press International, 1988), pp. 148–63: the quotations are on pp. 160–1.
29 I. R. Christie, *Stress and Stability in Late-Eighteenth Century Britain* (Oxford, Oxford University Press, 1984).
30 G. Best, 'The Making of the English Working Class', p. 278, *Historical Journal* 8:2 (1965), pp. 271–81; E. P. Thompson, *The Making*, pp. 916–17.
31 H. T. Dickinson, *Liberty and Property: Political Ideology in Eighteenth-century Britain* (London, Weidenfeld & Nicholson, 1977), paperback edition (London, Methuen, 1979); A. D. Harvey, *Britain in the Early Nineteenth Century* (London, Batsford, 1978); J. C. D. Clark, *English Society, 1688–1832* (Cambridge, Cambridge University Press, 1985); L. Colley, *Britons. Forging the Nation, 1707–1837* (London and New Haven, Yale University Press, 1992).

1

Sedition and treason, 1792–1820

The impact of the revolution in France

When news reached Britain of the political crisis in France in the summer of 1789, it was generally welcomed. The French king had supported the American republicans in their successful war against the British Crown and anything which might weaken his position was morally and diplomatically desirable. Whigs, Dissenters and parliamentary reformers in Britain interpreted the demands of the Third Estate – and subsequently of the National Assembly – as reasonable, embodying the constitutional aspirations enshrined in the Glorious Revolution of 1688. Edmund Burke was untypical in discerning as early as March 1790, in the debate on Fox's motion to repeal the Test and Corporation Acts, the dangers of abstract reasoning and the demand for natural rights common to both English Dissenters and French revolutionaries.[1] This argument he developed at length and published in November 1790 as *Reflections on the Revolution in France and on the proceedings in certain societies in London relative to that event*. The 'certain societies' included the London Revolution Society, a Whig dining club set up to commemorate the 1688 Revolution, at which Dr Richard Price, a leading Dissenter, had spoken in November 1789 in praise of the French Revolution which in his view had pointed the way forward for the incomplete revolution of 1688. Burke's publication was a manifesto of conservatism that was to grow in relevance and influence as reports from France appeared to fulfil his predictions and betray the optimism of the reformers.

Reactions to the French Revolution were not static, and over the next few years perceptions were continually revised as fears and hopes at home reflected the changing scene in France with its increasingly extreme impulse to innovation in church and state, leading from modest constitutional reform in 1789 to the flight and arrest of the king in June 1791 and the imposition of a new constitution in September. Worse was to follow: the declaration of war against Austria in April 1792; growing lawlessness in Paris which culminated in the September massacres; the trial of the king in December and his execution in January 1793 followed in February by war between France and Britain; the systematic use of Terror as an instrument of state during the period of Jacobin rule from June 1793 to the fall of Robespierre in July 1794; the abandonment of Christianity; and the increasing military threat to France's neighbours. These events explain the attitude of the government, that all reform was a revolutionary threat, as well as the willingness of extreme reformers to believe that the world really could be made anew. As Lafayette said and Thomas Paine quoted approvingly: 'For a nation to be free, it is sufficient that she wills it.'[2]

In the first phase of reaction to the revolution, the lines of dispute, as drawn up by Burke, lay between Church and Dissent, arising out of the defeat of Fox's motion to give equal citizenship to religious Dissenters in Britain. This was a right already conceded in France on the eve of the revolution and helps explain the Francophile outlook of English Dissenters. Their defeat in March was the first signal for Church and King celebrations, and in Manchester the original Church and King Club was formed as a dining club in jubilation at the defeat of Fox's motion. The reformers responded in October with the Manchester Constitutional Society. Though set up on the initiative of Thomas Walker, an Anglican Whig merchant, many of its members were leading Dissenters and this, and similar societies that were formed elsewhere over the next few months, were usually associated with Dissent. In Norwich, for example, the Revolution Society, which like its namesake in London grew out of the 1688 centenary, was identified with the elite of Rational Dissent in the city. These men, and their counterparts in Birmingham, Derby, Nottingham, Bristol and many other provincial towns and cities, were often leading intellectuals in their communities, the philosophers of the English Enlightenment. In their reform societies they identified themselves with France where liberties denied to British reformers were being conceded. On the second anniversary of the fall of the Bastille in July 1791, Church and King mobs attacked their homes and chapels in Nottingham, Manchester and Birmingham where the rioting directed against Joseph Priestley was especially ferocious.[3]

Thereafter, the terms of the debate began to change as the revolution in France grew more extreme. In March 1791, Paine published the first part of his *Rights of Man*, a scornful attack on Burke's defence of the British constitution. At the same time, as in France, the social base of the reform movement in Britain expanded beyond the elite to include lesser merchants, shopkeepers and even artisans. In London, the Society for Constitutional Information (founded 1780) became more radical and encouraged the formation of similar societies in the provinces to agitate for parliamentary reform. In Sheffield, the local Society for Constitutional Information recruited its members from among small masters and artisans; and in January 1792 the London Corresponding Society (LCS) began to meet, with Thomas Hardy, a Scottish shoemaker, as secretary.

The avowed aim of these and other popular societies remained the reform of Parliament but they identified themselves (and were identified by the government) with French ideas and the extremist views expressed in the second part to Paine's *Rights of Man*, published in February 1792. This work went beyond the programme of the moderate reformers to call for a sweeping reconstruction of the British constitution and a redistribution of wealth through taxation. Paine now replaced Dissent as the principal object of attack by Church and King loyalists. A Royal Proclamation was issued in May against seditious writings, and proceedings were begun against Paine. Loyalist forces were rallied by the Association for the Preservation of Liberty and Property against Republicans and Levellers, organised in November by John Reeves. As Louis XVI was brought to trial in December so too was Paine, on a charge of seditious libel. Tried in his absence – for by this time he was in France, ironically arguing in the Convention for the life of the king – Paine was found guilty. Whatever their intentions, reformers who now identified themselves with Paine could be deemed seditious by association and, once war had broken out with France, those who praised France could even be represented as traitors. Looking back from the year 1795, the *Annual Register* rewrote the history of 1791 in the most alarmist terms which tell us more about attitudes in 1795 than 1791:

> The publication of Mr. Burke's sentiments on the French revolution, and the subsequent answer to [*sic*] Mr. Paine, in his celebrated performance, styled the Rights of Man, were the first signals to the ministerial and popular parties in this country, to

engage in that violent and acrimonious contest, which is not yet terminated. These two famous performances revived, as it were, the royal and republican parties that had divided this nation in the last century, and that had lain dormant since the Revolution in 1688. They now returned to the charge with a rage and animosity equal to that which characterized our ancestors during the civil wars in the reign of King Charles the First; and it remained a long time in suspense, whether this renewed contest would not be attended with the same calamities: so eager were the partizans of the respected tenets contained in those performances, to assert them with unbounded vehemence.[4]

Plots, real or imagined, 1793–95

A growing suspicion of French intentions and the growing presence of French exiles in London in the autumn of 1792 created the first insurrection scare later that year. At the end of November extra troops were brought into London and defences at the Tower and Bank of England were strengthened. After a lengthy cabinet meeting on 1 December a new Royal Proclamation was issued and the militias were called out in ten counties – a measure warranted only by threat of invasion or insurrection. The Foxites were sceptical and claimed that the idea of a plot was a government device to consolidate its own power and suppress the liberties of the British people. News of what the government feared was leaked to the press just before Christmas: there had been a serious threat of insurrection which had successfully been prevented by prompt government action. The propertied and political classes were left to imagine what had so narrowly been avoided: the Gordon Riots in London in 1780 were still fresh in their memories, and the September massacres in Paris had come too close for comfort.

On what were these fears based? There is very little on the public record, but the Home Office files show that through much of November and into December alarmist reports were being received of Frenchmen armed with daggers on the road from Harwich to London, of quantities of muskets in private hands in the capital, of potentially dangerous unrest in Newcastle-under-Lyme and an actual disturbance in Dundee where a liberty tree was planted. Two reports from a French royalist emigré, Dubois de Longchamp, were particularly worrying. As the Prime Minister himself later admitted, the evidence for a French plot was only hearsay, yet the reports were sufficiently convincing for the government to take swift action. So, the historian is left with inconclusive evidence of an insurrection that did not happen. What we can say is that the government did not invent the evidence or the apparent seriousness of the situation. If it over reacted, it did so on reasonable grounds.[5]

One serious feature of the situation continued to alarm the government: the connection between the plotting and arming of a small minority, inspired and possibly aided by the French, and openly seditious pro-French talk in the popular debating societies. So the government was understandably nervous when, on 11–13 December, in the midst of this scare, the Scottish Friends of the People, organised by a young pro-French lawyer called Thomas Muir, summoned a Convention in Edinburgh with some 160 delegates from 80 societies in 35 towns. The word Convention was associated not only with the over-throw of James VII and II in 1689 but more immediately with the French constitution of 1792, an identification which was evident in the language used by the delegates.[6] The government immediately began proceedings for sedition against some of the leading members of the Friends of the People, and Thomas Muir was pursued on a charge of high treason. He was subsequently tried in August on the lesser charge of sedition but was still sentenced to fourteen years' transportation to Botany Bay.[7] Thomas Palmer, an outspoken reformer and Unitarian minister from Dundee, received seven years the following month. The Convention was briefly reconvened in April 1793, then met again in November, attended by delegates from the LCS amid the outrage caused by the savage sentences passed on Muir and Palmer. The government's response was to close down the Convention and to arrest its secretary, William Skirving, and the two English delegates, Joseph Gerrald and Maurice Margarot. They met the same fate as Muir.

The deteriorating international situation and continued evidence of seditious activity at home prompted the government to act next against reformers in England. At a meeting called by the LCS at Chalk Farm in London on 14 April 1794, a further Convention was demanded and language adopted that filled the government with alarm.[8] A month later, on 12 May, leading reformers – fourteen members of the LCS including Thomas Hardy and John Thelwall, and six members of the Society for Constitutional Information, including

John Horne Tooke, were arrested. The government was convinced that treasonable activity was rife, and a Secret Committee of the House of Commons produced the evidence for it in a lengthy report, sufficient to persuade Parliament to suspend *Habeas Corpus* on 23 May. A second report in June and further events in Scotland confirmed the government's resolve. However, when the treason trials came to court in October, Hardy, Horne Tooke and Thelwall were all acquitted and the cases against the others were dropped.[9]

The evidence for a revolutionary threat during these years was published in the early summer of 1794 in the two *Reports of the Committee of Secrecy*. Much of what they revealed was already public knowledge and hardly treasonable, but other information made available to the committee in private, including what historians can now read in unpublished files in the Public Record Office (PRO), shows clearly why the government believed it had cause for concern. The adversarial situation in Parliament and at the various trials was not such as to encourage an impartial review of the evidence. Government and prosecuting counsels needed to make their case, whether they believed it as much as they said or not. Conversely, the beleaguered Whig opposition in Parliament and defendants aiming to avoid transportation had an interest in stressing the harmless and constitutional nature of their ideas, organisations and literature. So what should the historian make of the view that there was a serious threat of revolution in the early years of the revolutionary wars with France?

Seditious language was frequently reported and did undoubtedly occur. Whether arising from loose talk or calculating rhetoric, this was dubiously legal and in the prevailing international situation alarming to the government. But such talk was hardly treasonable, which is why the treason trials of 1794 failed to secure any convictions. Seditious and potentially subversive words were, however, turned into deeds in Scotland in 1794, as the second *Report of the Committee of Secrecy* set out in chilling detail for the benefit of the House of Commons in June 1794. The aim of the prosecution was to implicate the LCS in these events north of the border. They failed, but the Scottish threat was no false alarm.

Following the break-up of the Convention in Edinburgh, a Committee of Union had been formed, of which Robert Watt was a leading member. On 5 March 1794, a secret Committee of Ways and Means was appointed with the ostensible object of meeting secretary

Skirving's debts but actually with a deeper purpose. The Home Secretary, Henry Dundas, sent a series of letters to the Prime Minister in which he gave an account of what he had discovered. The Sheriff's officers had obtained a warrant to search Watt's house for embezzled bankrupt stock. There they found twelve pike heads and two battle-axes. A further search of two blacksmiths' premises produced more spears and axes. One of the men arrested now

> confessed, that these weapons were the first of a very large number and quantity, actually ordered to be made, and intended to be privately dispersed among the members of the various societies throughout Scotland, styling themselves Friends of the People, and who appear to be at present employed in taking measures for calling together another British Convention of delegates to be held in England. An order has been given from one town alone in Scotland, for a large quantity of weapons of the nature described; no less a number than 4,000 has been mentioned, and more are intended to be distributed in Edinburgh. Emissaries appear also to have been dispatched, within this fortnight or three weeks past, to the manufacturing towns in the west of Scotland, for the purpose of sounding the inclinations of such of the inhabitants there who are known to be members of these societies; and there is reason to believe, from information received from various different quarters, that these persons have by no means been unsuccessful.[10]

Paisley was said to have been ready for rebellion, and there were reports of night-time assemblies for practising the use of arms. The men behind this conspiracy were 'the principal and most active members of the British Convention'.

These letters were laid before the Committee of Secrecy, which was also told that Watt had been in correspondence with the London Corresponding Society. Indeed, at the trial of Hardy the prosecution suggested a connection between these events in Edinburgh, evidence of arming in London and the manufacture of arms in Sheffield. The plan, it was claimed, was to start a rising in London, Edinburgh and Dublin to replace Parliament with the Convention. The rising in Edinburgh was to begin with a fire in the Excise Office. This would draw off the troops from the castle and the conspirators would then attack the troops, seize the castle, and take over the banks and other public buildings; the judges and magistrates would be arrested, farmers would be ordered to bring their grain to market, gentlemen would be confined to within three miles of their homes, and the king would be required to dismiss his ministers and dissolve Parliament. Much of the evidence for this plot came from government spies. The only hard evidence was the dozen pikes found in Watt's house but this was enough to convict him and he was executed on 15 October. His co-conspirator and treasurer of the Committee of Ways and Means, David Downie, was pardoned and the London jury clearly did not believe the prosecution's attempt to implicate Thomas Hardy in Watt's plot.[11]

How seriously should this plot be taken? Evidently, if there really were plans for a rising not only in Scotland but also involving London and Dublin, this would indeed have been serious. On the other hand, Watt was a former government spy and he may have been acting as an *agent provocateur*, in which case the plot could have amounted to very little.[12] The government's case at the trials in both Scotland and London was that the aim of those behind the Convention was not to demand a reform of Parliament but to overturn the Constitution and replace Parliament with a popularly elected Convention. The government could not afford to ignore this possibility, given the deteriorating situation at home and abroad in 1794.

If there was little direct evidence against leaders of the LCS, others in that organisation were certainly acting suspiciously. John Philip Francklow, a tailor and an assistant secretary of the LCS in 1793, together with John Williamson, a shoemaker, formed an association in Lambeth for LCS members to learn the use of arms following the trial and transportation of Maurice Margarot.[13] Members of the LCS were widely believed to be implicated in almost any subversive activity detected in the capital. In 1795, for example, riots occasioned by recruitment to the militia were thought by the London magistrates to be 'the result of a deliberate system originating with the corresponding societies for the purpose of overthrowing the government'.[14] Taken together with Watt's plans in Scotland, there seemed a real possibility that the government's intelligence network had exposed the tip of a dangerous iceberg of subversive activity rather than simply the ill-considered posturing of a few hotheads, however much the defence and the Whig opposition might seek to present it in this light.[15]

The most dangerous aspects of the alleged conspiracy were its

Irish and French connections. In Scotland these went back to at least December 1792 when Thomas Muir had been in secret contact with the Committee of Public Safety in Paris and delegates from the United Irishmen had attended the Scottish Convention. In April 1793, while in Belfast attempting to evade arrest, Muir was made an honorary member of the United Irishmen, and in November of that year an avowedly republican society of United Scotsmen was formed in Glasgow on the Irish model.[16] In Ireland, the French Revolution had reinforced the desire of Irish patriots to make the Parliament granted in 1782 truly representative of the Irish people, both Protestant and Catholic, independent of Britain; and it was this alliance of confessions which had led to the formation in Belfast in October 1791 of the Society of United Irishmen, led by a Protestant, Theobald Wolfe Tone. Adopting the language and sentiments of Paine's *Rights of Man*, the United Irishmen demanded full religious and political rights.

Their expectation of gaining either by constitutional means was disappointed and their demands came to look more sinister once war had broken out in 1793. Lord Edward Fitzgerald, a leader of the United Irishmen and cousin to Charles James Fox, had corresponded with Paine in 1792 about possible French support for a revolution in Ireland, but when the French sent an agent to Ireland in May 1793 he was not impressed by the state of preparedness among the Irish. The extent to which reformers in Britain and Ireland might become implicated in French attempts at subversion emerged the following year when the Reverend William Jackson, an Irish-born clergyman and a member of the Anglo-Irish community in Paris, was sent over to England by the French government to ascertain how much support there might be for a French invasion. He found very little, but the mission had already been penetrated by government spies and when Jackson went on from England to Ireland to meet with the leaders of the United Irishmen he was accompanied by a spy and *agent provocateur*, John Cockayne. Jackson was arrested on 28 April 1794 and committed suicide in the dock when he was brought to trial for high treason a year later.[17]

The significance of Jackson's mission lies not so much in its existence – at a time of war, both sides were anxious for accurate information about the enemy – as in its conclusion that there was little support in England for a French invasion. Wolfe Tone in 1796 thought this true also of Scotland.[18] While both Irish and Scots looked to France to assist their efforts, the French expected the domestic revolutionaries to lay for themselves the foundations for a successful invasion. So to break this vicious circle of inaction as each waited for the other, the temptation was for the United men, and especially their representatives in Paris, to exaggerate their state of readiness at home in order to encourage a French invasion. Both the French and British knew that the weakest link in Britain's defences was always going to be Ireland, and the British were fortunate when an initial invasion fleet of thirty-five ships and nearly 15,000 troops commanded by General Lazare Hoche was dispersed by bad weather off Bantry Bay in December 1796. The first French force actually to reach shore landed at Fishguard in Wales in February 1797, precipitating a run on the Bank of England and the suspension of cash payments.

The exposure of Jackson's mission gave the government grounds for suppressing the United Irishmen in May 1794. Up to this point they had been a very Whiggish body, hoping for another 'Glorious Revolution' with the French playing the part of the Dutch in 1688 but not staying to become king. Thereafter the growth of extremist factions within the society made it more radical as the political situation in Ireland deteriorated following the dismissal of the new Whig Lord Lieutenant, the fourth Earl Fitzwilliam, in March 1795, after only a few weeks in office. This ended all hope of legitimate reform. Wolfe Tone left for America and then headed for France to seek French aid. At the same time what had been a Presbyterian-led organisation uniting reformers of both confessions increasingly became an expression of Catholic constitutional aspirations. This polarisation of attitudes in Ireland was furthered in 1795 by the rise of Protestant Orange loyalism. By 1796 the transformation of the United Irishmen was complete.[19]

The situation in Britain also deteriorated in 1795 as bread prices rose in the first subsistence crisis of the war. Opposition to the war and Pitt's government was fuelled by economic hardship. Membership of the LCS recovered from the set-backs of the previous year and reached new heights – perhaps as many as ten thousand. Public meetings in London were addressed by John Thelwall, the largest being in Copenhagen Fields on 26 October when 100,000 to 150,000 people were said to be present. A hostile crowd greeted George III on his way to open Parliament on 29 October and one of his coach windows was broken by a stone (or bullet) thought to have been fired from an air gun. A few weeks earlier the government had been informed of a 'pop-gun plot' to shoot a poisoned dart at the king from an air gun disguised as a walking stick, but this idea was fabricated by a spy.[20] In response to this alleged evidence of practical republicanism, a Royal Proclamation was issued and two Acts rushed through Parliament: the Treasonable Practices Bill, to make it easier to convict publishers of treasonable and seditious writings even if no treasonable or seditious act had occurred; and the Seditious Meetings Bill, to prevent mass meetings such as those being convened by the LCS and addressed by Thelwall. These measures, and an improvement in the economic situation, then subdued the mass popular movement for reform.

United Irish, English and Scotsmen, 1795–1803

The ending of the French Convention and the beginning of the Directory in October 1795 marked a watershed between the most revolutionary phase of the French Revolution and the subsequent wars of nationalist expansion. While this strengthened anti-French feeling among all but a minority of extremists in Britain, the drain on British resources made Pitt's policy highly unpopular and threatened to destabilise the Ministry.[21] At the same time the repression of the reform societies in 1795, their consequent decline, and the collapse of open and constitutional reform movements, induced a sense of desperation which reinforced the arguments of the most subversive. Whatever the real nature of the threat before 1795, it was greatly increased thereafter.

The crisis in the spring of 1797 which followed the Fishguard landing was made worse by mutiny in the navy. This began at Spithead in April with a demand for more pay and the removal of unpopular officers, but then spread to the Nore where the mutineers blockaded the Thames; some ships in the fleet at Plymouth was also affected. A combination of concessions to the men and punishment for the leaders brought the mutinies to an end by June. Then in October, as Austria made peace with France, Bonaparte assembled his army of invasion within sight of the English coast. It remained there until May 1798 when he turned instead to Egypt.

Meanwhile, the United Irishmen were threatening internal subversion. Wolfe Tone reached Paris in February 1796 intending to establish a United Irish mission to work with the French for an invasion of Ireland, but after Hoche's unsuccessful attempt in December 1796, events in Ireland itself pushed the Irish into premature rebellion. Relations between the government and the Protestant community on the one hand, and the Catholics on the other, deteriorated rapidly as members of the Protestant Orange Order, formed in 1795, joined the yeomanry to attack the Catholic 'Defenders'. The latter were members of an illegal terrorist organisation formed to defend Catholics in their struggle for civil rights and agrarian justice. A working alliance established in 1795–96 between the mainly urban United Irishmen and the mainly rural and more popular Defenders brought together political and economic grievances in a revolutionary drive against the Protestant ascendancy. The brutal suppression of Catholics in Ulster by the British army and the forces of Orangeism drove Catholics south and across into Britain where some of their number formed local units of United Britons or joined the LCS. Links between Irish exiles in Paris and Britain with subversive forces in Ireland were maintained by a Catholic priest, James Coigly (or O'Coigly), who was arrested together with Arthur O'Connor of the United Irishmen, John Binns of the London Corresponding Society and two others as they prepared to cross from Kent to France in 1798. Coigly was carrying an incriminating Address from the 'Secret Committee of England' assuring support for a French invasion to maintain 'the sacred flame of liberty'. He was tried in May and executed on 12 June 1798.

The French invasion, which had been expected in April, did not arrive. On 23 May the Dublin leadership of the United Irishmen gave the order to rise. Ulster failed to do so but Catholic Defender insurgents held their own against the British army and militia in the southeast, enjoying initial victories at Wexford and elsewhere before suffering a major defeat at Vinegar Hill on 21 June. It was another month before ruthless repression finally broke the rebels. When the French finally landed their expeditions in August, September and October 1798, they were too late.[22]

The response of the British government to this year of conspiracy, mutiny, rebellion and threatened invasion was to arrest leaders and break up popular societies, driving the extremists still further under ground. Following Coigly's arrest, between 18 and 22 April virtually all the leading members of the United Irishmen in Britain and the LCS, including its entire general committee, were arrested and, *Habeas Corpus* having been suspended again on 21 April, most were kept in prison until 1801. Further arrests in March and April 1799 culminated in July in 'An Act for the more effectual Suppression of Societies established for Seditious and Treasonable Purposes, and for better preventing Treasonable and Seditious Practices', namely the United Scotsmen, United Irishmen, United Britons, LCS and all other societies which corresponded, took secret oaths, kept no list of members, or which had branches capable of independent action.[23]

The prisoners held without trial were released when the *Habeas Corpus* Suspension Act lapsed in March 1801. They then resumed their activities. A coup was planned in London, but the arrest of its alleged leader, Colonel Despard of the United Irishmen, in November 1802 and his execution the following spring put an end to the attempt. In Ireland, Robert Emmet's badly co-ordinated and premature rising in July 1803 was easily suppressed. His failure to persuade others to join him before a French invasion force was ready, was a mark of the success of the British government's policy of repression in 1798.

The mutinies, invasions and armed uprisings which filled these years between 1795 and 1803 would suggest that revolution was not merely possible but likely. However, in view of the limited success enjoyed by the insurrections, the extent of this threat has been much debated. Although the government's sense of crisis was understandable, it could be argued that the extremists were lent credibility only by the repressive nature of the government's reaction. The isolation of the violent fringe would have rendered them powerless had the suppression of legitimate forms of opposition not driven some reformers to take desperate measures to preserve what they regarded as 'liberty'. Only perhaps in Ireland is it conceded that a large section of the people was disaffected and, in sentiment at least, willing to see the overthrow of British government. The realisation that measures had to be taken both to control Ireland and to make timely but neutered concessions to Catholics brought Pitt to introduce the one major constitutional reform of this period – the Act of Union with Ireland, which came into force at the beginning of 1801.

The seriousness of the threat

Even more so than in the early 1790s, an estimate of how serious the situation was in Britain itself depends on the weight given to the government's sources of information.[24] If they are credible, then the situation was indeed serious. The word 'spy' is often used in a derogatory sense. It implies a casual, amateur, individualistic and probably unreliable person. Undoubtedly some of the government's informers were spies in this sense. But to call them 'intelligence agents' is to imply organisation, professionalism, co-ordination and reliability, and there was much of this too in the 1790s. Though local magistrates might be prone to alarmism, some of it induced by the activities of the government's own agents operating unknown to those responsible locally for the maintenance of law and order, at the centre ministers were not wholly 'duped and deluded by their spies', as Sheridan suggested in 1795.[25]

The government had several sources of information. The Home Office, with its permanent under-secretaries, Evan Nepean and John King, sometimes employed its own special agents, the most prominent of whom was James Walsh. Another channel of information flowed through the seven London police offices, created in 1792 on the model of Bow Street, each of which had a stipendiary magistrate attached. Bow Street was the most important of these offices because here the police function of the court was undefined by legislation and finance came from unitemised expenditure in the civil list. A small secret service had been based on Bow Street since the 1780s and during the 1790s the second magistrate, Richard Ford, was the key figure co-ordinating a domestic secret service. This was a development of the local and informal system – which still continued – whereby information was gathered throughout the country by magistrates who had their own favourite informers. Government special agents received a regular salary. These individuals were thus spared the temptation to invent evidence in order to earn their pay and their information was usually more reliable. The information so gathered was co-ordinated by the Aliens Office at the Home Office, originally created by the Aliens Act of 1793 to keep an eye on French refugees, but from 1794 when William Wickham became superintendent it was used to oversee all the government's intelligence-gathering activities.[26]

Though some of this information was doubtless suspect or

exaggerated, much was of a high quality and the government relied upon it in the formulation of policy. By its very nature such information was sensitive and its sources could continue to be effective only so long as they remained unacknowledged. Some of the government's best sources of information, George Lynam, William Metcalfe, John Groves – all prominent members of the London Corresponding Society – became useless once their work had been made public. So the interpretation put upon events by the Secrecy Committees of the House of Commons in 1794 and 1799 looks more extreme than the evidence presented appears to warrant, not because the evidence was lacking but because it could not be acknowledged. Unpublished reports in the Home Office papers show that the Secrecy Committees did indeed know more than they admitted which was still less than ministers themselves knew. Of twenty-two bundles of evidence submitted by the government to the Committee of Secrecy in 1799, only five were read out. There was more than enough evidence to justify the legislation and arrests by which the radical movement was suppressed.[27]

Irish and French agents, for example, almost certainly did attempt to exploit the naval mutinies in 1797. Given the importance of the navy to British defences it would have been remarkable had the French not sought to do so. Though the mutinies were undoubtedly provoked by and supported largely for economic reasons, political forces were also at work, not least because some 15,000 of the 114,000 sailors in the navy in 1797 were Irish, the result of pressing convicts into the navy including many United Irishmen and Defenders. Another source of potential support for political discontent came from the quota system, introduced in 1796, which enlisted into the fleet reluctant young men not from seafaring backgrounds, such as urban artisans who were likely to have taken part in the popular political societies. Unlike the Irish, the object of their mutiny was not revolution but an end to the war and the reform of Parliament. Whether they were fighting the French, the Dutch or their own commanders, they did so in the name of English liberty.[28]

Active groups of reformers existed in both Portsmouth and the Medway towns, where missions had been undertaken respectively by John Binns and John Gale Jones of the LCS early in 1796.[29] Aaron Graham, one of the London stipendiary magistrates, was sent to Portsmouth after the outbreak of mutiny to investigate the extent of the rumoured political connection. He was unable to find any firm evidence of radical involvement from the shore, but it was true that Valentine Joyce, the leader of the mutiny, was a radical, that radicals in the port were active, and that pamphlets were sent to the ships. At their subsequent trials, political views and statements in favour of peace were attributed to some crew members.[30] Both John Bone, the LCS secretary, and Robert Watson of the LCS were in Portsmouth during the mutinies, supposedly to form popular societies, but Bone claimed at a meeting of the LCS on 25 May that Watson had gone to Portsmouth to foment mutiny on his own initiative and not as a representative of the LCS; Watson counter-claimed that Bone had undertaken unsanctioned treasonable activities. We now know from Watson's subsequent activities in United Irish circles and with Colonel Despard that he *was* a revolutionary.[31]

Following his mission to Spithead, Graham and another stipendiary magistrate, Daniel Williams, were next sent to interview prisoners from the Nore mutiny. Again, they found it difficult to gather hard evidence but they strongly suspected connections between the popular societies and leaders of the mutiny. This would not have been enough to secure a conviction in a civil court so the charge against Richard Parker and the other leaders was switched from treason, which would have been tried at the Assizes, to mutiny which was easier to prove before a court martial.[32]

The involvement of the corresponding societies in the mutinies, especially in an official capacity, must remain open to doubt, although individual radicals in the fleets and on shore probably did play some part in turning economic discontents into a demand for peace. The involvement of the United Irishmen can be asserted with more confidence. Though they did not know of the mutinies before they happened, they did then attempt to exploit them. There were, for example, cells of United Irishmen both in the fleet and in Portsmouth, and Dublin sent a special envoy to work with United Irishmen in England to prolong the mutiny at the Nore. Though some Irish sailors responded to this intervention, the English generally did not and even when they favoured peace they did not support an instruction issued by the United Irishmen for the mutineers to take their ships over to the French. A plan to divide the fleet, with only some ships going over to the French, was recognition that the extremists would not be able to sway every crew. In the end, as the mutinies collapsed, only a few of the extremists fled to France; others, including Richard Parker, were hanged.[33]

This Irish dimension to anti-war and, to a lesser extent, pro-French feeling was deeply worrying to ministers, particularly when evidence began to emerge during 1798 of a wider conspiracy to bring down the ministry, end the war and liberate Ireland. The background to this conspiracy was the dispersal of United Irish forces from Ulster in 1797 and the reinforcement of Irish communities in Britain with discontented refugees. Central to the scheme was James Coigly, and a section of the United Irish leadership including Arthur O'Connor. Coigly was born in Armagh in 1761 and, after ordination in 1785, went to Paris for his theological training. After the revolution he fled back to Ireland where he probably became involved with the Defenders at a time when agrarian, sectarian and political tensions were increasingly leading to violence in Armagh. These disturbances reached a peak in 1795 following the recall of Earl Fitzwilliam, and Coigly's parents were among the many victims of the Orange mob. All the while Coigly himself was being drawn more deeply into radical politics across the line dividing sympathetic pastoral care from radical activism. Following the failure of the Bantry Bay expedition in December 1796, he associated with the United Irish extremists led by Fitzgerald, O'Connor and Samuel Neilson, who were determined to plot an independent Irish rising to encourage the French to undertake a fresh invasion. By 1797 he was important enough to be reported on by one of the government's agents who was a member of the United Irishmen and in June of that year he joined those of his fellow Irish who, fearing arrest and the Orange mob, took the boat to England. Here he became a link between Dublin, Paris and the Irish communities in Britain. He travelled in the English Midlands, established contact with Manchester where the corresponding society had converted into a republican organisation known as the United Englishmen, and formed links also with the United Scotsmen. He then went to London where he met Irish republicans such as Valentine Lawless and Colonel Edward Marcus Despard, and also John and Benjamin Binns, leading members of the extreme faction within the LCS. At a meeting in London of delegates from both England and Scotland, 'the chief revolutionary committee of England' drew up a manifesto in support of a French invasion and Coigly conveyed this to Paris before returning to Dublin by way of London. He then returned to London to mature the plot before setting out with Arthur O'Connor, John Binns, John Allen and Jeremiah Leary for France. But the government was aware of their plans and as they sat at breakfast in the King's Head, Margate on 28 February 1798, they were arrested.[34]

Told in this way, it would seem that Coigly was at the heart of a serious plot with considerable support amongst the Irish community in Britain which could well have achieved its objective of persuading the French government to make a further invasion attempt. Yet, at the subsequent trial, only Coigly was found guilty, and that only on the evidence of the Address found in his pocket. No serious evidence of conspiracy was produced against the others despite all that the government's agents had been observing and reporting of their activities – Leary had wisely disposed of directly incriminating evidence down the privy at the King's Head. In his autobiography, Francis Place recalled how he had attended some of the London meetings at which Coigly was present but thought little of the conspiracy: 'A more absurd and ridiculous project never entered the heads of men out of Bedlam.'[35] He thought that the Committee of Secrecy which reported in 1799 grossly exaggerated the scale and extent of support for the revolutionary committee. Their *Report* alleged that for at least the past two years the real object of the LCS had been to form a republic with French assistance. John Ashley, a member of the committee in 1794 and secretary of the LCS in 1795–96, 'was now acting as their agent at Paris, and had recently given them hopes of the succour of a French army'. Meetings had been held in London 'to contrive the means of procuring arms, to enable them to co-operate with a French force, in case of an invasion'. One of these meeting places was a cellar in Furnival's Inn, which

> gradually became the resort of all those who were engaged the most deeply in the conspiracy. It was particularly attended by Arthur O'Connor and O'Coigly, previous to their attempt to go over to France; and by the persons chiefly instrumental in carrying on correspondence with the Irish conspirators; and secret consultations were repeatedly held there, with a view to projects, which were thought too dangerous and desperate to be brought forward in any of the larger societies. Among these plans, was that of effecting a general insurrection, at the same moment, in the metropolis and throughout the country, and of

directing it to the object of seizing or assassinating the king, the royal family, and many of the members of both Houses of parliament.[36]

Though mass political assassination seems unlikely, the men at the Home Office were better informed than Francis Place, and they checked their information carefully. Having first been alerted by a Catholic priest from Stonyhurst in Lancashire that there were 20,000 United Englishmen in Manchester, the Home Secretary (the Duke of Portland) asked a leading Manchester magistrate, Thomas Butterworth Bayley, to check this claim. He was able to persuade a leading member of the local corresponding society, Robert Gray, to turn paid informer. Gray confirmed that the United Irishmen had indeed infiltrated the Manchester Corresponding Society and he was the source for the information provided to the committee that a society of United Englishmen had been established in Manchester before 1797.

At the beginning of that year it consisted of about 50 divisions and had grown to about 80 during 1798. Since each division contained between 15 and 36 members, this put their total numbers in the Manchester area at between 1,200 and 2,880 – about a tenth of what had originally been reported. These United Englishmen had attempted, unsuccessfully, to win over the troops but they had established 'an extensive district' around Manchester, managed by 'a very zealous and active committee' which 'frequently sent delegates to various parts of Yorkshire, Derbyshire, Nottinghamshire, and Cheshire' and also corresponded with 'the most distant parts of England as well as to Edinburgh and Glasgow'. There was a second central society in Liverpool which was in correspondence with other parts of England, and with Scotland and Ireland. At the same time attempts were made in Scotland to form a society of United Scotsmen on the same plan, the intention being 'to separate Scotland as well as Ireland from England, and to found, on the ruins of the established government, three distinct republics of England, Scotland, and Ireland'.[37]

Eleven United Englishmen were arrested, including one of the leaders, James Dixon, who stated that in fact only twenty-five divisions had been set up, thus reducing the total numbers involved in the Manchester area to under a thousand, but he did attest to the secret communications network. So, although the size and readiness of the organisation would appear to have been exaggerated by Coigly, the London committee and Robert Gray, it was true that support for the United Irishmen was being organised in Britain.[38]

Why then was this evidence not used at the trial of Coigly and the others? Edward Thompson, who was one of the first historians to take this mass of secret government evidence seriously, plausibly argued that it was not in the government's interest to reveal all that it knew but only sufficient to serve its purpose.[39] Informing was not a popular trade and informers preferred the anonymity of a written or verbal report to the public exposure of an appearance in the witness box; and a good spy would be useless once he had been produced in court.

One of the key agents was Samuel Turner, a lawyer, a United Irishman and member of the Ulster Revolutionary Committee. It was he who supplied the information leading to the arrests at Margate, and when he fled to join the community of Irish exiles in Hamburg he continued to supply information on activities there. Using the alias of 'Richardson' or 'Mr R' (Lord Edward Fitzgerald's wife was called Pamela, as was the heroine in Samuel Richardson's 1740 novel, *Pamela*), he supplied the British government with information for eight years and his cover was never broken. If he had given evidence against O'Connor he could not have done this.

Similarly successful was James Powell, assistant secretary to the LCS, who began working for the government in 1795. He was probably the source of the information supplied in April 1798 which implicated some members of the LCS in the United English/Irish plot which brought about the arrest of the leaders of the corresponding society. Powell was included among those arrested: it would have looked suspicious for him not to have been as he was a noted extremist. 'Powell was honest, but silly,' thought Francis Place, totally taken in by the spy as he helped him escape – to Hamburg! He was still working for the government when he returned in 1802 and the nature of his true work was never exposed. In correspondence he was 'Mr P'. A third spy whose name was not revealed even to the Committee of Secrecy, was George Orr who fled to England before the Irish rebellion and then proceeded to Hamburg where he reported on and followed Napper Tandy, founder of the United Irishmen in Dublin, and another leader of the extremists.[40]

With information such as could be gained from men like these, the government had good reason to believe that a widespread and potentially dangerous plot existed, involving not only Ireland and France, but Britain itself, and Pitt's fury at not being able to convict Arthur O'Connor provoked him into a foolish duel with the Foxite MP and Irishman, George Tierney. The government suspected that the Foxite opposition was not so innocent of the conspiracy as they liked to pretend. Suspicion had already been aroused during the Spithead mutiny when Samuel Whitbread, a Foxite MP, was reported attending a pre-arranged meeting in Purfleet with a leader of the mutiny. How far the Foxites were prepared to go in their anxiety to bring about the fall of Pitt's administration, end the war and secure English liberties is unclear. Fox was, after all, Lord Edward Fitzgerald's cousin and Arthur O'Connor had been noticeably active in Whig circles in London at the same time as he was conspiring with Coigly. Sir Francis Burdett's friendship with O'Connor was especially suspicious. The Foxites gave evidence of O'Connor's good character at his trial, when the government already knew him to be a traitor.

How much the Foxite Whigs knew or were prepared to take advantage of can only be surmised, and the evidence is only circumstantial. The Foxites were certainly in a difficult position after 1795 and genuinely seem to have feared that Pitt was a threat to constitutional liberty.[41] The Foxite secession from the House of Commons in November 1797 coincided with Grattan's secession from the Irish Parliament and appeared to be co-ordinated. Lord Lansdowne thought that 'secession means rebellion, or it is nonsense' and William Wilberforce thought of the Foxites that 'a conviction of their weakness alone prevents their taking up the sword against the government'. What did Fox know when he wrote in March 1798 that 'no good can ever be done now, but by ways in which I will never take a share, and for which I am as unfit, as I am indisposed to them'? Why was Lady Holland concerned lest Holland House be thought 'a *foyer* for Jacobinism'? Is it just coincidence that the papers of the leader of the Whigs, the fifth Duke of Bedford, were destroyed after his death in 1802 and that Lord Holland destroyed Lord Stanhope's political correspondence relating to this time? Nothing can be proved, but if the Foxites were aware of the plans of the United Irishmen and were contemplating exploiting the political instability which might follow an invasion to save English 'liberty' from Pittite repression, the Margate trials were enough to warn them off. The exposure of Coigly silenced them as effectively as the suspension of *Habeas Corpus* enabled the government to silence Binns and others, against whom it was now unnecessary to bring evidence to secure their imprisonment.[42]

The fall of Pitt in 1801, occasioned by the refusal of the King to contemplate repealing anti-Catholic legislation after the Act of Union, brought about the political conditions in which the prisoners could be released, among them Colonel Despard. His subsequent activities need to be placed in the context of this earlier attempt to rouse Britain to support an Irish rising, though the fact that Britain was at peace with France between March 1802 and May 1803 removed both the war-weariness and the immediate threat of a French invasion which had made the situation during 1797–98 so dangerous. After 1798, the revolutionary organisation built up by the United Irishmen and their British supporters was severely weakened but the United Irishmen still maintained an Executive Directory linked to both France and London where the Irish community had been augmented by a fresh influx of refugees following the defeat of the 1798 rising. The extent to which an underground revolutionary organisation was maintained has been documented from the Home Office papers by Marianne Elliott: William Duckett in Hamburg had contacts with the French government; Patrick Finney organised the Irish in London where a National Committee had been formed by early 1801; in Lancashire and Cheshire, former United Britons were ready to resume their activities and when one of the most prominent local leaders, William Cheetham, was released from gaol in 1801 he continued where he had left off. The government set up a new Committee of Secrecy, suspended *Habeas Corpus* again and arrested thirty radicals whom they had good reason to suspect of treasonable activity. Though Napoleon had little time for republican conspirators, his government encouraged them as a useful adjunct to his greater aim of defeating Britain.

The Peace of Amiens only temporarily interrupted this strategy. The release of prisoners when the *Habeas Corpus* Suspension Act again expired fuelled preparations for a new conspiracy and magistrates' spies reported increased activity and organisation in the industrial districts of both Lancashire and the West Riding. Although the Lord Lieutenant of the West Riding, Earl Fitzwilliam, was sceptical and despite good reasons not to believe everything reported by Thomas Hirst, whom the government had provided as a spy, other and more reliable sources of information, such as that provided by Charles Bent, a Manchester tailor employed as a spy by Colonel Ralph Fletcher of Bolton, show Fitzwilliam to have been too complacent.[43]

Irish activity quickened during the summer and autumn of 1802 in the hope that a French invasion would follow the expected breakdown of the peace. So the arrest of Colonel Despard at the Oakley Arms in Lambeth in November 1802 can be seen as a pre-emptive strike by the government in circumstances where Despard's committee were winning some support among the Guards and was possibly in a position to begin a rising in London that would then have been taken up in the industrial north. Had the full plan been allowed to mature until 1803, when Napoleon's invasion army was again assembled and Ireland was ready to rebel, the danger to British security could have been considerable. By acting to stop Despard in November 1802, the government did not have to admit publicly the extent of subversion in the country, but it lost the opportunity of bringing the most dangerous leaders to trial without putting valuable informers in the witness box and thus ending their usefulness. The alternative of suspending *Habeas Corpus* as in 1797 was not available because Addington's government needed the support of the Foxites to resist opposition demands for a renewal of the war. So, the 'Despard conspiracy' was presented and prosecuted in isolation from the main events of which it formed but a small part.[44]

Luddism

Magistrates and ministers alike feared that republicanism and subversion might get mixed up with economic grievances. The decision in 1799 to make combinations of workmen illegal had placed societies organised for economic purposes in the same illegal category as political societies. 'The republicans are drinking Mr Pitt's health,' reported one spy, concerned about a union of industrial and political discontents.[45] Some historians have dismissed this fear as groundless, and the nature of the relationship between political protest and economic discontent is not easy to establish. But governments in the decades after the French Revolution continued to feel anxious that the troublesome minority of revolutionaries might achieve a following by appearing to offer solutions to the grievances of the lower classes in times of economic hardship. It was no coincidence that the political crisis of 1795 came in a year of record bread prices, supplying a ready audience for Thelwall's inflammatory speeches. Similarly, one of the most disturbing things about the turn of events during 1801–2 was the possible connection between revolutionary politics and industrial unrest in the West Riding and Lancashire.[46] Local magistrates such as Colonel Ralph Fletcher of Bolton and Joseph Radcliffe of Huddersfield grew alarmed at what their spies were telling them and even Fitzwilliam, the phlegmatic Lord Lieutenant, asked for reinforcements of regular troops – just in case.[47] Bread prices in 1801 were twice what they had been in 1797 and remnants of the United Irish were reported still active.

A major source of discontent in the north of England was the introduction of new machinery into the textile industries to help manufacturers meet the rising demand for cloth and to reduce their reliance on organised groups of skilled workers. In the cotton industry, where the factory system was well-established for spinning, the main industrial disputes were over hours and conditions of work for the (mainly) child and female labour force, while for the predominantly male handloom weavers the question was one of wages, as manufacturers ignored apprenticeship, recruited new workers (including many Irish) and attempted to drive down wages to factory levels. The failure of Rose's Bill, which would have introduced some regulation of handloom weavers' wages, led to a major strike in Lancashire and Cheshire in 1808 when, according to a local magistrate, Blackburn was 'in a state approaching to that of a general insurrection in consequence of a dispute betwixt the weavers and their employers on the subject of wages'.[48] The small gains made at this time were wiped out by the next depression in 1811.[49]

In the Yorkshire woollen industry, where the factory system was still in its infancy, the master clothiers passed resolutions in 1806 urging Parliament to protect the domestic system by enacting that no individual or firm should own more than 5 looms or 160 spindles or employ children other than those who had served a seven-year apprenticeship.[50] The response of Parliament was to do nothing until 1814 when the apprenticeship clause of the Statute of Artificers (1563) was repealed. Apprenticeship was also a cause of a strike by all 80 croppers at Benjamin Gott's woollen mill in Leeds in 1802 when Gott attempted to circumvent the apprenticeship regulation by indenturing boys over the age of 14. His real aim was to break the croppers' union, for the croppers controlled the last stage in the production of woollen cloth and so could regulate the output of the whole trade. On this occasion 80 croppers were able to force one of the biggest capitalists in the industry to back down.[51]

The position of the croppers was being undermined by the introduction of new machinery, invented in 1787, to both raise and shear the nap on woven and fulled cloth enabling a man and a boy to do in a day what a skilled cropper had formerly done in a week. Textile workers in the east Midlands stocking industry were similarly under pressure at the beginning of the nineteenth century, as employers resorted to using large numbers of apprentices and wide knitting frames in an effort to increase output and cut costs. Although many of the problems arising from changing methods of production had been developing for most of the previous century, they reached crisis point in 1811 as high bread prices coincided with a collapse in markets.[52]

The reason for the recession lay in international relations and economic warfare with Napoleonic France. In 1807, Orders in Council were issued which required all neutral shipping trading with France to call first at a British port and pay duty. This led to a deterioration of relations with the United States, a collapse in British exports to the United States and war between the two countries in 1812. The loss of the American market coming on top of the exclusion of Britain from French controlled ports left unwanted goods piling up in warehouses. Employers retrenched by cutting wages and laying off labour. At the same time the price of bread climbed to a peak three times that of before the war.

Against this background a new and intense phase of machine-breaking began, starting in Nottinghamshire in the spring of 1811. Rioting and frame-breaking were widespread over the winter of 1811–12, presenting a severe threat to law and order as the anonymous 'General Ludd' made his appearance in threatening letters. One newspaper correspondent from Nottingham wrote that, 'The insurrectional state to which this country has been reduced for the last month has no parallel in history, since the troubled days of Charles the First', echoing language used by the *Annual Register* back in 1795 of the impact of the French Revolution.[53]

The movement and the name of 'Luddism' spread to the West Riding where shearing frames were just beginning to take hold in the smaller communities of the Colne and Calder valleys to the south and west of Leeds. In February 1812 machines were smashed in a finishing shop less than a mile from Milnsbridge House, home of the vigilant magistrate Joseph Radcliffe. Other attacks followed in the district and threatening letters were received by prominent mill-owners and magistrates. The laws were tightened against Luddism: machine breaking was made a capital offence in February 1812 as was the taking of unlawful oaths in May. Two mill-owners were singled out by the Luddites: William Horsfall, who had installed some of the new machines in his mill at Marsden and who was an outspoken member of the 'Committee for Suppressing Outrages' formed in Huddersfield; and William Cartwright, who was also fitting new shearing frames at his Rawfolds mill in the Spen valley between Bradford and Dewsbury. On 11 April 1812 about 150 Luddites attacked Rawfolds mill. They were repulsed by an armed guard and two of their number were killed. A week later an attempt was made on Cartwright's life and on 28 April Horsfall was murdered as he rode home to Marsden: he had promised to ride up to his saddle girths in Luddite blood and they had extracted their revenge.[54]

This murder intensified the efforts of the authorities to find out who was responsible but, unlike the 1790s, in this period the magistrates were remarkably deficient in secret intelligence. They picked up rumours but found hard evidence difficult to obtain despite rewards of £2,000 being offered for the apprehension of the guilty. Arrests were finally made for the murder. The government was anxious to hold an exemplary trial before the winter and so pressed ahead with inadequate evidence. As a consequence 'clemency' was granted to some of those arrested because little evidence had been gathered against them, but George Mellor, William Thorpe and Thomas Smith were all convicted of murder on the evidence of their accomplice, Benjamin Walker, and they were hanged at York on 8 January 1813. Eight days later fourteen more were hanged for their part in the attack on Rawfolds mill and other property.[55]

The third scene of Luddite activity was the Manchester area, culminating in an arson attack on a cotton steam loom factory at Westhoughton on 28 March 1812, but here the unrest took an apparently different form from that in the east Midlands and Yorkshire. In the Midlands, acts of violence against property were sustained over several years, the last great outburst being an attack on John

Heathcote's lace factory at Loughborough in June 1816. In the West Riding the violence was more intense but also more short-lived, lasting less than a year. In Lancashire there is more evidence of political activity, spilling over into violence: more evidence, partly because political organisations, however clandestine, were as in the 1790s easier for spies to penetrate than oath-bound Luddite gangs; and partly because of Ralph Fletcher's industrious spy, John Bent.[56] But when Joseph Nadin, deputy constable for Manchester, arrested thirty-eight workers for administering an illegal oath at a meeting in a Manchester public house, their subsequent prosecution on the evidence of the thirty-ninth person present failed to secure a single guilty verdict thanks to the vigorous defence conducted by the Whig lawyer, Henry Brougham.[57]

Most historians have dismissed Luddism as a serious revolutionary threat, while admitting that it constituted a grave challenge to civil peace, private property and even life itself. Violence is in itself no more a proof of a revolutionary conspiracy than its absence demonstrates the lack of such a conspiracy. What can be shown, however, is that there were allegations and rumours and some circumstantial connections between the economic violence of Luddism and men who wished to change (and if not change, then of necessity overthrow) the political system.

The grievances that spilled over into Luddism were first expressed politically in petitions to Parliament for the enforcement of protective legislation, not only the wages clause of the Statute of Artificers (repealed in 1813) and the apprenticeship clause (repealed in 1814), but also the law prohibiting the use of gig-mills which were incorporated into the new shearing frames (repealed in 1809). It was the refusal of Parliament to listen to these petitions that fuelled the anger of Luddism. The 'Friends of Liberty' meeting on Steeton Moor near Keighley in April 1801 had rejected the idea of petitioning Parliament for redress of grievances, asking whether they should continue to submit to 'a Majority of mercenary Hirelings, Government pimps – Corn dealers – Place men – Pensioners – Parasites, &c, and yourselves Starving for Bread? – No, let them exist not one Day longer, we are the Sovereignity'.[58] It is hard to know how representative this group was in 1801, but by 1811 events had done a great deal to reinforce their sentiment.

In Nottinghamshire, there was even a suspicion that Gravener

Henson, leader of the Framework Knitters' Union which petitioned Parliament in vain, might be General Ludd; it is more probable that some of his frustrated followers, particularly those from the depressed country areas around Nottingham, resorted to violence as a response to parliamentary inaction.[59] In Yorkshire, George Mellor and other Luddites in York Castle awaiting trial joined a petition for parliamentary reform, but that does not provide a reason for their being Luddites. But many of those associated with the Luddites were also reformers. Foremost among these in Yorkshire was John Baines of Halifax, a hatter and a republican of twenty-three years' standing, who was tried at York for administering a Luddite oath to John McDonald, a police spy, a couple of days before that became a capital offence, earning him seven years transportation instead of a hanging.[60]

A threatening letter sent by the Yorkshire Luddites to a Huddersfield factory master in 1812 shows something of their thinking. It began with the usual threats against machinery but then expanded in politics. However unrealistic this section of their letter was, it indicates the relationship between the failure of the petitioning movement and Luddism and also the ease with which industrial grievances could spill over into political hatreds.

> The immediate cause of us beginning when we did was that Rascally Letter of the Prince Regent to Lords Grey and Grenville which left us no hope of a chance for the better, by his falling in with that damned set of Rogues Perceval & Co to whom we attribute all the miseries of our Country but we hope for assistance from the French Emperor in shaking off the Rottenest, wickedest and most Tyrannical Government that ever existed, then down comes the Hanover Tyrants and all our tyrants from the greatest to the smallest, and we will be governed by a just Republic, and may the Almighty hasten those happy times is the wish and prayer of Millions in this Land, but we wont only pray but we will fight, the Red Coats shall know when the proper times come, we will never lay down our arms till the House of Commons passes the act to put down all the machinery hurtful to the Commonality and repeal that to the Frame Breakers but we Petition no more, that wont do, fighting must.[61]

With this perspective in mind, we can now review the evidence about Luddism and politics in Lancashire and Cheshire, much of which comes from the spy John Bent. Malcolm Thomis sees him as 'wild and imaginative' and his employer, Ralph Fletcher, as revealing an 'unbelievable naïveté'.[62] John Dinwiddy, on the other hand, thought him prone to exaggerate those matters about which he did not have direct knowledge but possibly 'giving fairly accurate accounts of proceedings in Manchester about which his employer might be suspected of having other intelligence'.[63] The extent of this Luddite activity became clear when General Maitland, in charge of the troops enforcing law and order in Lancashire and Cheshire, decided to apply the provisions of the Illegal Oaths Act which offered immunity to those who admitted their guilt. Hundreds rushed to take advantage of the indemnity in July and August 1812 – over eight hundred came forward in the last week in August in Stockport and Hyde alone.[64] This suggests widespread illegal organisation in Lancashire in the summer of 1812, coinciding with a spate of attacks on factories. Clandestine violence and open petitioning were taking place side by side, with some of the same people participating in both. Some of the thirty-eight alleged oath takers arrested by Nadin, tried and acquitted, who claimed they were innocent parliamentary reformers, later came forward under the indemnity to be 'untwisted' of their illegal oaths. This on its own would not make their illegal behaviour revolutionary in a political sense and much of the evidence suggests the oath was not overtly political.

However, some of the evidence points to a political oath calling for 'a general reform and general change'. Weaver informant, Humphrey Yarwood, came to understand that 'something further than the destruction of steam looms or machinery was intended', and Thomas Wood of Mottram was told when he took the oath 'that there was to be a revolution, and that all who were not for it, would be killed; and those who were for it, were to take the oath'.[65] If these statements are then put in the context of the evidence for United Irish activity in the area a decade earlier, Lancashire Luddism may appear not quite so purely economic after all. The same argument can be applied to Yorkshire. Although most of those convicted of machine breaking were workers in the woollen industry, mainly croppers, oath taking was more widespread, extending eastwards to Leeds and south to Sheffield.[66] In Barnsley, a weaver later gave information that 'The Luddites have in view ultimately to overturn the System of Government, by Revolutionising the Country.'[67]

However, this did not amount to the national network of revolutionary conspiracy that Bent imagined it to be. And, despite the lingering possibility in Luddite and other minds of links with the United Irish and the renewed possibility of a French invasion in 1812, Dublin Castle was not alarmed in the way it had been in the later 1790s.[68] If there were to be a threat of revolution on the Irish model in 1812, it was more likely to take the form feared by Sir Francis Wood, Vice-Lieutenant for the West Riding, who thought that the general lawlessness and collecting of weapons that was spreading in Yorkshire in the summer of 1812 could lead from robbery to assassination (which it did) and then 'end as the same Course of Outrage ended in Ireland, in open Rebellion against the Government of the Country; – The Similarity of our present State to that of Ireland strikes every one who witnessed the Transactions of 1797 and 1798 in that Country'.[69] This was perceptive. The assumption that there is a dividing line, however thin, between economic and political activity, is a rationalisation that lies in the historian's rather than the contemporary's mind. The hungry and desperate worker whose livelihood was at risk did not pause to categorise his motives or clarify his objectives, and what had begun as economic protest and direct action of an industrial nature could easily drift towards political subversion given the right conditions. Had the industrial counties presented the same face in 1801–2, with a French invasion imminent and Ireland preparing to rise, unrest on the scale experienced in 1812 might indeed have posed a serious revolutionary threat.

The post-war crisis, 1817

The immediate post-war years, 1815–21, proved as difficult as any during wartime itself, as unemployment and high bread prices coincided with renewed political discontent. Lord Sidmouth feared, 'We must expect a trying winter, and it will be fortunate if the Military establishment which was pronounced to be too large for the constitution of the country shall be sufficient to preserve its internal tranquillity.'[70] In 1817 the price of wheat rose to heights previously unknown except in the crisis years of 1800–1 and 1812–13. Though this undermined the relevance of the Corn Law of 1815, which protected domestic agriculture from foreign imports when the price was below 80 shillings a quarter, this protectionism became a symbol for reformers of the way in which the old order represented in Parliament always looked after its own. During the wars, the armed forces of Britain had been increased to 400,000 men (with as many again in the reserves) compared with about 60,000 in 1791.[71] As the military establishment was reduced to peace-time levels, thousands of men trained in the use of arms were discharged on to the labour market. At the same time, sectors of the economy that had expanded to meet war-time demand – in the production of uniforms, munitions and ships – now had surplus capacity. Added to this came the strains of technological redundancy. The number of shearing frames in Yorkshire had increased in the past decade from under a hundred to over fourteen hundred, and in October 1817, 3,625 croppers (of whom only 860 were in full employment) petitioned Parliament for help.[72] In Lancashire, the number of handloom weavers continued to rise while their wages continued to fall.[73]

At the same time the ending of the war re-invigorated the demand for parliamentary reform which had been kept alive by campaigners such as Major Cartwright, political organisers like Francis Place in Westminster, and a minority of Whig politicians such as Sir Francis Burdett. During the war, to demand reform implied a lack of patriotism and Cartwright, Place and Burdett had each at some point been suspected of seditious activity, but all three and their like had wisely avoided direct involvement with the extremist and illegal revolutionary fringe. The same was true of William Cobbett who was probably the most popular journalist of the reform movement. He had been imprisoned for two years in 1809 for a seditious libel on 'the borders of high treason' in his *Political Register* in which he had condemned the use of German mercenary troops to flog mutinous militiamen.[74] After the war he issued the *Register* in a cheap edition at twopence a week, in which he denounced Luddism and advocated political reform as the means to redress grievances. He was widely read, his paper reaching an initial circulation of 40,000, stimulating a legitimate and popular movement for political reform in London and across the troubled industrial areas of the Midlands and the north. Popular societies sprang up as in the early 1790s, often called Union Societies, or Hampden clubs after the style of the London Hampden Club established by Major Cartwright, but appealing to a lower social class. There were twenty-one such societies in Lancashire alone at the beginning of 1817.

Other influences were also at work, but it is hard to tell how wide-spread or influential they were. Chief among them were the followers of Thomas Spence, whose natural environment was the clubs and taverns of London which the loyalist pamphleteer, William Hamilton Reid, had recognised as hotbeds of subversive republicanism in the 1790s, and where Despard had found support.[75] Spence was a revolutionary land reformer who had sold his tracts in London and inspired a band of dedicated followers during the lean years of the reform movement after 1799. These followers regrouped after Spence's death in 1814 under the leadership of Thomas Evans, one-time secretary of the London Corresponding Society in its revolutionary phase after 1797, whose house had been a base for United English planning in 1798. On release from prison in 1801, Evans had resumed his revolutionary activities until the exposure of Despard's plot had brought him greater discretion. Thereafter he was to be found with other old 'Jacobins' in the 'free-and-easy' atmosphere of London tavern life. Their historian, Iain McCalman, has constructed a list of some of their number in 1811–12: they included several former United Englishmen and Irishmen, arrested during 1798–99 and plotters with Despard in 1802.[76] Around 1810–11 they were joined by Maurice Margarot, returned from Australia, and Arthur Thistlewood who visited Paris with Evans's son in 1814 where they met up with John Ashley, formerly of the LCS, and other members of the Anglo-Irish community of revolutionary exiles.[77]

Leading members of Evans's Society of Spencean Philanthropists at the end of the war included Arthur Thistlewood, 'Dr' James Watson and Thomas Preston. Thistlewood was the illegitimate son of a Lincolnshire farmer. He had been a lieutenant in the Yorkshire militia and then gambled himself into debt in London where Place suspected him of being a paid informer. Watson was a surgeon–apothecary from Cheshire whose businesses repeatedly failed in London, as did his marriage, and who eked out a marginal existence. Preston was a master shoemaker similarly fallen on hard times, and also with a failed marriage.[78] These men might be compared to that political 'low life' identified by Robert Darnton in Paris before the 1789 Revolution.[79] Well-fitted to be their leader after 1814, Thomas Evans is described by McCalman as 'a marginal, restless artisan, an incorrigible revolutionary, a tavern *bon vivant* and balladeer, a radical black-mailer and smut-pedlar; yet at the same time, an ambitious, conscientious father, an aspiring self-improver, a moderate Westminster activist, a *philosophe-manqué* and . . . a fervent millenarian.'[80]

The concept of millenarianism is important for understanding the revolutionary outlook of this group. Since the French Revolution, the prospect of a new world and a new beginning had given rise to a number of millenarian sects. Some of them, like that attached to Richard Brothers in 1795, had political implications; others, like the followers of Joanna Southcott, were apolitical, though this cannot be said of all Joanna's successor prophets. Speakers fired with biblical language and apocalyptic visions filled pulpits and inspired crowds, especially in London. From the 1790s to at least the 1830s, radical millenarianism could pose a real threat because it inspired a brand of fanaticism which did not respond to the rationalities governing normal political behaviour, such as the calculation of likely success and the deterrent effect of punishment. One such preacher was the ex-Methodist tailor, Robert Wedderburn, a discharged black sailor who may have been present at the Nore in 1797. By 1818 he was a leading Spencean and his Hopkins Street chapel, where he moved after breaking with Thomas Evans in April 1819, was a centre for revolutionary plotting.[81]

By 1816 the Spenceans were divided into two groups. The mainstream, followers of Evans, adhered to Spence's revolutionary plan for the redistribution of the land but did not espouse revolutionary methods. The minority, among whom Thistlewood and 'Dr' Watson and his son (also James) were the leading figures, were more in the Watt or Despard tradition, looking to create a revolutionary spark which would fire the country.[82] Their hope in 1816 was to achieve this in alliance with the most popular radical speaker of his day, Henry Hunt. Hunt hoped to exploit the Spencean connection with tavern radicalism to extend his own political base in his competition for support with Cobbett and other radical leaders.[83] So when Preston invited leading reformers, including Hunt, Cobbett and Burdett, to address a meeting to be held on Spa Fields in north London on 15 November 1816, Hunt alone accepted but on conditions which enabled him to keep control of the meeting. Nothing daunted, Thistlewood and the younger Watson decided to mount an attack on the Tower of London on the morning before Hunt's next Spa Fields meeting on 2 December. Despite the efforts of Thistlewood's associate, John Castle, to persuade Hunt to become involved, he refused. This was wise, for Castle was a government agent who later gave evidence against the conspirators. Thistlewood and young Watson led a crowd of about five thousand through London, raiding gun shops on the way to the Tower. Rioting went on all day, but little was achieved other than the arrest of most of the leaders. Remarkably they were released on bail, as if the government wanted to give them the opportunity for further revolutionary activity (monitored by Castle) in order to justify the kind of repression of free speech which would not otherwise be acceptable in peacetime.[84] They did not have to wait long. On 28 January the events of 1795 were repeated. A projectile, supposedly a bullet, broke a window in the Prince Regent's coach on his way to open Parliament. Then, on 8 February, Thistlewood and his co-conspirators were arrested and committed to the Tower on a charge of high treason. On 4 March *Habeas Corpus* was suspended. The Seditious Meetings Act of 1795 was revived on 14 March and it was made a treasonable offence to attempt to persuade soldiers and sailors to break their oaths. Magistrates were reminded to suppress all blasphemous and seditious literature.

The severity of this reaction has to be put in the wider context, not only of the riot in London, but also of its effect in the rest of the country, especially in the industrial Midlands and north where Luddites disturbances were of very recent memory. Fitzwilliam felt that the public temper at a riotous public meeting in Sheffield was 'the offspring of a Revolutionary spirit', though this worried him less than if it had been the product of distress. Nevertheless it was enough for him to vote with the government for the repressive legislation.[85] One of the men who had come from the north to London for the second Spa Fields meeting was Joseph Mitchell, a journeyman printer from Liverpool who since 1816 had been operating as a radical missionary in Lancashire. He reported back to a meeting at Middleton near Manchester in December, which nominated him and William Benbow, a local shoemaker, as delegates to visit the distressed areas of Lancashire and Yorkshire. At a further meeting of Lancashire reform societies on 1 January 1817, Samuel Bamford, a young weaver, was chosen to represent Middleton at a national gathering of reformers at the London Hampden Club. Bamford's recollections of events over the next two years provide a graphic insight into the twilight world of conspiracy which linked London and the northern industrial communities. His autobiography, however, is not an untainted source. It was written in a didactic spirit in the late 1830s and early 1840s as a warning to Chartists not to indulge in violence and to beware of spies, and it carefully represented the author as an innocent and rather naive participant in events which he did not fully understand.[86]

In London he was met by Benbow, who was already in the capital 'agitating the labouring classes at their trades' meetings and club-houses'.[87] He also met Mitchell, with whom he looked up a friend in the Foot Guards. They just happened to have with them copies of Cobbett's *Register* and Hone's *Political Litany* (1817), which they read out to the troops and gave them to read – an act shortly to be made illegal. Mitchell and Benbow also introduced Bamford to the Spenceans, including the elder Watson and Thomas Preston; he later recalled that 'Mitchell and Benbow had cultivated a rather close acquaintance with these men'. On his return to Lancashire, Benbow began organising a march of weavers to London to petition the Prince Regent, the so-called 'Blanketeers'. None of this was illegal, but Bamford was right to observe that it was on the illegal side of what Cobbett, Hunt, Cartwright and the other legitimate popular reform-ers were advocating: the whole idea, he thought, 'was one of the bad schemes which accompanied us from London, and was the result of the intercourse of some of the deputies with the leaders of the London operatives – the Watsons, Prestons, and Hoopers'.[88]

The Blanketeers gathered in the rain, about five thousand strong, on St Peter's Field, Manchester, on 10 March. The Riot Act was read and two of the leaders were arrested before no more than six or seven hundred set out for London, only to be turned back before they got as far as the county boundary. It is likely that this march was intended to be a mass demonstration to gain support along the route and so put pressure on the government in London, rather than the gathering of a revolutionary army to overawe the capital, but it is also true that the men were desperate and angry, powerless rather than passive in their suffering. The day after the St Peter's Field meeting a stranger called on Bamford and his friends with a plan to march on Manchester, divert the military, raid the garrison for arms, fire the houses of marked individuals and release the prisoners; they would make 'a Moscow of Manchester'. Bamford wisely (in retrospect) ignored the man; he was probably an *agent provocateur*. Others were not so careful and a group of delegates who gathered at Ardwick Bridge to hear news of risings elsewhere was informed on and arrested at the end of March.[89]

The suspension of *Habeas Corpus* enabled the government to terrorise suspects and scatter any incipient cells of revolution. Bamford has left a graphic account of what this could mean:

> Personal liberty not being now secure from one hour to another, many of the leading reformers were induced to quit their homes, and seek concealment where they could obtain it. Those who could muster a few pounds, or who had friends to give them a frugal welcome, or who had trades with which they could travel, disappeared like swallows at the close of summer, no one knew whither.[90]

Twenty-three prominent radicals were arrested; others, including Cobbett, fled. Mitchell ominously 'moved in a sphere of his own, the extent of which no man knew except himself'.[91] In London in April he met up with Charles Pendrill, first arrested in 1798 and a veteran of the Despard conspiracy, who was about to flee to Philadelphia. Pendrill introduced Mitchell to his friend, William Oliver, and on 23 April, Mitchell and Oliver set out on a provincial tour which culminated in a delegate meeting in Wakefield at which a rising was planned for 26 May 'to cause a finishing blow to be levelled at the boroughmongers'.[92] Mitchell was arrested on 4 May, leaving Oliver as the only London representative available to take part. Unknown to Bamford, and indeed to Mitchell himself, the latter's movements were not at all secret – Oliver was reporting everything to the Home Secretary. Oliver's method of working is illustrated in the following sworn deposition:

> about 11 or 12 Weeks ago, invited Walker the Painter to Dinner: found at his Lodgings two strangers, Mitchell & Oliver – after dinner Walker intimated that those two friends of his had expressed a desire to have conversation with you – W & I went to meet them, we four then went 2 Miles out of town, & went into a publick House at Mirfield – the two strangers stated themselves advocates of Parl[iamen]t[ar]y Reform, but Oliver signified that as the H of Cs *notified* [inserted above (probably not inclined)] to listen to Pet[ition]s on that subject, O said Force must be used – that he had instructions from his friends in London to come into this country to sound the minds of the

People on that subject, and that he should appoint meetings to mature the Plan and then communicate to his friends in London. He signified that the physical Force was in the Hands of the People, & that his friends in London were confident of success, if things were properly organized according to his wish; on that account he shd visit the different manufacturing towns, & he should appoint meetings to determine how to act.[93]

But, as Edward Thompson argued, this does not mean that Oliver fabricated or caused the whole provincial conspiracy single-handed. Although he reported it to be 'a weak and impractical scheme',[94] the delegates and their plans for a rising were real enough. Those who brought Bamford news of the Wakefield meeting were the veteran Paineite, Thomas Bacon from Pentrich, and William Turner from nearby South Wingfield.[95] What is true, is that Oliver, as the London delegate, now took charge. The date for the rising was switched to 9 June, and the government was ready. Ministers did not need the additional information about the collection of weapons which informers sent to the Home Office.[96]

Whatever the rumours and allegations of widespread plotting, the actual rising took place in only two places, both of them former centres of Luddite violence. The danger may possibly have seemed greatest in the West Riding, but here the authorities accidentally made a pre-emptive strike when a local magistrate arrested ten delegates at Thornhill Lees, not knowing that Oliver had arranged the meeting. This provoked fewer than a hundred cloth workers from the Holme Valley, including desperate croppers led by George Taylor, said to be a veteran of the Rawfolds attack, to march on Huddersfield on the night of 8 June. A sworn deposition relating to the planning of this insurrection gives some sense of the atmosphere of the times, and also of links back to Luddism:

> Riley has sometimes talked to me about their plans he said that the rising was to be in the Night time, and to be general through the Kingdom wherever they had formed a Union all Communication was to be stopped, the Coaches were to be stopped, the Magistrates were to be seized and kept as Hostages until there was a regulation at London – Riley frequently said to me – 'you see Buckley that Petitioning is of no use we are like to do something else.' Riley told me that Veevors had laid down a plan for seising the Military in Huddersfield and that there was

a list of the Quarters where the Soldiers were billeted at, that they were to divide into Parties and go and surprize them before they were aware – he said men like me that had been Soldiers must March off to Sheffield the first day after the great Heads were secured – I asked what was to become of the Families of Men like me? and he said that such as him who stopt at home, would take care of them and that they should not want – he has an old Halbert which he said had been used in Ludding time and I might have it if I would join them. I recollect that when Riley brought me the Lead and Bullet Moulds, he said that he wanted the Lead casted into Bullets and that somebody would want them at the time Rising if I did not, and that they would be ready – he said it would begin the Monday following and that he wished it was over – he said that altho' he himself did not know the use of Arms, yet he would do what he could to assist it.[97]

On the night of Sunday, 8 June, they rose and were dispersed by the yeomanry just short of the town on the bridge over the River Colne at Folly Hall.[98]

The next night, a similar rising took place in the vicinity of Pentrich in Derbyshire to the west of Nottingham. About 400 men armed with guns and pikes set out from the villages around Pentrich to march on Nottingham where they expected to be joined by other bands of revolutionaries, including 16,000 from Nottingham itself. They would then attack the barracks and seize the town before taking boats down the Trent to Newark, with the eventual aim of reaching London where the forces promised by Oliver would overthrow the government. Their 'captain' was Jeremiah Brandreth, a framework knitter from Sutton in Ashfield, though the actual planning was probably the work of Thomas Bacon who, with a warrant already out for his arrest, did not take part in the rising itself. The armed band got as far as Giltbrook, about thirteen miles from the start of the march and still eight miles short of Nottingham. Here, those who had not already thought better of this midnight outing in the rain fled at the sight of soldiers on horseback. Over eighty arrests were made during the next few weeks and as a result of the trials in October, three men, including Brandreth, were hanged; eleven, including Bacon, changed their pleas to guilty and were transported for life and three others for fourteen years; and six were gaoled. The prosecution centred its case, as with

Despard's conspiracy, on the actual rising for which the evidence was easy to present, and not the extensive plot behind the rising centred on Bacon. To have exposed this would have meant putting Oliver in the witness box. Already the treason trials against Thistlewood, Watson, Hooper and Preston had foundered because the jury would not convict on an informer's evidence; and the exposure of Oliver by the *Leeds Mercury* on 14 June had resulted in the acquittal of those arrested after the Folly Hall rising. By abandoning the idea of prosecuting Bacon first and trying Brandreth instead, there was no problem in securing guilty verdicts and exemplary punishments.[99]

The Folly Hall and Pentrich risings can be regarded as the last flickers of Luddism in its desperate, violent and political phase. While awaiting transportation for life, George Weightman told the gaol chaplain of a conversation with Brandreth about the latter's part in a Luddite attack at Basford; many years later, Weightman himself was recalled as 'a young man whose face would be familiar to the Luddites of the West Riding' at delegate meetings at the St Crispin Inn, Halifax, the old haunt of John Baines.[100] Machine-breaking could sit alongside the Jacobin politics of Baines and Bacon; armed attacks on mills and masters could grow into revolutionary plots, assisted by – but not necessarily originating with – agents employed by local magistrates and the government.

From Peterloo to Cato Street and Bonnymuir

The Thistlewood group was encouraged rather than intimidated by the collapse of the case against them following their attempt to seize the Tower of London in December 1816. They discussed plans for another rising in the capital, to take place in October 1817, and in February 1818 plotted to assassinate the Home Secretary, Lord Sidmouth, and other members of the government.[101] Finally in May, when Thistlewood challenged Sidmouth to a duel, the authorities thankfully put him in gaol for a year. The rest of the group, led by the Watsons, modified their tactics and continued their mission more openly in association with Henry Hunt. They made considerable progress, particularly in Lancashire.

On his release in May 1819, Thistlewood resumed his conspiratorial approach along with Preston, William Davidson and other associates who frequented Robert Wedderburn's Hopkins Street chapel.[102] They hoped to exploit a meeting in Smithfield chaired by Hunt on 14 July 1819 to commemorate the thirtieth anniversary of the fall of the Bastille but, as in 1816, Hunt was able to retain control and thwart the revolutionaries. He was determined to divert the energies of the reform movement away from conspiracy towards an open policy of platform agitation, based on the strategy of the mass meeting.[103] The government, however, did not see the clear distinction between the two. Any assembly calculated to strike terror 'in minds of ordinary firmness' was unlawful, which meant in effect that local magistrates could declare unlawful any public meeting which they felt to be a threat; and they could order any such meeting to disperse by reading the Riot Act. Since one aim of Hunt's strategy of the mass platform was to demonstrate force of numbers, potentially striking terror in the minds of ordinary citizens, Hunt's constitutionalism was therefore at best on the margins of legality.

Furthermore, on 30 July a Proclamation had been issued against seditious meetings, which included meetings to coerce Parliament. For this reason the magistrates banned a proposed meeting in support of parliamentary reform planned for 9 August 1819 at St Peter's Field, Manchester, at which Hunt was to be the main speaker. When he moved the meeting to the following week, the magistrates ordered his arrest at the start of the meeting, sending in the troops to effect this. What followed, as the Manchester and Salford Yeomanry lashed out with their swords, contrary to military discipline, killing eleven people and injuring hundreds, has entered the folk history of radical protest and was quickly dubbed the 'Peterloo' massacre.[104]

Hunt's strategy was confrontational but not revolutionary. However, the meeting was held against a background of social tensions which were potentially revolutionary. Joseph Johnson of the Manchester Patriotic Union Society had written to Hunt on 3 July 1819, inviting him in very ambivalent language to come to Manchester to address the meeting:

> Trade here is not worth following. Everything here is almost at a stand still, nothing but ruin and starvation stare one in the face. The state of this district is truly dreadful, and I believe nothing but the greatest exertions can prevent an insurrection. Oh, that you in London were prepared for it!

Though Johnson did not know it, James Norris, the Manchester stipendiary magistrate, had written to Lord Sidmouth on 30 June with an almost identical assessment of the situation.[105] Most ominous were reports of armed drilling on the moors at night and the military-style discipline shown by those who attended the mass meetings.

The real danger came after news of the massacre spread, first to the Lancashire and Cheshire communities represented at the meeting and then, within a couple of days, to the rest of the country. Fear and anger, coming on top of economic hardship and thwarted political demands, produced a revolutionary cocktail and it is a measure of Hunt's stature that he was able to restrain the crowds who treated him as a hero while he was on bail awaiting trial for seditious conspiracy. Even so, there is evidence of further arming at public meetings which the magistrates dared not disrupt in open confrontation with the crowd. In their defence, those accused of bearing such weapons claimed that they were carried for self-protection, and not for illegal aggression. Peterloo turned out to be a disaster for the authorities as the radicals now seized the moral high ground. John Gale Jones later recalled his reaction to the news:

> From that fatal day when the sword was drawn and war declared against the people of England, by the bloody and unavenged massacre of the defenceless men, women and children of Manchester, I was one of those, who made up their mind that all further praying and petitioning ought to be at an end, that the *time for Reform was past and the hour of Revolution come*.[106]

At one meeting held near Burnley in November to protest at Peterloo and to advocate parliamentary reform, the crowd marched to music in an orderly fashion, carrying sticks and banners. But when someone – in panic or mischief-making – raised the cry that the soldiers were coming, 'many persons' produced pike-heads from up their coat sleeves, which they tied to their sticks ready to repulse their attackers.[107] Elsewhere events could not be presented in so innocent a light and the government took new powers by the so-called Six Acts on 1 January 1820 to ban meetings of more than fifty people, suppress or tax out of their market blasphemous and sedition publications, and prohibit unauthorised military training.

There were three main theatres of action during the winter of 1819–20: London, the textile districts in the north of England, and the

Glasgow area of western Scotland. Of the three, events in London were, despite appearances, the least threatening. Here, Thistlewood continued with his plots to overthrow the government by some bold revolutionary *putsch*, following which popular risings would occur elsewhere. The tone was set at Wedderburn's chapel. According to one informer at a meeting in October:

> Principal Speaker was Wedderburn, who dwelt chiefly on the late Affair at Manchester; that the bloody Revolution had begun in blood there, & must now end in blood – that the Prince Regent had lost the Confidence of & affection of his People, but being supported by the army & surrounded by his vile Ministers, nothing short of the People taking arms in their own defence, could bring about a Reform & prevent the same bloody scenes taking place at the next Smithfield Meeting, as had taken place at Manchester, for his own Part old as he was, he was learning his exercise as a Soldier & could be on[e] if he fell in the cause, for he would rather die like Cashman, if he could but have the satisfaction of plunging a Dagger in the heart of a Tyrant. That the next meeting, on 1 Nov would be such a General Meeting throughout the Country as well as London that then only was the time *'therefore all come armed or its of no use and be sure you bring plenty of Ammunition with you'*.[108]

Even discounting Wedderburn's pulpit rhetoric, this message created a mood of heightened expectation on both sides, but on 1 November only forty armed men gathered in London and so the revolution was postponed until 15 November and this was later deferred until 24 November. The revolutionaries were committed to their course but were unable to muster sufficient numbers to turn words into deeds. Preparations were then made for a rising in reaction to the Prince Regent's speech from the throne announcing repression, beginning with simultaneous meetings in London, Scotland, the north and the Midlands on 13 December. Thistlewood's numbers in London, however, were too small and when this failed he turned to an alternative plan to assassinate the ministers at a cabinet dinner. This would be followed immediately by a number of simultaneous attacks on key targets throughout London.

Several dates were fixed and postponed. Matters were finally brought to a head by a spy and *agent provocateur*, George Edwards, leading to the arrest of the group in Cato Street on 23 February 1820 as they prepared to set out on their mission to destroy the cabinet. One of their number turned King's evidence so the government did not have to use Edwards as a witness and risk the jury again refusing to convict. Thistlewood, Davidson and three others were found guilty and executed in May; five others changed their pleas to guilty and were transported. What had become an increasingly marginal activity, involving neither the mainstream radicals who followed Hunt nor the orthodox Spenceans who followed Thomas Evans, finally appeared to have been put to rest.[109]

What did stir the people of the capital was not republican revolution, but the cause of Caroline whom George IV and his ministers wished to exclude from her position as Queen. The riotous demonstrations that accompanied the attempt to carry a Bill of Pains and Penalties through Parliament brought to the capital scenes which in Manchester or Glasgow would have been called revolutionary – and which in Paris would probably have *been* revolutionary. There was some repetition of these events the following August at Caroline's funeral and there the matter ended – with a few broken windows – but the ministry survived. And yet, of all the anti-government demonstrations of this period, this was the only one to be supported by a section of the propertied classes and indeed leadership from the Whig opposition, daring to do in the name of royalty what it may have wished to do (but dared not) in the name of peace in 1797. The disturbances were greater than any London had seen since the Gordon Riots of 1780. Thistlewood had missed his opportunity, but he was dead and other key radical leaders were safely in gaol.[110]

Thistlewood's belief in the possibility of simultaneous meetings was not wholly misplaced. Lord Sidmouth was aware in early March that 'an expectation prevailed among the disaffected in the northern parts of the Kingdom that an important blow would be struck in London, previous to the expiration of the month of February'.[111] But Lancashire was weakened by divisions between the Huntite majority and the conspiratorial minority followed by the arrest of key figures on 22 December, and only Yorkshire and Scotland actually rose in the early spring of 1820. One link between these places was James Brayshaw of Leeds, a Paineite republican and Freethinking Christian, who proposed a motion (which was carried) in favour of arming at a meeting in Leeds to protest at the Six Acts in December 1819. He later blamed the attempted rising in Yorkshire on James Mann, another

Leeds radical and supporter of Hunt who had been one of those arrested at Thornhill Lees in 1817.[112] Brayshaw was also active in the west of Scotland, having visited the area in 1819 to spread radical union societies such as those formed in the Manchester area in 1818. He was there again in March 1820, visiting Strathaven, Paisley and Parkhead where he stayed with James Wilson, an old radical and noted extremist whose involvement with the reform movement went back to the Friends of the People in 1792. It was here that Brayshaw probably helped draft an Address which was pasted up in Glasgow on 1 April to signal the start of the Scottish insurrection.

The background to this series of alarming and violent events was widespread depression and hardship among the weavers of Lanarkshire, Renfrewshire, Dunbartonshire, Stirlingshire and Ayrshire, but this was politicised through the union societies and led to organised protest meetings following Peterloo. Paisley was particularly disturbed and there was serious rioting between 11 and 18 September, with gun shops looted and property attacked. Mass meetings continued throughout the autumn, amid rumours of arming and preparations for a rising. As a precaution, the yeomanry paraded in Glasgow on 13 December, Thistlewood's first date for simultaneous meetings. Three hundred armed men who had marched into Kilsyth on their way to Glasgow disbanded and went home on learning that Glasgow was quiet. Charles Hope, Lord President of the Court of Session, wrote to Lord Melville on 17 December that, 'the people are rife for rebellion as ever, and only in sullen and sultry silence waiting for a more convenient opportunity'.[113] The unrest appears to have been co-ordinated by a shadowy Committee for Organising a Provisional Government comprising twenty-eight men, one of whom, John King, may have been a spy. On 22 February, the night before the Cato Street arrests, this entire committee was arrested. The effect was to spur on a determined minority. Historians are divided over whether or not the events which followed were encouraged by spies who, like Edwards in London, were officially or otherwise determined to flush the conspirators out by leading them to their own destruction.[114]

On the night of 1 April, the Address prepared by Wilson, Brayshaw and others was pasted up on the streets across the industrial districts of western Scotland so that on the morning of Sunday, 2 April crowds of weavers, spinners and other workers could read the call for a general strike and threats of armed resistance. The army, yeomanry and police were put on the ready and prayers were offered for deliverance from civil war. The strike was remarkably solid in the Glasgow area, through a combination of persuasion and intimidation, but it lasted less than a week. The threatened uprising was less coherent and lasted scarcely longer.

On the night of 4/5 April a small contingent of thirty-five men, led by John Baird and Andrew Hardie, set out to collect weapons from striking workers at the Carron ironworks. They were caught by the cavalry on the moor near Bonnybridge, where they stood their ground and fought, but the 'Battle of Bonnymuir' was an unequal contest. Eighteen prisoners, some of them wounded, were taken, including Baird and Hardie. The following night there was to have been an attack on Glasgow, but only James Wilson's contingent of about twenty-five armed men from Strathaven rose and they melted away when they realised that no one else was marching on Glasgow. Further arrests followed, and weapons and ammunition were seized as the authorities sought to dismantle the disillusioned and defeated remnants of the revolutionary movement, but still sporadic unrest continued into the summer. In all, eighty-eight people were charged, of whom all but thirty fled or went into hiding. They were outlawed. Of the remainder, two were acquitted and twenty-four were sentenced to death. The death penalty, however, was carried out only in the cases of Wilson, Baird and Hardie. The others were transported. In 1835, a young Scot called Peter Mackenzie wrote a book in which he claimed that the spy, Alexander Richmond, was behind the events of 1820. Richmond sued for libel and lost. Though the evidence was by no means certain, the government then granted an absolute pardon to those it had outlawed and exiled in 1820. Historians still differ over how large a part was played in the rising by spies, but the persistent unrest and numbers of weapons subsequently recovered would suggest that, if spies and *agents provocateurs* were involved, they did no more than bring into the open a genuine and widespread conspiracy to levy war against the King.[115]

Coincidences of date suggests that the Scottish insurrection was not conceived in isolation from events in England. Indeed the *Leeds Mercury* believed that the fall of Huddersfield was to have been the signal for a simultaneous rising 'throughout all the manufacturing districts in the Kingdom, extending even to Scotland'.[116] On the night before the Address was placarded in Scotland, the men of

Huddersfield, whose Luddism had been at the heart of similar unrest in 1812 and who had also responded in 1817, were rumoured to be ready once more to answer the call. Contingents from the Calder and Spen Valleys were to assemble at the old Luddite meeting place where the River Colne joined the Calder and then march on Huddersfield. The magistrates sat up all night in the principal hotel overlooking the market place, surrounded by infantry and cavalry. When a beacon on Castle Hill outside the town gave the signal, only about two hundred insurgents had gathered, so they quickly abandoned their attempt, agreeing to reconvene on 11 April at Grange Moor where an earlier generation of rebels had gathered in 1801.[117] The Grange Moor plan, conceived in Barnsley, was betrayed to the magistrates and when the Barnsley contingent of about three hundred arrived on Grange Moor, instead of a force of some three thousand like-minded men from Huddersfield, Leeds, Wakefield and Sheffield, the moor was deserted. The insurgents ran for their lives, even before a detachment of yeomanry and dragoons arrived from Huddersfield.[118] In Sheffield, John Blackwell's simultaneous attempt to storm the barracks and seize weapons came to nothing when his followers decided to postpone the event. Blackwell was arrested next day. In all, twenty men were charged with high treason and others with lesser offences. Those found guilty were transported.[119]

Conclusion

There seems little doubt that revolutionary conspiracies did exist in Britain at various times in the thirty years following the revolution in France. More contentious is the interpretation given to these events: their scale and significance. Where outbursts occurred, these were generally small, involving a few hundred men at most, usually poorly armed and badly led. The nature of the government's reaction, however, suggests a greater threat to public order than actually materialised. Were they just being cautious? Did their sources of information mislead them? Did the government's over-reaction cause them to drive legitimate reformers into the arms of the subversive minority, thus strengthening the latter and giving them credibility? Or were ministers rather better informed than sceptical historians have sometimes liked to think?

Much of the evidence is circumstantial. The individual historian must use judgement to interpret the evidence offered by reports from spies or statements given by witnesses in court who had turned King's evidence to save their own skins – two of the principal sources for what was going on. Taken as a series of isolated incidents, the case for a sustained revolutionary impulse is not strong, but it is easier to accept the general drift of the evidence, however weak, suspect and implausible some of it might be, than to believe that all we are examining in these years is no more than a series of coincidences.

The continuities are striking but not surprising. With a limited number of obvious meeting places to choose from, their frequent use might be expected. The same could be said of people. If the source of unrest lay in prevailing industrial conditions, then the same areas and the same sorts of people might be expected to respond in similar ways at similar points in the economic cycle, and the same individual names might emerge from a limited pool of local leadership. Does all this amount to anything more sinister than the obvious?

Edward Thompson set the terms of the historical debate in *The Making of the English Working Class*, beginning his argument in chapter 14, 'An Army of Redressers', with the assertion that 'Between Despard and Brandreth there stretches the illegal tradition. It is a tradition which will never be rescued from its obscurity.'[120] The memory of such a tradition was recorded in the late nineteenth-century journalism of Frank Peel's *The Risings of the Luddites, Chartists and Plug-Drawers* (1880), which contained family and community memories and values handed down not only from the 1790s to the 1820s but beyond to Chartism. This tradition linking Despard to Brandreth was described by Thompson as an 'underground' tradition, implying perhaps the deliberate and concealed tunnelling of the miner or mole.[121] My preference is for the less precise 'underworld' used by McCalman: an environment in which all kinds of subversive cultures could knock against one another and thrive, generating from time to time surges of rebellious energy which drew upon ideas and personalities nurtured in the warmth of village ale houses, city taverns and artisan workshops.

The story of the whole makes greater sense than the sum of the parts. When John Blackwell led his attack on the local militia armoury in Sheffield on 14 April 1812 he might have been expressing his anger at the price of bread that year, though if so he would have done better to attack a bakery. Certainly, he was to be found leading a food riot demanding 'Bread or Blood' on 3 December 1816, the day that news of the Spa Fields riot would have reached Sheffield. But the suspicion that Blackwell was not just a food rioter is increased when we then find him attempting to attack the barracks in Sheffield on 11 April 1820, the day appointed for the Grange Moor rising.[122] Perhaps he was just an eccentric troublemaker, but if so he was not the only one. The arrest of William Wolstenholme on 29 May 1817, a delegate at a secret meeting conspiring to join the insurrection on 10 June, might seem melodramatic had he not earlier boasted of being 'a Despard's man' and been a member of a secret revolutionary committee in Sheffield broken up by the authorities in November 1802.[123] Among incriminating papers found in Yorkshire in 1802 was a declaration of aims also found when Despard was arrested in London the same year, though this may be no coincidence since both took their wording from the United Britons' declaration reported to the House of Commons in 1801.[124] But what are we to make of three Luddite 'twisters in' of 1812, Craven Cookson, Stephen Kitchenman and William Thompson of Barnsley, turning up on Grange Moor in 1820?[125] The 'Jacobins' of 1792 might well have been peaceful parliamentary reformers, but John Baines's later connection with the Luddites suggests that either he had become more radical and incautious with age, the reverse of the usual trajectory, or the divisions between what made a man a reformer or a revolutionary, a politician or an economic protester, were neither hard nor fast. The same point can be made about Thomas Bacon of Pentrich and James Wilson of Strathaven. If these men were prepared to resort to violence in one context, were they far from it in another? Apparently random stitches of evidence may in this way be knitted with a little imagination into a garment of some substance, a revolutionary underworld feeding sporadic outbursts and an ever-present threat demanding sustained vigilance from magistrates and ministers.

Notes

1 See the debate on Fox's motion to repeal the Test and Corporation Acts, *Cobbett's Parliamentary History*, House of Commons, 2 March 1790, cols. 432–3.

2 T. Paine, *Rights of Man*, part 2 [1792], chapter 5, second paragraph. Repeatedly quoted in the early nineteenth century, the full quotation reads, 'For a nation

to love liberty, it is sufficient that she knows it; and to be free, it is sufficient that she wills it': see the running title caption for the *Chartist Circular* (28 September 1839–2 July 1842).

3   Goodwin, *Friends of Liberty*, pp. 138–58.

4   *Annual Register* (1794), History of Europe, p. 266.

5   C. Emsley, 'The London "Insurrection" of December 1792: Fact, Fiction, or Fantasy?', *Journal of British Studies*, 17:2 (Spring 1978), pp. 66–86.

6   For the history of the concept of the Convention in this period, see T M. Parssinen, 'Association, convention and anti-parliament in British radical politics, 1771–1848', *English Historical Review*, 88:3 (July 1973), pp. 504–33.

7   For Muir's subsequent escape and remarkable adventures, which confirm that he was a revolutionary then if not before, see P. B. Ellis and S. Mac a' Ghobhainn, *The Scottish Insurrection of 1820* (London, Gollancz, 1970), reissued (London, Pluto, 1989), pp. 67–9, 79–81, 84.

8   M. Thale (ed.), *Selections from the papers of the London Corresponding Society, 1792–1799* (Cambridge, Cambridge University Press, 1983) (hereafter *LCS*), pp. 135–41 (Report from spy Groves, 14 April 1794; spy Gosling's 'Information', 11, 15 April 1794; Report from spy Taylor, 15 April 1794).

9   A. Wharam, *The Treason Trials, 1794* (Leicester, Leicester University Press, 1992).

10 'Second Report from the Committee of Secrecy of the House of Commons respecting seditious practices', *Cobbett's Parliamentary History*, House of Commons, 6 June 1794, cols. 696–8. See also Goodwin, *Friends of Liberty*, pp. 334–7.

11 *Trial of Thomas Hardy for High Treason*, pp. 62–3 in J. Bell, *Bell's Reports of the State Trials for High Treason* (London, Bell, 1794); Wharam, *Treason Trials*, pp. 95–100; H. W. Meikle, *Scotland and the French Revolution* (Edinburgh, Maclehose, 1912), reprinted (New York, Augustus Kelley, 1969), pp. 150–3.

12 C. Emsley, 'The home office and its sources of information and investigation, 1791–1801', p. 551 in *English Historical Review*, 94:3 (July 1979), pp. 532–61.

13 Thale (ed.), *LCS*, p. 83 (LCS General Committee, 19 September 1793); p. 91 (note on government paraphrase of report from spy Lynam, 5 November 1793); p. 131 (note on summary of Report from spy Nodder, 7 April 1794); pp. 155–7 and 165–8 (spy Gosling's 'Information', 9 and 16–17 May 1794).

14 Quoted in Stevenson, *Popular Disturbances*, pp. 168–9.

15 See the debates on the *Habeas Corpus* Suspension Bill, *Cobbett's Parliamentary History* (1794), House of Commons, 15–17 May 1794, cols. 497–573; on Sheridan's motion for the repeal of the *Habeas Corpus* Suspension Act, ibid. (1795), House of Commons, 5 January 1795, cols. 1062–1130; and on the continuation of the *Habeas Corpus* Suspension Act, ibid., House of Commons, 15–28 January 1795, cols. 1144–93.

16 Ellis and Mac a' Ghobhainn, *Scottish Insurrection*, pp. 58–9, 63, 72.

17 Goodwin, *Friends of Liberty*, pp. 322–4; Elliott, *Partners in Revolution*, pp. 62–7.

18 Berresford and Mac a' Ghobhainn, *Scottish Insurrection*, pp. 72–3.

19 The most complete treatment of Ireland is provided by Elliott, *Partners in Revolution*; see also her 'French Subversion in Britain in the French Revolution' in C Jones (ed.), *Britain and Revolutionary France: Conflict, Subversion and Propaganda*, Exeter Studies in History No. 5 (Exeter, University

of Exeter, 1983), pp. 40–52; and 'Ireland and the French Revolution' in H. T. Dickinson (ed.), *Britain and the French Revolution, 1789–1815* (London, Macmillan, 1989), pp. 83–101. Also, M. Duffy, 'War, revolution and the crisis of the British empire' in M. Philp (ed.), *The French Revolution and British Popular Politics* (Cambridge, Cambridge University Press, 1991), pp. 118–45.

20 Emsley, 'The home office', pp. 551–2.

21 For general background and the difficulties of the ministries during these years, see C Emsley, *British Society and the French Wars, 1793–1815* (London, Macmillan, 1979), pp. 41–98.

22 Goodwin, *Friends of Liberty*, pp. 428–38; Wells, *Insurrection*, pp. 64–130.

23 39 Geo III, cap. 79.

24 This subject is discussed in B. Porter, *Plots and Paranoia: A History of Political Espionage in Britain, 1790–1988* (London, Unwin Hyman, 1989), pp. 24–40; and Hone, *Cause of Truth*, pp. 65–82.

25 Sheridan's speech in the debate on his motion for repeal of the *Habeas Corpus* Suspension Act, *Cobbett's Parliamentary History*, House of Commons, 5 January 1795, col. 1068; see also his speech on the *Habeas Corpus* Suspension Bill, *Cobbett's Parliamentary History*, House of Commons, 17 May 1794, col. 544.

26 Hone, *Cause of Truth*, pp. 65–82; Emsley, 'The home office', pp. 532–65.

27 Hone, *Cause of Truth*, p. 51.

28 The most thorough investigation of the naval mutinies is in Wells, *Insurrection*, pp. 79–109; see also Goodwin, *Friends of Liberty*, pp. 407–11 and Elliott, *Partners in Revolution*, pp. 134–44.

29 Thale (ed.), *LCS*, pp. 341–9 (Reports from spy Powell, 5, 12, 22 February 1796).

30 Wells, *Insurrection*, pp. 92–8.

31 Thale (ed.), *LCS*, pp. 396–8 (Minutes of General Committee, 25 May 1797); Goodwin, *Friends of Liberty*, p. 437; Elliott, *Partners in Revolution*, pp. 141–2.

32 Wells, *Insurrection*, pp. 93–5.

33 Wells, *Insurrection*, pp. 102–4.

34 D. Keogh (ed.), *A Patriot Priest. The Life of Father James Coigly, 1761–1798* (Cork, Cork University Press, 1998); Wells, *Insurrection*, pp. 121–8; Elliott, *Partners in Revolution*, pp. 174–83.

35 F. Place, *The Autobiography of Francis Place*, ed. M. Thale (Cambridge, Cambridge University Press, 1972), p. 178.

36 'Report of the Committee of Secrecy of the House of Commons relative to the Proceedings of different Persons and Societies in Great Britain and Ireland Ingaged in a Treasonable Conspiracy', *Cobbett's Parliamentary History*, House of Commons, 15 March 1799, col. 600.

37 'Report of the Committee of Secrecy', *Cobbett's Parliamentary History*, cols. 602–4.

38 Goodwin, *Friends of Liberty*, pp. 438–42; Wells, *Insurrection*, pp. 124–5.

39 Thompson, *The Making*, p. 636.

40 Hone, *Cause of Truth*, pp. 61–3; Thale (ed.), *LCS*, p. 426 (Deposition from spy [Powell?], *c.* 15 April 1798); Place, *Autobiography*, p. 180.

41 F. O'Gorman, *The Whig Party and the French Revolution* (London, Macmillan, 1967), p. 235.

42 Hone, *Cause of Truth*, pp. 42–7 and for Burdett's later association with Despard, see pp. 113–14. The quotations are as given by Hone.

43   M. Elliott,'The "Despard Conspiracy" reconsidered', *Past & Present*, 75 (May 1977), pp. 46–61; Wells, *Insurrection*, pp. 232–37.

44   Wells, *Insurrection*, pp. 237–52; Elliott, *Partners in Revolution*, pp. 285–97; Smith, 'Irish Rebels', pp. 81–3.

45   PRO, PC 1/44A, fo 161, 'R. F.' to Privy Council, 8 August 1799, as quoted in J. Foster, *Class Struggle and the Industrial Revolution* (London, Weidenfeld & Nicholson, 1974), p. 38.

46   Wells, *Insurrection*, pp. 226–37.

47   E. A. Smith, *Whig Principles and Party Politics. Earl Fitzwilliam and the Whig Party, 1748–1833* (Manchester, Manchester University Press, 1975), p. 246.

48   T. D. Whitaker to Lord Sidmouth, 17 September 1808, as quoted in Stevenson, *Popular Disturbances*, p. 231.

49   Dinwiddy, *Radicalism and Reform*, p. 375.

50   PP (1806) 268, *Minutes of Evidence taken before the Committee appointed to consider the State of Woollen Manufacture in England*, pp. 448–9 (6 June 1806).

51   R. Reid, *Land of Lost Content: The Luddite Revolt, 1812* (London, Heinemann, 1986), pp. 46–7.

52   Reid, *Land of Lost Content*, pp. 41–5; Thomis, *Luddites*, pp. 47–65.

53   *Leeds Mercury*, 26 December 1811, as quoted in Reid, *Land of Lost Content*, p. 60.

54   In addition to Reid, Thomis and Dinwiddy, cited above, the most influential and controversial study of Luddism comes in Thompson, *The Making*, pp. 569–659. Useful local studies of Yorkshire Luddism are J. A. Hargreaves, '"A Metropolis of Discontent": Popular Protest in Huddersfield, *c.* 1780–1850', pp. 195–204, in E. A. H. Haigh (ed.), *Huddersfield. A Most Handsome Town: Aspects of the History and Culture of a West Yorkshire Town* (Huddersfield, Kirklees Cultural Services, 1992), pp. 189–220; and A. Brooke and L. Kipling, *Liberty or Death. Radicals, Republicans and Luddites, 1793–1823* (Honley, Workers History Publications, 1993). The enthusiasm of the latter can be offset by the scepticism of B. Bailey, *The Luddite Rebellion* (Stroud, Sutton Publishing, 1998).

55   *Proceedings under the Special Commission at York* (Leeds, Baines, 1813), pp. 70–1.

56   Possibly the same person as, or related to, the Charles Bent employed in 1802. For John Bent, a buyer and seller of waste cotton, see PRO, HO 40/1(8), fos 40–5, Statement of Humphrey Yarwood, 22 June 1812.

57   Dinwiddy, *Radicalism and Reform*, pp. 382–6; Reid, *Land of Lost Content*, p. 201.

58   Sheffield Archives, Wentworth Woodhouse Muniments [hereafter WWM], F45a/12, Copy of Resolutions of the Friends of Liberty, 10 April 1801, for a meeting on Steeton Moor on 20 April 1801, sent to Earl Fitzwilliam by J. R. Busfield, 14 April 1801.

59   R. A. Church and S. D. Chapman, 'Gravener Henson and the Making of the English Working Class', pp. 137–45 in E. L. Jones and G. E. Mingay (eds), *Land, Labour and Population in the Industrial Revolution* (London, Arnold, 1967), pp. 131–61.

60   Reid, *Land of Lost Content*, pp. 211–12, 252–5.

61   PRO, HO 40/1(7), fo 18, copy of a letter sent to Mr Smith, a Huddersfield master, 1812.

62   Thomis, *Luddites*, p. 91.

63   Dinwiddy, *Radicalism and Reform*, pp. 378–9.

64 Dinwiddy, *Radicalism and Reform*, p. 386.

65 PRO, HO 42/123, Statements of J. Taylor and T. Whitehead, 7 May 1812, HO 40/1(8), fos 40–5, Statement of H. Yarwood, 22 June 1812; and Deposition of Thomas Wood [August 1812] printed in F. Raynes, *An Appeal to the Public containing an account of service rendered during the disturbances in the north of England in the year 1812* (London, John Richardson and Baldwin, Cradock and Joy, 1817), p. 92, all as quoted in Dinwiddy, *Radicalism and Reform*, pp. 388–9.

66 Dinwiddy, *Radicalism and Reform*, pp. 392–3.

67 WWM, F46/122, Deposition of Thomas Broughton, 26 August 1812.

68 Elliott, *Partners in Revolution*, p. 362.

69 PRO, HO 40/1, fo 224, F. L. Wood to Earl Fitzwilliam, 17 June 1812.

70 Lord Sidmouth to Lord Sheffield, 1 November 1817, as quoted in Stevenson, *Popular Disturbances*, p. 207.

71 Emsley, *British Society*, pp. 11–12, 133.

72 Reid, *Land of Lost Content*, p. 275.

73 D. Bythell, *The Handloom Weavers. A Study in the English Cotton Industry During the Industrial Revolution* (Cambridge, Cambridge University Press, 1969), pp. 99–104; G. Timmins, *The Last Shift: The Decline of Handloom Weaving in Nineteenth-century Lancashire* (Manchester, Manchester University Press, 1993), p. 28.

74 Hone, *Cause of Truth*, p. 197.

75 W. H. Reid, *The Rise and Dissolution of the Infidel Societies in this Metropolis* (London, Hatchard, 1800) was a tract by an ex-radical turned loyalist.

76 McCalman, *Radical Underworld*, pp. 19–20.

77 McCalman, *Radical Underworld*, pp. 7–25.

78 McCalman, *Radical Underworld*, p. 49.

79 R. Darnton, 'High Enlightenment and the low life of literature in pre-revolutionary France', *Past & Present*, 51 (May 1971), pp. 81–115.

80 McCalman, *Radical Underworld*, p. 49; see also Hone, *Cause of Truth*, pp. 223–37.

81 McCalman, *Radical Underworld*, pp. 50–72, 124–39; D. Worrall, *Radical Culture: Discourse, Resistance and Surveillance, 1790–1820* (Hemel Hempstead, Harvester Wheatsheaf, 1992), pp. 165–200. For millenarianism in general, see J. F. C. Harrison, *The Second Coming: Popular Millenarianism, 1780–1850* (London, Routledge & Kegan Paul, 1979) and C. Garrett, *Respectable Folly: Millenarians and the French Revolution in France and England* (Baltimore, Johns Hopkins University Press, 1975).

82 T. M. Parssinen, 'The Revolutionary Party in London, 1816–20', *Bulletin of the Institute of Historical Research*, 45:111 (May 1972), pp. 266–82.

83 For Hunt's relationship with the Spenceans, see Belchem, *'Orator' Hunt*, pp. 54–70.

84 Belchem, *'Orator' Hunt*, pp. 58–70; Hone, *Cause of Truth*, pp. 263–6.

85 Smith, *Whig Principles*, pp. 334, 336; Hone, *Cause of Truth*, p. 265.

86 S .Bamford, *Passages in the Life of a Radical* [1844], ed. W. H. Chaloner (London, Cass, 1967), chapters 2–7, 12–13, and 26. See also Thompson, *The Making*, pp. 713–26.

87 Bamford, *Passages*, p. 15.

88 Bamford, *Passages*, p. 31.

89 Thompson, *The Making*, pp. 714–15.

90   Bamford, *Passages*, p. 42.

91   Bamford, *Passages*, p. 44.

92   Bamford, *Passages*, p. 156.

93   WWM, F45/177, Deposition of John Dickinson, linen draper of Dewsbury, sworn before J. P. Heywood, 16 June 1817.

94   Thompson, *The Making*, p. 717, following Cobbett's Petition to the House of Commons and the Deposition he obtained from William Stevens in America, both printed in *Cobbett's Weekly Political Register*, 33:18 (16 May 1818), cols. 539–64.

95   Bamford, *Passages*, pp. 155–8.

96   The fullest account of the Pentrich rising is J. Stevens, *England's Last Revolution: Pentrich, 1817* (Buxton, Moorland Publishing Co., 1977).

97   WWM, F45/189–91, Information and Examination of John Buckley, sworn before Benjamin Haigh Allen, 18 July 1817.

98   Hargreaves, 'Metropolis of Discontent', p. 205.

99   Stevens, *England's Last Revolution*, pp. 11–108; and map on pp. 26–7.

100 Stevens, *England's Last Revolution*, p. 103; F. Peel, *The Risings of the Luddites, Chartists and Plug-Drawers*, 4th edition [text of 3rd edition of 1895, with a new introduction by Edward Thompson] (London, Cass, 1968), p. 285.

101 Prothero, *Artisans and Politics*, pp. 91–2.

102 McCalman, *Radical Underworld*, pp. 132–3.

103 Belchem, *'Orator' Hunt*, p. 57.

104 The best account is D Read, *Peterloo: The 'Massacre' and its Background* (Manchester, Manchester University Press, 1958).

105 The text of both letters is given in J. Macdonnell (ed.), *Reports of State Trials, new series vol. 1, 1820–1823* (London, HMSO, 1888), Appendix B, cols. 1372–3.

106 Letter from John Gale Jones, *Republican*, 6:5 (28 June 1822), p. 138. Emphasis in original.

107 Trials of John Knowles, James Morris, George Dewhurst and others at Lancaster Assizes, 1820, in Macdonnell (ed), *State Trials*, cols. 497–608.

108 PRO, HO 42/197, fo 384, 11 October 1819, as quoted in Worrall, *Radical Culture*, p. 170. Emphasis in original. Cashman had been executed for his part in the Spa Fields riots in 1816.

109 Worrall, *Radical Culture*, pp. 178–200; Prothero, *Artisans*, pp. 116–31.

110 Prothero, *Artisans*, pp. 132–55; J. Stevenson, 'The Queen Caroline Affair' in J. Stevenson (ed.), *London in the Age of Reform* (Oxford, Blackwell, 1977), pp. 117–48. See also his *Popular Disturbances*, (London, Longman, 1979), pp. 199–203. For a summary of the significance of the affair, see R. McWilliam, *Popular Politics*, pp. 7–13.

111 Devon CRO, Sidmouth Papers, Sidmouth to B. Bloomfield, 3–4 March 1820, as quoted in Stevenson, *Popular Disturbances*, p. 198.

112 Belchem, *'Orator' Hunt*, pp. 130, 155; Thompson, *The Making*, p. 725.

113 National Library of Scotland, MS 10, Melville Papers, Charles Hope to Lord Melville, 17 December 1819, as quoted in Ellis and Mac a' Ghobhainn, *Scottish Insurrection*, p. 131.

114 Ellis and Mac a' Ghobhainn, *Scottish Insurrection*, pp. 34–5, 140–1. For a different reading of the evidence, see Thomis and Holt, *Threats of Revolution*, pp. 62–84.

115 Ellis and Mac a'Ghobhainn argue persuasively from a range of primary sources but their lack of detailed footnotes makes it hard to check their interpretation which is imaginative and highly emotive; Thomis and Holt (*Threats of Revolution*, p. 79) are hightly critical, commenting that circumstantial evidence offers 'some slight support to the view advanced at the time and later that the Scottish rebels, like their English predecessors of 1817, were the victims of *agents provocateurs*', but adding, 'The documentary evidence does not support this view; nor do the known facts support the latest extravagant version of the *provocateur* thesis, that the rebels were Scottish nationalists who were led into a trap by the machinations of the Westminster government and its agents.'

116 *Leeds Mercury*, 8 April 1820

117 *Leeds Mercury*, 8 April 1820; *Manchester Observer*, 8 April 1820, drawing on *Leeds Intelligencer* account; Brooke and Kipling, *Liberty or Death*, pp. 75–90; Thompson, *The Making*, p. 776; Hargreaves, 'Metropolis of Discontent', p. 206; Peel, *Risings of the Luddites*, pp. 307–8.

118 *Leeds Mercury*, 15 April 1820; *Manchester Observer*, 15 April 1820; Thompson, *The Making*, pp. 776–7; Hargreaves, 'Metropolis of Discontent', p. 206; Peel, *Risings of the Luddites*, pp. 308–12; F. J. Kaijage, 'Working-class Radicalism in Barnsley, 1816–1820', pp. 122–3 in S. Pollard and C. Holmes (eds), *Essays in the Economic and Social History of South Yorkshire* (Sheffield, South Yorkshire County Council, 1976), pp. 118–34.

119 F. K. Donnelly and J. L. Baxter, 'Sheffield and the English Revolutionary Tradition', pp. 108–9, in Pollard and Holmes (eds), *Essays*, pp. 90–117.

120 Thompson, *The Making*, p. 515.

121 Thompson, *The Making*, p. 923; see also A. W. Smith, 'Irish Rebels', pp. 78–85.

122 Donnelly and Baxter, 'Sheffield', pp. 99, 107

123 Donnelly and Baxter, 'Sheffield', pp. 100–10.

124 J. R. Dinwiddy, 'The "Black Lamp" in Yorkshire, 1801–1802', *Past & Present*, 64 (August 1974), pp. 119–20.

125 Dinwiddy, *Radicalism and Reform*, p. 393. Peel was to claim that it was Cookson and Kitchen[man] who betrayed the Grange Moor rising in 1820: *The Risings of the Luddites*, pp. 311–12.

Revolution or reform, 1830–32

Between 1830 and 1832 Britain underwent major constitutional change during a period of economic hardship, with unrest in both agricultural and industrial areas. At the same time, a new series of revolutions on the Continent reminded politicians of the impermanence of political regimes, as the Restoration settlement of 1814–15 was torn up first in Paris and then in Brussels. The July 1830 revolution in Paris was a clear warning of what might happen when an intransigent and reactionary government was faced with a strengthened opposition party, supported by popular pressure on the streets fuelled by economic discontents.

In Britain, where the Duke of Wellington's Tory ministry had been weakened by the secession of the ultra-Tories after Catholic Emancipation, George IV died on 26 June. The change of monarch necessitated a general election, in the middle of which came news of the revolution in France on 29 July. A month later, the first threshing machine was destroyed in what was to become known as the 'Swing' riots. The Duke refused to contemplate reform, leading the Whigs to compel his resignation on 16 November and to introduce their reform proposals, thus precipitating a political crisis which was not resolved until June 1832. By this time, not only had large parts of the south and east of England been engulfed by riots, but Merthyr Tydfil, in south Wales, had fallen to an insurrection which lasted three days; Bristol had suffered major destruction of property; Nottingham castle had been burnt down; middle-class political unions had prepared to form their own National Guard, and working-class political unions had again talked of arming and revolution. During May 1832 there had seemed a genuine possibility that, had Wellington played a Polignac and formed a ministry to serve a reactionary king, then William IV might have suffered the fate of Charles X and the last of the Bourbons would have been followed by the last of the Hanoverians.

The Reform Bill crisis

There was a variety of possible approaches to constitutional change in Britain between 1790 and 1850. At one extreme, revolutionaries demanded a complete renewal of the constitution; at the other were those who wanted Parliament merely to be reformed so that certain specific social and economic measures could be carried to remedy the grievances of the people; and in the middle were those who wished to maintain the existing framework of the constitution but with a franchise widened to recognise the political rights of all (males) who paid taxes. The most common position was based on a combination of the second and third positions, extending parliamentary representation as a right but linking it to the need to remedy specific grievances. On two occasions, however, a fundamental change was made to the constitution, and in each case the reason was Ireland.

The first was the 1801 Act of Union between Britain and Ireland, carried as a result of government policy and not by popular demand. The second was the 1829 Catholic Relief Act (usually called Catholic Emancipation) which admitted Catholics to the Union Parliament at Westminster and finally broke the link between Protestantism and the British state. This latter was not achieved without a struggle and resulted from the re-organisation of Irish popular politics in the 1820s by Daniel O'Connell. Although he abandoned the methods of the United Irishmen, his Catholic Association of 1823 was nevertheless revolutionary in intent. Its combination of a formidable, nation-wide organisation and the support given to it by a peasantry notorious for their propensity to civil disorder and rural terrorism, led the government to ban the Association by name in 1825. By the simple device of renaming it the New Catholic Association, O'Connell continued.

Matters were brought to a head in 1828, when he was elected to Westminster at a by-election in County Clare. The Duke of Wellington's government gave way and carried the Catholic Relief Act, using all the 'corrupt' devices known to unreformed ministers to force their will on a reluctant House of Commons. Robert Peel later explained his change of approach: whereas formerly he had 'much doubted whether the removal of the disabilities complained of would restore tranquillity to Ireland', in 1828 there were 'circumstances which the time is not yet come to disclose, which convinced me there would be more danger in continuing to resist these claims than in yielding to them'.[1] By this he appears to have meant that he had information of a real threat of major disorder in Ireland if the government continued to resist. Two conclusions were apparent from O'Connell's success. One, reached by outraged Tory Protestants, was that the House of Commons needed reforming to make it more representative of British Protestant opinion. The other, reached by parliamentary reformers, was that a peaceful, organised mass movement, backed by the unspoken threat of force by numbers, could compel a hostile Parliament to concede fundamental constitutional change. O'Connell went on to inspire the formation of the Birmingham Political Union (BPU) at the end of 1829 and to be associated with the beginning of the movement for the People's Charter in 1837.[2]

O'Connell's peaceful revolution not only destroyed the remnants of the Protestant Constitution: it split the Tory party which had formed the core of administrations since the French Revolution, it made reform an election issue, and it gave the Whigs the chance to take the initiative and introduce reform. The years 1830–32 therefore provided a unusual opportunity for change. The movement for reform in the country was, for once, campaigning *for* the implementation of government policy, not against it.

Earl Grey's first Whig ministry, which introduced the first Reform Bill in March 1831, was a minority government supported by disillusioned Tories. Although the terms of the Bill fell far short of the universal manhood suffrage demanded by the extremists, its proposals for the abolition of many rotten and nomination boroughs, and transfer of seats to new boroughs as well as subdivided counties, went further than many of the propertied classes had expected. The Bill passed its second reading by only one vote. Amid mounting tension in the country, Grey asked the King to dissolve Parliament and call a General Election. This was most unusual, but not without precedent – the King had prematurely ended parliaments in 1784, 1806 and 1807 – but for ministers to take the initiative and go to the country seeking support on a single issue – in effect a plebiscite – was revolutionary. Grey received the support he sought and was now able to confront the two unelected parts of the legislature, the Lords and the King, with the will of 'the people'. So long as the government remained in control of the situation, the revolution from above was likely to proceed peacefully; but, in relying on public support to rally wavering supporters and put pressure on the Lords and King to acquiesce, Grey knew he was riding the back of a tiger.

Twice his opponents threatened to push him off. In October 1831, the House of Lords rejected the Reform Bill by 41 votes; and in May 1832 the King refused Grey's request to create a Whig majority in the House of Lords and so the government resigned. The King then called on the Duke of Wellington to form an administration. In the event, Wellington failed to form an administration and instead persuaded opponents of the Bill in the Lords to abstain. Parliament was thus peacefully reformed. The property base of the House of Commons was extended without altering the overall balance of power or yielding anything of substance to those who wanted fundamental constitutional change. The Whig version of history, whereby revolutions were to be directed peacefully by themselves from above, was confirmed; only, they no longer spoke of revolution but simply of Reform.

Political unions and urban riots

The Whig view of the Constitution was aristocratic. That is, it identified the Lords as occupying the sensible middle ground between the dangers of democracy (the Commons) and autocracy (the King). Whig aristocrats were the safest and surest means of providing enlightened government for the benefit of all. But from the later eighteenth century an alternative view was growing which identified the middle ground as that existing between the old landed and political classes represented in Parliament on the one hand, and the propertyless majority on the other.[3] This new middle 'class' was quite narrowly defined although it claimed to lead and speak for the whole 'people'. It was urban and drew on the commercial and manufacturing classes whom David Ricardo (1772–1823), the political economist, identified as those deriving their incomes from profits in his threefold division of society into rent, profit and wages – landlords, capitalists and workers – but it did not necessarily include lesser middle men such as shopkeepers and small employing artisans whose politics were often 'working class'.

This political – and, to a lesser extent, economic – middle can be called a middle class provided this phrase is not confused with the *bourgeoisie* of later Marxist theory. It thought of itself in economic terms as leading the industrious classes: that is, all who worked and added to the country's wealth as opposed to the idle rich, whose rentals were the first charge on their profits (which excused low wages), and whose political places and pensions were funded by the taxes paid by the honest and industrious. Occupying the moral high ground between aristocratic vice and vulgar licence, this middle class led the popular demand for reform of the political system in 1830–32. Though some who spoke with the more democratic voice of the people did not share the middle class's image of itself, only when the 1832 Reform Act had drawn a line through the reformers, including the 'middle class' among those directly represented in Parliament and excluding the rest, did democratic leaders finally create a separate political movement among those with little or no property, and appropriate to themselves the phrase 'working classes' now that the 'middle classes' had joined the exploiting rich. Though it is easy with such language still in the process of formation to slip into the parallel socialist language which has since dominated the writings of historians, it is important to remember that in the early nineteenth century this language of class was primarily political, employed for propagandist purposes to persuade reformers to support a moderate 'middle class' or extremist 'working class' stance, irrespective of actual economic class.

The first political unions were middle-class affairs, set up in the major and largely unrepresented urban centres of Britain to demand an extension of the franchise and separate representation for urban interests. Political unions in Birmingham, Leeds, Manchester, Newcastle upon Tyne and London took the lead in articulating public opinion through the local press and mass meetings to put pressure on the government to persist with its programme of reform. Their image and strategy demanded they speak on behalf of the whole outraged community. In Birmingham, where the first union was founded in December 1829, it was a 'Political Union for the Protection of Public Rights' – a 'General Political Union between the Lower and the Middle Classes of the People'.[4] In London, the National Political Union was not 'a Union of the Working Classes, nor of the Middle Classes, nor of any other Class, but of all Reformers, of the masses and of the millions. The *National Political Union*, is essentially a Union of the People.'[5]

This degree of co-operation across such a wide political and social spectrum proved hard to maintain and, during 1831, rival democratic unions were formed in some cities, notably the National Union of the Working Classes (NUWC) in London, which explicitly rejected the middle class view of itself and reform. As Philip Brown pointed out, these democratic unions were able to draw on a tradition of political thought and organisation reaching back to the French Revolution and, as then, they presented the greatest potential threat of revolution in that their demands went beyond anything Whig ministers were pre-pared to contemplate.[6] But to judge by their ambiguous language and actions, the middle-class unions could also be seen as a threat in 1831–32.

The reaction to the impending defeat of the first Reform Bill in March 1831 was a sign of what was to come. The *Annual Register* voiced the concerns of the conservative classes and captured the mood of impending revolution:

> Everywhere, the political unions boasted of the numbers whom they could bring into the field. The chairman of that of Birmingham openly declared, that they could supply two armies, each of them as numerous and brave as that which had conquered at Waterloo, if the king and his ministers should require them in the contest with the boroughmongers – under which appellation were comprehended all who differed from them in opinion.

The paper went on to ask, with some rhetorical sarcasm, 'In what ways were the armies to support ministers against an anticipated vote of the House of Commons?' and then answered itself in language drawing on the Cromwellian nightmare of the seventeenth century to which conservatives usually appealed in such circumstances. In fact, as the *Register* admitted, the real reason for the talk of armies was to force opponents into making a concession to reform.[7]

By going to the country to increase his majority in the House of Commons, Grey defused the situation.

The reality of the violence became apparent in October, when Grey's Second Bill was rejected by the House of Lords. Even though the leaders of the political unions drew back from carrying out their threats, the popular mood was less easily contained. The Lords had rejected the Bill by 41 votes and it was quickly noticed that 21 bishops had voted against the measure and only 2 for it. The bishops had, in effect, determined the fate of the Bill. The anger of the mobs was turned against known opponents of Reform, especially bishops.

Demonstrations were held in London during which the windows of the houses of prominent opponents of the Bill were broken, and the Dukes of Cumberland and Wellington, and the Marquis of Londonderry were assaulted in the street. In Derby, the mob released prisoners from the gaol and had to be quelled by the army after two days of disturbances. While the cavalry was in Derby, in Nottingham another mob broke into the Castle, home of the Duke of Newcastle, and burnt it to the ground. In the House of Commons, Sir Charles Wetherall, Recorder of Bristol, used these incidents to mount a Tory attack on Lord John Russell and the government. Wetherall's arrival in Bristol on 29 October then became the signal for a worse outbreak of rioting. The Mansion House (including its wine cellar) was sacked and the troops failed to contain the mob who rioted unrestrained for three days: the Mansion House, Excise Office, Customs House, 4 toll houses and 3 prisons were destroyed, along with the Bishop's palace and 42 houses and warehouses. Parts of Queen's Square were reduced to ruins. The casualty list was greater than at Peterloo.

The exact number is unknown but a conservative estimate was 12 people killed and nearly 100 injured, although the latter figure could have been up to 400; 180 individuals were committed for their part in the riot and 50 were charged with the capital offences of rioting and burning, of whom 5 were eventually executed. It was the worst urban disorder since the Gordon Riots of 1780.[8]

This extensive rioting did not constitute a revolution but it was the sort of behaviour out of which revolutions could be made. More ominous was what was happening in Birmingham. Peace, law and order were the watchwords of the Political Union but there was a growing movement in the wake of the Bristol riots for the formation of a French-style National Guard to secure property, which would in effect be a private army of citizens under the control not of the magistrates but the Political Union. Although no one was to be armed by the Union there was nothing to prevent individuals from arming themselves in self-defence. The Duke of Wellington was convinced that this was a proposal for an armed association comparable to that of the United Irishmen, and the government persuaded Thomas Attwood to drop the plan.[9] At the same time a Royal Proclamation was issued against political unions adopting a military-style organisation.[10] Whether this proposal was ever seriously intended has been questioned by Attwood's biographer. The unions needed the Whig ministers as much as the ministers needed the unions in their struggle to carry their Bill. So long as Grey remained in charge at Westminster, peace, law and order were secure.[11]

When Grey's government resigned in May 1832, therefore, the resolve of the political unions was tested as they sought to imply revolution without actually precipitating it. There was widespread talk of withholding taxes, and normally law-abiding newspapers screamed in fury. The *Dispatch* declaimed:

> '*Reform or Revolution*' is the cry of every man who deserves the name of Englishman. The idea of twenty-four millions of free men submitting to a denial of their undoubted rights by less than two hundred beings called Peers, is utterly out of the question. The only wonder is, that the people have so long submitted to the delay of their new Magna Charta. The time has at length arrived when Englishmen are called upon to act – to show their strength – to teach these insolent and ignorant aristocrats that with all their boasted wealth and empty titles, they are but dust in the balance, compared with the mighty energies against which they have dared to array themselves.[12]

The paper was of course, referring only to Tory peers, not to Whigs, and in higher Whig circles Lord Milton, heir to Earl Fitzwilliam, actually began withholding his taxes, later justifying his action with typical Whig logic: '*Illegal* it may have been . . . *unconstitutional* I do not think it was, for it is consistent with the spirit of the constitution that the subject should refuse his taxes when the government acts in such a manner as to forfeit its claim to obedience.'[13]

When men of property could claim that their understanding of the constitution was above the law, and that there was a constitutional right to bear arms in self defence, then revolution might indeed be near at hand.

This is what Francis Place thought. The fear which he appears to have shared with many in the political unions was that if the Duke of Wellington were given a free hand, he would use troops to suppress the reform movement. Under these circumstances liberty would need to be defended as in 1642 and 1688. As a lesser evil to the financial panic and economic ruin which this would bring, Place and his co-conspirators devised a plan of economic action to prevent the Duke forming a government, and on 12 May the London Political Union issued its celebrated placard, 'TO STOP THE DUKE GO FOR GOLD'. Despite Place's recollection that the intention was to avoid revolution, he must have known that a financial crisis would not only affect the proper-tied classes but also, by causing widespread economic dislocation and unemployment, threaten further civil unrest. This has led some histo-rians to conclude that the reformers were playing a dangerous game of bluff. If so, it appeared to work, for three days later Wellington advised the King to send for Lord Grey and the crisis was soon over.

We shall never be sure whether Place and the others would actu-ally have been prepared to precipitate a financial crisis but it is clear from the way in which Place represented the episode that he regarded the alternative as worse. On Sunday 20 May Place sat down to review the events of the past few days and record his assessment of them:

> The impending mischief has passed over us, thanks to the inlightened [sic] state to which large masses of the people have attained; thanks indeed to their foresight, the steady conduct of their leaders and the unlimited confidence the people felt in themselves, and that which they placed in the men who came forward in the common cause. But for these demonstrations a revolution would have commenced, which would have been the act of the whole people to a greater extent than any which had ever before been accomplished. Now, relieved from all present apprehension, the Sunday was indeed a day of repose, of solid gratulation, and satisfaction to the people generally, in every rank and station.

Place attributed this state of affairs to the 'middle class' who had steered a moderate and sensible course between the extremes of aris-tocratic reaction and popular licence.[14] He was aware that the latter still remained a threat, as he continued:

> Here let us hope the turmoil will end. We were within a moment of general rebellion, and had it been possible for the Duke of Wellington to have formed an administration, the King and the people would have been at issue, it would have been soon decided, but the mischief to property, especially to the great Landowners and the Fundholders – and personally to immense

numbers would have been terrible indeed. . . . Happily the general demonstration of resistance compelled the Duke to withdraw and made it necessary for the king to recal [sic] Earl Grey to office, with the assurance of means to carry the Reform Bills unimpaired and unmutilated in their principal clauses. The bold honest discreet men who took the lead during the eleven days from the 7th to the 18th of the month have saved the country.[15]

Whereas Place was always ready to regard the revolutionary threats of others as foolish or empty, he did not see his own involvement in this light. Thus May 1832 was for him the moment when revolution was avoided only by timely concession. Many historians from all points of the political spectrum have come to a similar judgement. Edward Thompson, who was not a historian to trust Francis Place's judgement, wrote: 'In the autumn of 1831 and in the 'days of May' Britain was within an ace of a revolution which, once commenced, might well . . . have prefigured, in its rapid radicalization, the revolutions of 1848 and the Paris Commune.'[16] His reason for this belief lay in the activities of the popular political unions which were gaining ground in 1831 and were prepared to support the middle-class effort, if at all, only as a first step towards a real reform.

So far as the government's perceptions were concerned, the most immediate threat came in London, from the NUWC, founded in April 1831 by radicals schooled in the literature of Paine, Spence, and socialists such as William Thompson and Robert Owen. Some of their speakers, like John Gale Jones, were veterans of the 1790s; others, like William Benbow, had emerged as extreme radicals after 1815. At the heart of their organisation were the publishers and editors of the 'blasphemous and seditious press' which, in response to the reform agitation, had revived in open defiance of the restrictive stamp legislation which had suppressed them at the end of 1819. The most influential of these men was Henry Hetherington whose *Poor Man's Guardian* led the way in the 'war of the unstamped'. These extreme radicals met at various places in London but were identified with the Rotunda, a lecture theatre in Blackfriars where people like Robert Taylor ('the Devil's Chaplain'), Richard Carlile, and John Gale Jones performed for the benefit of their radical audiences, and police informers were sent with their notebooks to gather evidence for possible prosecutions and to keep a watchful eye and ear on what was happening there.

Very early in the crisis, two of the leaders were disposed of when Carlile was sentenced to two years for sedition in January 1831 and Taylor received a similar sentence for blasphemy in July.[17]

Place knew these people well, and appreciated the danger they posed not only to civil order and property but also to his own view of how a successful and peaceful revolution should be conducted. To begin with he did not think much of the organisation of the NUWC, but by late October, he had to admit that

> The influence of the union had become extensive, and was increasing, it was felt, acknowledged and acted upon in many places, especially in the large manufacturing towns, in Bristol and in the southern and south western parts of England.
>
> The resolutions passed at the weekly meetings of the Union in London, and the speeches made at these meetings being regularly published in the *Poor Man's Guardian* induced large numbers of the working people in the country to attribute an importance to the union it did not possess.

With this growth of provincial organisations came a dangerously exaggerated notion of their own strength and their capacity for conducting a serious revolution by physical force:

> The leaders of all these unions, with but a few exceptions had suceeded [*sic*] in persuading themselves that the time was coming when the whole of the working men would be ready to rise en masse and take the management of their own affairs, i.e. the management of the affairs of the nation into their own hands . . .
>
> There were, at this time, several delegates from Manchester, and some from other places in London. Most of these came to me and I conversed with them. So thoroughly satisfied were these men that in a very few months 'the people would rise and do themselves justice', that when I expressed my doubts, they became irritated, and on being pushed to extremities, they threw aside all disguise and declared their conviction that within a few months there would be a simultaneous rising of the whole working population, and then the proud tyrants who oppressed them and kept them out of their just rights would be taught a lesson, such a lesson as none before had ever been taught. They admitted it was probable that large numbers of their fellows would be slain in the contest which might, and probably would take place. A great many they said might perhaps be *'murdered'*,

but numbers would prevail and then ample revenge would be taken. They talked of the men they would lose as a matter of very small importance, a trifling sacrifice to obtain a great good, they said it would be of no importance to the great body, they would not be missed, and might as well be killed in so righteous a cause, as linger on in a life of privation and misery. I should be convinced by the circumstances which would take place that what they said was true. I need only wait until a commencement was made the result of which was certain.[18]

This was dangerous talk if the men of Manchester and elsewhere really believed it and were then prepared to act on their belief.

The popular or 'low' unions peaked in the late autumn of 1831 at the time of the Nottingham, Bristol and other riots when the middle-class political unions were planning their National Guard. The London leaders proposed a meeting in White Conduit Fields on 7 November to coincide with simultaneous mass meetings across the country. Those attending were advised to take pointed staves with them – for self defence: the memory of Peterloo ran deep, or was a ready excuse. A manual was published on street fighting, entitled *Defensive Instructions for the People. Containing the New and Improved Combination of Arms called Foot Lancers; Miscellaneous Instructions on the subject of Small Arms and Ammunition, Street and House Fighting, and Field Fortification*, by Colonel Francis Macerone. Although this cost five shillings, the *Poor Man's Guardian* obligingly printed extracts in a special number in April 1832.[19] It gave instructions on the use of staves against cavalry.

The White Conduit Fields meeting was postponed, however, after the Home Secretary had threatened to prosecute the organisers, and on 9 November the committee of the NUWC meeting at Benbow's house rejected a motion from one of the Rotunda leaders, George Petrie, to drill the people in military fashion. Nevertheless, police spies continued to inform the Home Office of extreme plans to arm the people and it was this knowledge, taken with the Birmingham plans, which led the government to recall Parliament early on 6 December and to issue the Royal Proclamation against the political unions.

Even so, the 'low' unions were not as easily brought into line as the middle-class unions. In Manchester a series of mass meetings was held between 28 November and 22 January in defiance of the

Proclamation, at which, it was alleged, there was a concerted plan 'to disturb the public peace, and by seditious and inflammatory speeches and otherwise to excite the subjects of our lord the King to insurrection and insubordination, and to subvert and overturn lawful and settled institutions of the realm'. The jury at the subsequent sedition trials disagreed, but did find the leaders guilty on a lesser charge of 'having riotously and tumultuously assembled together to disturb the public peace'.[20] The jury was probably right. There was much heated talk, and the placard summoning a meeting on 26 December had called for a National Convention, for which Benbow repeatedly pressed at meetings of the NUWC, but by December the worst appeared to be over. The peak of independent popular protest had come in the autumn when the middle-class unions held back in the face of popular violence, allowing the government to suppress illegality and proceed with moderate reform. By May 1832, when Place and others were willing to talk of revolution, popular support had been brought firmly into line behind the strategy of the middle class. The protests of the *Poor Man's Guardian* or Henry Hunt about the folly of supporting a Bill which did not give truly radical reform went largely unheeded until too late. The different nature of the two revolutionary peaks, and their failure to synchronise, considerable reduced the threat of these years. The undirected violence of October 1831 was alarming but largely negative; the potential for violence in May 1832 was real but never tested.

The Welsh rising, 1831

English concerns with the prospect of revolution in October 1831 and May 1832 should not obscure the fact that one major insurrection did occur, far more serious than the Bristol riots. Yet it resulted in no state trials for treason and of the twenty-eight people charged, most were only for riot. Five capital sentences were passed but only one man, Richard Lewis (*alias* Dic Penderyn) was hanged. In the raw, half-formed society of the Welsh valleys, Merthyr Tydfil was the largest town in Wales, with a population of about 27,000, a quarter of whom were iron workers. It was here that riot passed into insurrection during the summer of 1831.

The industrial workers of South Wales had a long history of

violent protest, partly generated by conditions in the valleys and partly responding to the wider British movement for revolutionary change. During the winter of 1816–17, a paper found in the Tredegar ironworks urged

> The Poor Workmen of Tredegar to prepare Yourselves with Musquets Pistols, Pikes, Spears and all kinds of Weapons to join the Nattion and put down like torrent all Kings, Regents, Tyrants, of all description and banish out of the Country, every Traitor to this Common Cause and to Bewry famine and distress in the same grave [*sic*].[21]

More specific was a paper found near Penydarren, dated 20 December 1816:

> everyone are required as soon as the news arrives of our preparing to take up arms to enforce these just demands, that all will hold themselves in readiness and Procure arms or some other weapons for either defence or annoyance as circumstances may require and to accomplish this you are recommended to observe that the Soldiers are every night dispersed about the Public Houses and in a defensive state so that when the time comes it would be an easy matter to take them and their officers firearms at a stroke and seize their arms, Horses and all, without any bloodshed: and you ought also to take every one of your Masters Prisoners as well.

The grievances were low wages and bad trade. The latter, together with high taxes, was blamed on the government. Thus economic conditions prompted political protest,

> so join hand and heart to overthrow tyranny and oppression and be a people at once free and happy therefore shout out with one voice down with all tyrants and oppressors and woe be to all that will take their parts [*sic*].[22]

So the mood which created the insurgencies at Spa Fields, Folly Hall and Pentrich had its counterpart in South Wales.

In the great south Wales strike of 1816, the most resolute resistance was shown in the east of the region, in Brecknockshire and Monmouthshire, and it was here that a particularly violent movement known as the 'Scotch Cattle' developed among ironworkers and colliers during the next few years. Though there were many subdivisions of workmen, the main social cleavage ran between a small middle class and a much larger working class distinguished by language and religion as well as manual labour. The Scotch Cattle was an illegal organisation which operated in a similar manner to the Luddites, beginning with threatening letters to intimidate employers, blacklegs and strike-breakers, and following up with damage to the property of those who were judged to have offended. The men's purpose was industrial, obtaining by terror what they lacked the industrial strength to achieve.[23]

Though few direct links can be suggested between the industrial violence associated with the Scotch Cattle and the reform movement of the early 1830s, the violent background of the Scotch Cattle helps explain the turbulent politics of the valleys throughout the 1830s. Following the defeat of the first Reform Bill in March 1831 there was rioting in several parts of Wales, notably in Carmarthen where there was sporadic unrest throughout May with a resurgence of violence in October,[24] but it was in Merthyr that the most alarming events occurred. Here on 9 and 10 May 1831, a pro-reform mob attacked the courtroom and then forced the release of prisoners. This gave the rioters confidence to go further. They took over a Reform meeting on 30 May in order to voice their local, mainly economic grievances, and then, amid increasing violence, shops were attacked in an attempt to secure the return of goods seized in settlement of debts. On Thursday 2 June the Riot Act was read and ignored. By midnight Merthyr was in the hands of the mob. The following morning an attempt at nego-tiation failed and the mob attacked the troops. In the gunfire that fol-lowed, at least sixteen rioters were killed. They dispersed to arm themselves and on 4 June managed to ambush and disarm a detach-ment of the Swansea Cavalry on its way to reinforce the troops in Merthyr. Violence continued in the town and surrounding area for several more days and it was not until 6 June, after 450 soldiers with fixed bayonets near Dowlais had cut off a supporting crowd advanc-ing from Monmouthshire, that the military finally gained the upper hand in Merthyr itself.

The nature of this Merthyr rising has been much disputed. Many of its ritualistic features were reminiscent of the Scotch Cattle, although the main area for Scotch Cattle activity was further east in Monmouthshire. Economic and employment issues were clearly important in the rioters' demands and the local liberal press naturally stressed these aspects of the affair, but two of the rising's most recent historians were agreed that economics and industrial relations were not the whole story. According to David Jones

> The Merthyr massacre was a unique popular disturbance, one which indicated the changing nature of society. Plunged into the economic and political turmoil of the 1790s and the post-war depression, the 'lower orders' of Merthyr Tydfil emerged during the reform crisis with a new awareness of themselves as a body or 'class' oppressed alike by employers, magistrates, and legislators.[25]

Less circumspectly, Gwyn Williams declared, 'from the beginning it was an *insurrection* designed to effect *Reform* and overthrow a social order'.[26] The symbol adopted by the leaders was the red flag of Reform, so the Tory press may not have been too fanciful in seeing the riots as the work of 'revolutionary forgemen, Jacobin moulders, democratic colliers, and demagogue furnace-men'.[27] Political preachers fanned the flames of rebellion no less than union organisers.

The idea of using an industrial strike to promote radical political reform was being advocated in London at this time by William Benbow and there was some support for this approach in Merthyr. Magistrates were therefore alarmed when, in August, the colliers' union spread across the Valleys, apparently in association with political clubs and protected by a secret oath. The employers responded with a lock out, supported by the magistrates who denied poor relief to union men and their families. The struggle was bitter and the climax of the workers' desperation coincided with the Bristol riots and preparations for simultaneous reform meetings on 7 November. 'This place is in a dreadful state', wrote one informant. 'The moment the news arrived of the disturbance at Bristol, the Union Clubs all met, what happened I know not. All is quiet but everyone is apprehensive. Thousands are out of employment and starving. The men know all that passes and are evidently plotting. They talk of revolution.'[28]

But despite the fears of the magistrates, nothing happened. Torrential rain and tight military precautions saw to that. Even more so than Bristol, Merthyr in 1831 demonstrated what could develop when economic and political grievances came together to overwhelm the inadequate local forces of law and order. It also demonstrated that, whatever the popular leaders might think and say, effective economic and political power ultimately lay not with the people, but with their employers and the military.

Rural unrest

Urban riots were worrying to local property owners but most were usually containable and the Home Office overall seems to have taken a relaxed attitude to all but the most alarming reports received from magistrates. Industrial unrest was a problem for the manufacturing classes and the occasional urban disturbance was as much to be expected as rioting at election time. If the severity of the government's reaction is a measure of the seriousness with which unrest was regarded, then things were very different in the countryside. Poaching and incendiarism were endemic. Where the image was of a paternalistic and deferential society, the reality was often an oppressed and resentful class of labourers, ill-paid, underemployed, and unable to escape the controlled environment of rural life for the anonymity and freedom of the town. Occasional outbursts drew attention to the unease beneath the calm. One such had swept through the Cambridgeshire Fens in 1816. No one has claimed that these riots were overtly political. Their long-term causes were enclosure, deteriorating conditions of labour and abject poverty; their immediate causes were the high price of bread and unemployment inflated by the return of militiamen from the war. The target was often the property of particular individuals – farmers and clergymen – whose conduct had been offensive to the popular sense of 'justice'. Rioting was widespread through the early summer of 1816, but centred on Ely and Littleport where troops opened fire to disperse the crowd. At the subsequent Special Assizes at Ely, twenty-four men were sentenced to death, of whom five were hanged, nine were transported and ten were sentenced to a year in gaol.[29]

This was a foretaste of the rural riots associated with the name of 'Captain Swing' in 1830–31. These latter riots were far more extensive, reaching through southern England from Kent as far as Dorset, and up the eastern side of England to Lincolnshire. The worse affected counties were Kent, Berkshire, Sussex, Hampshire, Wiltshire and Dorset in the south and Essex, Suffolk and Norfolk in the east. Cambridgeshire, which had been at the centre of the 1816 riots, was less affected and Littleport and Ely were quiet. The principal counties of industrial unrest – Nottinghamshire, Derbyshire, Lancashire, Cheshire and Yorkshire – were little involved. The main reasons for the outbreaks were as in 1816, but the situation was made worse by the introduction of threshing machines which threatened a major source of winter employment for agricultural workers. The outbreaks took the form of machine-breaking and arson, followed by wage riots and robbery.[30] As with Luddism, threatening letters were an important device to put preliminary pressure on farmers to get rid of their hated machines:

> this is to inform you what you have to undergo Gentelmen if providing you Don't pull down your messhines and rise the poor mens wages the maried men give tow and six pence a day a day the singel tow shilings. or we will burn down your barns and you in them this is the last notis [sic].[31]

Clerical magistrates were also objects of popular hatred. The following more literate letter, with its concluding echo of the prayer of general confession in the Book of Common Prayer, may include a pun rather than a spelling mistake:

> Your name is down amongst the Black hearts in the Black Book and this is to advise you and the like of you, who are Parson Justasses, to make your wills.
> Ye have been the Blackguard Enemies of the People on all occasions, Ye have not yet done as ye ought.[32]

Retribution, tempered with 'mercy', was swift. Hobsbawm and Rudé have calculated that 1,976 prisoners were tried by 94 courts in 34 counties. Of 252 death sentences, all but 19 were commuted; of 505 who were sentenced to transportation, 24 were reprieved; 644 were imprisoned; 7 were fined, 1 was whipped and 800 were acquitted or bound over to keep the peace. The totals indicate the extent and severity of the riots, but did this amount to a serious threat of revolution?

In one sense it did, in that in peasant societies throughout Europe, risings in the countryside were recognised as having the potential to destabilise the whole of society, and the role of the *jacquerie* in 1789 was not easily forgotten. But in the English case there is little evidence of direct involvement by rioters in political activities. The Royal Commission on the Poor Laws in 1834 found that in most instances the causes of the riots were economic: 300 cases being attributed to low wages and unemployment compared with 110 blamed on agitators and beer shops.[33] The latter figure is high, due more to beer shops than agitators. Out of 1,475 incidents counted by Hobsbawm and Rudé, only twenty-three were classified as 'political' and only an additional three were for 'sedition'. The only counties with more than two incidents under these headings were Cumberland, with three political cases and Lancashire with five. Neither of these was a 'Swing' county.[34] This is not to deny that there were small groups of radicals in villages who would have liked to turn the riots to political effect, and there is some evidence of urban radicals attempting to capitalise on the rural unrest.

The election campaigns of 1830, 1831 and 1832 took politics to almost every market town, if not every parish, in the country. One of the most celebrated cases was at Blandford in October 1831 where the Dorset county by-election resulted in a narrow victory for the Tory candidate, Lord Ashley, whereupon a mob attacked several houses, including the property of two lawyers who had acted for Ashley, and were prevented from burning down the parsonage only by the arrival of troops. Here local grievances and score-settling merged with anger at the failure of the reformers to carry the seat. Rural artisans, and urban artisans 'on tramp' were able to spread the political message sufficiently far to cause the magistrates some anxiety lest the grievances of the labourers should become infected with politics. Cobbett's reform lecture tour of Kent and Sussex in October 1830 was, therefore, viewed with suspicion, as were the Rotunda radicals when they took up the agricultural riots in their London lectures. Carlile issued an 'Address to the Insurgent Labourers', for which he was prosecuted for sedition and sentenced to two years in gaol; and Taylor wrote and produced a play called *Swing: Who are the Incendiaries?* which indirectly led to his prosecution for blasphemy.[35] Though the majority of the Rotunda audiences would have been from London, James Thomas Cooper, a Swing leader in Fordingbridge, Hampshire, cannot have been alone in attending the Rotunda when he was in London.[36] Also, radical literature was widely available in towns and villages. One report from Sussex claimed that the agricultural labourers were 'ripe for anything'.

> Moreover, they are all politicians. In one field 30 or 40 are set to work breaking stones; and in the midst of them on a heap of flints at meal times, one of the most learned of their number, may be seen reading aloud the *Morning Herald*, and expounding the clauses of the Reform Bill, in which they take a great interest, to his fellow workmen.[37]

In Dorchester, a hand bill was stuck around the town at the end of October 1831, denouncing those who had voted against the Reform Bill in the Lords and listing government pensioners.[38] 'I am very confident, that ever since the Reform Bill was first talked of in this neighbourhood, it has produced a great deal of disorder and immoral state of the population', claimed B. S. Escott of Somerset in 1837.[39]

The growth of labourers' friendly societies and chapels in the years after Swing confirms the capacity of rural workers to organise themselves, and the fact that one such group of labourers in Tolpuddle in Dorset could form a branch of the London-based Grand National Consolidated Trades Union in 1834 suggests that the interchange of ideas between town and country was not so improbable as the usual emphasis on the isolation of the rural worker might suggest. Even so, the culture and mentality of agricultural labourers were such as to make some forms of communication difficult. Arson and other acts of immediate response to grievances were the usual manifestation of discontent, whatever dark discussions might also go on in low beer shops beyond the reach of parson and licensing justices.

Remarkably, this rural culture flared into outright revolt once more in the later 1830s. As with Swing, the affair started in Kent, though this time it did not spread beyond three villages: Boughton, Dunkirk and Hernhill, situated between Faversham and Canterbury. The area had already seen Swing riots in 1830 and anti-Poor Law riots in 1835 but in 1838 an added ingredient was millenarianism. The Messiah was John Tom or Thoms, *alias* Sir William Courtenay, who on 20 May 1838 led his small group of between thirty-six and forty-eight disciples through the villages of north Kent as far west as Sittingbourne, before being confronted on 31 May in Bossenden Wood near Dunkirk by a detachment of the 150 men of the 45th Infantry sent to hunt them down. One soldier, a special constable and nine rioters were killed, including Courtenay. The latter had previously stood for East Kent in the general election of December 1832 and was a political demagogue with a radical appeal. But to the rioters, two-thirds of whom were labourers, he was the Messiah come to bring the Jubilee when all oppression would end and debts be cancelled.[40] One of those killed, was Edward Wraight, a sixty-year-old yeoman farmer who could both read and write; his son, of the same name, was taken prisoner. In answer to the question whether she 'really had believed that Thoms was our Saviour', the son's wife replied:

Oh yes sir, certain sure I did believe him; and good warrant I thought I had. William Wills, you see, sir, came one day to our cottage, and we had some ale; and, says he, 'Have you heard the great news, and what's going to happen?' – 'No,' says we, 'William Wills; what be it?' And he said, the great Day of Judgment was close at hand, and that our Saviour had come back again; and that we must all follow him. And he showed us in the Bible, in the *Revelations*, that he should come upon a white horse, and go forth and conquer; and sure enough, sir, the day after, as we were coming in our cart from market, we met the groom leading Sir William's white horse; and he told us that all the country would be up, for the great jubilee was to come, and we must be with 'em. And so, sir, you see, next day poor Edward certainly did go to join 'em, little thinking what was to happen. And the day after, as they were all passing by the house, I looked out, and Muster Foad was just at the tail of them. And I said, 'Do you, Muster Foad, believe he is our blessed Saviour?' – 'Oh, yes', he says, 'Mrs Wraight, for certain sure he is, and I'll follow him to the world's end.'

Asked whether his death had not convinced her that Courtenay was an imposter, she went on:

Not at once, sir; for we was told he would surely rise again; and, for certain, after poor Edward was taken prisoner, me and a neighbour sat up the whole of that blessed night reading the Bible, and believing the world was to be destroyed on the morrow.

Asked whether this was also the belief of her neighbours, she replied:

I can't say for all, sir, but many of them did. There was Mrs.—— opposite, who asked him to a tea-party; and she said afterwards to me, 'You may be sure he isn't one of us; he isn't like to us. To hear him talk, and see him, it's not at all like talking to a man. He sings the beautifullest hymns, and talks the finest words that ever you heard.'

Courtenay had also administered the sacrament and anointed his followers to make them invulnerable.[41]

The interviewer, Frederick Liardet, who was a barrister and supporter of the Central Society of Education, found this a 'strange infatuation', but it was strange only to an educated, urban member of the middle class. To the peasantry of Kent, this cultural reaction to socio-economic deprivation was perfectly natural. It also defied the logic of contemporary Chartists who saw the rising only as a response to the new Poor Law, just as it continues to defy the logic of historians accustomed to secular revolutions which are economic or political in inspiration. The contrast should be made between this account of a meeting in a Kent cottage and the deposition quoted earlier about the meeting near Huddersfield before the Folly Hall rising of 1817.[42] Culturally the two accounts were a world apart, and yet they amounted to the same thing: not a riot but a revolution, in which old forms of oppression were to be swept away. Courtenay was not far from the teachings of Spence which encouraged the revolutionary party in London from Spa Fields to Cato Street. As Liardet himself realised:

> Although the late disturbance was undoubtedly of a religious character, it must not be supposed that it was altogether unconnected with views of another nature. Thoms, taking advantage of the occasional distress of some of his auditors, did not fail to represent it as owing to the enormous masses of wealth accumulated by the few to the disadvantage of the many. In his addresses, he often hinted at a more equable distribution of property; and declared that, when he was put into possession of the power God intended to give him, no man should have less than fifty acres of land.[43]

Courtenay himself seems to have participated in this belief.

Conclusion

The uprising in Kent in 1838 gives an insight into the potential for revolutionary disturbances in Britain in the 1830s. At a time of rapid population increase, agricultural depression and deep cyclical industrial recessions, when industrialisation was transforming the social frameworks of communities on the coal fields of Britain, there was much inherent instability which on occasions spilled over from sporadic rioting into actual insurgency. The army was kept on the alert. At Bossenden Wood as many men were killed as at Peterloo; more at Bristol and Merthyr Tydfil. There was clearly a revolutionary situation in 1830–32: one which in France would have led to revolution. Reports suggest there were some people throughout the country who would have taken Britain down the same path.

Lord Camden, Lord Lieutenant of Kent, believed the incendiaries were 'those who wish Revolution in England, in order to create confusion & that in London, the main directors reside'.[44] Tricolour flags, symbol of the new French regime, were paraded in Henry Hunt's Preston, and an ex-metropolitan policeman was charged in Battle, Sussex, with wearing a cap with tricoloured ribbons and saying 'if they were minded, there would be a revolution here'.[45] The red flag flew in Merthyr. But in the end, revolution did not happen; or, rather, the constitutional revolution was contained within constitutional bounds by the middle-class political unions and the Whigs. The crisis of May 1832 was resolved peacefully, and the leaders of popular radicalism who had provided the reality of the threat of physical force felt betrayed by the Reform Act that followed. Out of this sense of betrayal, the Chartist movement was born.

Notes

1   Speech on the Reform Bill in 1832, quoted in *Annual Register* (1832), History of Europe, p. 39.
2   M. Brock, *The Great Reform Act* (London, Hutchinson, 1973), pp. 57–8.
3   D. Wahrman, *Imagining the Middle Class: The Political Representation of Class in Britain, c. 1780–1840* (Cambridge, Cambridge University Press, 1995).
4   Brock, *Great Reform Act*, pp. 59–60.
5   Handbill reproduced from the Place Papers, in D. J. Rowe, (ed.), *London Radicalism, 1830–1843* (London, London Record Society, 1970), p. 63.
6   Brown, *French Revolution*, pp. 193–7.
7   *Annual Register* (1831), History of Europe, p. 80.
8   *Annual Register* (1831), History of Europe, pp. 280–1; Chronicle, pp. 161–3, 171–8.
9   Wellington to Aberdeen, 22 November 1831, printed in A. R. Wellesley (ed.), *Despatches, Correspondence, and Memoranda of Field Marshall Arthur Duke of Wellington, K.G.*, continuation series, 8 vols (London, Murray, 1867–80), vol. 8, pp. 74–6.
10   *Annual Register* (1832), Chronicle, pp. 186–7.
11   D. J. Moss, *Thomas Attwood: The Biography of a Radical* (Montreal, McGill-Queen's University Press, 1990), pp. 205–9.
12   Quoted in *PMG*, 1:49 (19 May 1832), p. 398.
13   Northampton CRO, Fitzwilliam Papers, F(M) 732, Letter Book, Lord Milton to Denis O'Bryen, 29 November 1832, quoted in D. J. Gratton, 'Paternalism, Politics and Estate management: the fifth Earl Fitzwilliam (1786–1857)', Ph.D. thesis, University of Sheffield, 1999.
14   This view was echoed in Whig histories: see J. R. M. Butler, *The Passing of the Great Reform Bill* (London, Longmans, Green & Co., 1914), p. 137.

15   BL, Add MSS 27795, fos 26–9, Place Papers, Sunday, 20 May 1832, as printed in Rowe, *London Radicalism*, pp. 94–5.

16   Thompson, *The Making*, pp. 898–9.

17   J. H. Wiener, *Radicalism and Freethought in Nineteenth-Century Britain: The Life of Richard Carlile* (Westport, Greenwood, 1983), pp. 164–90.

18   BL, Add MSS 27791, fos. 333–5, Place Papers [October 1831], as printed in Rowe, *London Radicalism*, pp. 51–3.

19   *PMG*, 1:44, supplementary no (11 April 1832), pp. 345–52.

20   *Annual Register* (1832), Chronicle, pp. 38–9.

21   PRO, HO 40/5/5, fo 22, paper sent by Edward Thomas Fitzgerald, Capt. 25th Foot to Lord Sidmouth, from Abergavenny, 22 December 1816.

22   PRO, HO 42/158, fo 304, Copy of a Paper Found near Penydarren on Monday 27 January 1817. This is reprinted in D. V. J. Jones, *Before Rebecca* (London, Allen Lane, 1973), pp. 231–3.

23   Jones, *Before Rebecca*, pp. 86–113.

24   Jones, *Before Rebecca*, pp. 117–32.

25   Jones, *Before Rebecca*, p. 158.

26   G. A. Williams, *The Merthyr Rising* (London, Croom Helm, 1978), p. 224.

27   Quoted in Jones, *Before Rebecca*, p. 133.

28   Quoted in Williams, *Merthyr Rising*, p. 219.

29   A. J. Peacock, *Bread or Blood: A Study of the Agrarian Riots in East Anglia in 1816* (London, Gollancz, 1965).

30   E. J. Hobsbawm and G. Rudé, *Captain Swing* (London, Lawrence and Wishart, 1969), Appendix 1, pp. 262–3.

31   PRO, HO 52/10 (Sussex), fo 412, letter from Fulking near Hove, sent to Home Office 12 November 1830. There is a facsimile in Hobsbawm and Rudé, *Captain Swing*, p. 175.

32   PRO, HO 52/7 (Hampshire), fo 231. There is a facsimile in Hobsbawm and Rudé, *Captain Swing*, p. 177.

33   Hobsbawm and Rudé, *Captain Swing*, pp. 57–9.

34   Hobsbawm and Rudé, *Captain Swing*, Appendix 1, pp. 262–3.

35   Wiener, *Radicalism and Freethought*, pp. 165–6, 174–7.

36   R. Wells, 'Rural Rebels in Southern England in the 1830s', p. 135 in C. Emsley and J. Walvin (eds), *Artisans, Peasants and Proletarians, 1760–1860* (London, Croom Helm, 1985), pp. 124–65.

37   'State of the Rural Population', *Brighton Gazette*, 31 May 1832.

38   Mary Frampton's *Journal*, 6 November 1831, quoted in E. A. Smith, *Reform or Revolution? A diary of Reform in England, 1830–2* (Stroud, Sutton, 1992), pp. 105–6.

39   PP (1837) 464, 30, *Report from the Select Committee of the House of Lords appointed to inquire into the State of Agriculture in England and Wales*, June 1837, Q 4956.

40   B. Reay, *The Last Rising of the Agricultural Labourers: Rural Life and Protest in Nineteenth-century England* (Oxford, Clarendon Press, 1990).

41   F. Liardet, 'State of the Peasantry in the County of Kent', p. 90–1, *Central Society of Education Papers* 3 (London, Taylor and Walton, 1839), pp. 87–139.

42   See above, pp. 49–50.

43   Liardet, 'State of the Peasantry', p. 133.

44 PRO, HO 52/8 (Kent), fos 248–50, Camden to the Home Office, 12 November 1830.
45 G. Rudé, 'English Rural and Urban Disturbances 1830–1831', pp. 96–7, *Past & Present*, 37 (July 1967), pp. 87–102.

3

Chartism,
1837–48

The first Chartist crisis, 1839–40

The Chartist movement began as a peaceful pressure group, organised in London by some of the more moderate leaders of the London trade unions, former members of the NUWC and supporters of the unstamped press. In June 1836 a group of these men set up the London Working Men's Association (LWMA) to advance the cause of democratic radicalism by the peaceful means of education, moral improvement and reasoned pressure for further political change. Their approach showed the unmistakable influence of Francis Place and they had the support of several Radical Members of Parliament, including Daniel O'Connell. Their secretary, William Lovett, who was a former co-operative socialist and trade union official, was a model of rational moderation. It was this group that drew up the political programme for radical change expressed in the six points of Universal Suffrage, No Property Qualifications, Annual Parliaments, Equal Representation, Payment of Members and Vote by Ballot. Though the individual points of this programme had been around for at least two generations, taken together they summed up what was needed to make the Reform Act of 1832 effective for working men. Not only did all men need the vote, thus asserting individual political rights as opposed to the idea of the representation of interests, but to make that effective it would have to be possible for anyone to be elected, irrespective of property or income, it would be necessary for every vote to count equally with every other vote, the right to vote must be rescued from the threat of illegitimate pressure from employers or landlords, and those elected must be accountable.

There was no mention of women, or direct attack on the monarchy or the House of Lords. Nevertheless, this package of ideas would have revolutionised political life. As the Irish lawyer and one-time editor of the *Poor Man's Guardian*, James 'Bronterre' O'Brien, put it in 1837, 'Knaves will tell you, that it is because you have no property that you are unrepresented. I tell you, on the contrary, it is because you are unrepresented that you have no property.'[1] Thus the values of 1832 were reversed and that implicit challenge to property which had made Paine's *Rights of Man*, Part 2 so threatening, was again spelt out. Behind these radical political proposals lurked the threat of social revolution. But the methods chosen to achieve the end were strictly constitutional. A draft parliamentary Bill was drawn up which sought to implement the Six Points and also to rectify a number of administrative problems and anomalies created by the 1832 Reform Act.[2] Like the Reform Act, this was presented as a new Magna Carta: the People's Charter.

This constitutional approach was reinforced from Birmingham where former members of the Political Union were also disillusioned with the failure of the 1832 Reform Act to transform aristocratic politics to the extent they had hoped. So Thomas Attwood and others returned to the tactics of 1832, calling mass meetings in support of a National Petition for further change. In its bid for popular support, essential for the strategy of mass pressure to seem realistic, the BPU now declared for universal suffrage. The Charter was published on 8 May 1838, the National Petition on 14 May, and the two were merged at mass meetings in Glasgow on 21 May and Birmingham on 6 August. The strategy now was, as in earlier campaigns, to hold a series of mass meetings throughout the country to elect delegates to a Convention in London, the overt purpose of which was to oversee the presentation of the Petition to the House of Commons, but with the threat always implicit in the notion of a Convention that it might constitute an alternative and more legitimate version of the House of Commons.

Had the London Working Men's Association (LWMA) retained its dominant place in this campaign for radical reform, Chartism would never have become the movement that it did, but as the mass movement grew it was able to draw on other traditions, agitations and leaders with different ideas and approaches. In London, there were many radicals with roots in Paineite and Spencean radicalism who were unhappy with the moderation of the LWMA. Some of them, organised initially in the East London Democratic Association, reconstituted themselves in May 1838 as the London Democratic Association in opposition to the moderates. Their most outspoken leader, George Julian Harney, had three times been imprisoned in the war of the unstamped, and romantically regarded himself as playing Marat to O'Brien's Robespierre in a re-enactment of the French Revolution. He and others like him had to look outside London for election to the Convention.

Despite the enormous size of London as a centre of population and manufacturing, with long traditions of radical protest, early Chartism was not primarily a London movement: its origins as a mass movement lay in the provinces which had, with increasing frequency since the days of Luddism, taken the initiative in movements of popular protest. Chartism was a blend of political programme and economic discontents generated in the industrial Midlands and north of England, fused in the severe trade depression which began to affect Britain in late 1836 and which continued with intermissions until the summer of 1842.

The oldest industrial district of the north was around the mouth of the river Tyne, where the economy had been stimulated by the demand for sea-borne coal for London. There was a long tradition here of turbulent industrial relations, among the colliers who dug the coal and the keelmen who conveyed it from the shore to waiting ships. In 1792 and again in 1819, major strikes had occurred which governments had feared might lead to revolution. In the later 1830s, this region was again to the forefront of what was known as 'physical force' Chartism, in contrast to the 'moral force' of the LWMA. The engine which drove the physical force approach was partly economic, with a severe depression at the rather outdated iron works at Winlaton where idle hands could be turned to the manufacture of pikes; and ideological, with the production of an uncompromising newspaper, the *Northern Liberator*. This was started by an American, Augustus Hardin Beaumont, who seems to have believed his own language of revolutionary violence. In November 1837 he called for 'five hundred thousand democrats in arms' and in January 1838 he sold his paper and went on a lecture tour to raise a force of five hundred to fight for the rebels in Canada, a task which his premature death prevented him from realising.

Beaumont's successors at the *Northern Liberator* were Robert Blakey, a subtle logician (who was to become Professor of Logic and Metaphysics at Queen's College, Belfast, in 1849) and Thomas Doubleday, a romantic poet and secretary of the Northern Political Union. Although initially more discreet, advocating arming only in self defence, in January 1839 this amounted to advice on how to make cartridges and barricades and information about the ready availability of hand grenades. Thomas Ainge Devyr, an Irish journalist (and son of a United Irishman) working on the paper, many years later recalled shells being manufactured in the rooms above the *Liberator* offices in Newcastle. Harney was unsurprisingly elected to the Convention as a delegate for Newcastle, along with another extremist, 'Dr' John Taylor of Ayr. The *Liberator* was finally silenced in 1840 by a crippling fine on Blakey for publishing a paper on the 'National Right of Resistance to Constituted Authorities'.[3]

In spite of the revolutionary voices and activities on Tyneside during the early years of Chartism, other forces minimised the potential danger. The economy of the area was generally buoyant, the Winlaton iron workers being untypical. The major industry, coal mining, was effectively unionised and conflict could be institutionalised within industrial relations; and the new Poor Law, which was to cause problems elsewhere, was introduced with less confrontation and greater discretion in the north-east. The *Northern Liberator* had an extensive circulation beyond Tyneside and sought to bring national and international perspectives to bear, but it was not entirely successful. Although Newcastle was to remain a centre of republican thought, and supported international revolution in the 1850s through the efforts of Joseph Cowen junior, it did not rise in 1839 and was not thereafter a major centre of Chartist activity. Iron working districts were always of concern to the government, whether at Winlaton, Carron in Scotland, Low Moor outside Bradford, Sheffield, Birmingham, the Black Country, or the valleys of South Wales, for it was here that the manufacture of arms for illicit purposes might be expected and revolution might become a cottage industry for unemployed workers, but the market for such weapons was more often to be expected elsewhere.

The textile producing counties of the east Midlands, northwards from Leicestershire through Nottinghamshire and into Derbyshire, across to north-east Cheshire, south-east Lancashire, and over the Pennines into the West Riding of Yorkshire were those associated with the greatest history of turbulent radicalism. Here the recurring problems of the domestic outworkers, mainly weavers, reached a climax as their earning power fell and bread prices rose in the late 1830s. These familiar causes of unrest merged with others, some old, some new. Fresh immigration from Ireland brought renewed bitterness born of despair in the famine years; and in Bradford technological redundancy hit the wool combers of the worsted industry as hard as it had destroyed the croppers of the woollen industry earlier in the century.

The social forces which created the Chartist movement began in the factory districts of Lancashire, Cheshire and, especially, the West Riding in 1830 (rather than 1838), with the movement to secure the enforcement of protective legislation in cotton factories and its extension of protection to Yorkshire worsted mills and other sections of the textile workforce. The majority of workers in factories were women and children but large numbers of men were employed as handloom weavers, kept on to supply surplus capacity to meet the demand for output in an industry notoriously vulnerable to booms and slumps. Not only was their employment uncertain, but their rates of pay were fixed by the cost of producing a piece of cloth on a power loom, not the time taken to produce a piece by hand.

The campaign for shorter hours in the factories was presented in humanitarian language as one to protect women and children from exploitation, but it was also aimed at driving up factory costs to increase the income of domestic workers. The problems of the textile districts centred on families, in which women and children were exploited in order further to exploit fathers and husbands. Although some of the children employed in factories went on to other forms of employment, and did so increasingly in times of economic expansion, some were not so fortunate and the depression of 1837–42 caused much hardship. A tinder-box of discontent was created which, as in 1812, 1817 and 1819, could easily be lit by the sparks of revolutionary oratory and the dedicated plotting of men who saw no other way of achieving reform. In the small mill towns and face-to-face communities of the textile districts, Chartism straddled the boundary between constitutional protest and insurrection.

The latter was personified by two men, neither of them Chartists: Richard Oastler, son of a leader of the Methodist New Connexion in Leeds, who adopted the position of Tory Anglican paternalist squire in his post as steward for the Thornhill estate at Fixby, between

Huddersfield and Halifax; and Joseph Rayner Stephens, a former Wesleyan Methodist minister in Stalybridge, the son of the Wesleyan superintendent minister in Manchester in 1819 who had praised the magistrates for their actions at 'Peterloo'. Oastler led the campaign for factory reform, later also taking up leadership of West Riding opposition to the Poor Law Amendment Act of 1834; Stephens, expelled from the Wesleyan ministry for advocating the disestablishment of the Church of England, led the anti-Poor Law movement in Lancashire and Cheshire and was a prominent speaker on early Chartist platforms across the north of England. These campaigns were whipped up into mass movements of working people convinced by practical experience of the 'Whig betrayal' in 1832. This phrase referred not only to the fact that the 1832 Act did not deliver the promised change in politics, but also to the legislation which followed. This seemed to favour the interests of newly enfranchised urban and manufacturing elites, not 'the people'. The coercion of Ireland, the attack on trade unions, and the 1833 Factory Act which in part met the humanitarian issue without helping male adults, were all parts of this betrayal, but the measure which hurt most of all was the Poor Law Amendment Act of 1834, enforced in the factory districts in 1837 as the depression deepened.

The orchestrated violence which greeted the attempt to implement the Act showed the strength and ferocity of public feeling. By force of numbers, rate payers were intimidated and meetings disrupted, delaying and in some cases preventing the implementation of the Act. A great anti-Poor Law rally on Peep Green, midway between Leeds, Bradford, Halifax and Huddersfield at Whitsuntide 1837 was followed by a campaign of intimidation, led in Huddersfield by Oastler, which on 5 June prevent the newly-elected Poor Law Guardians from choosing a clerk and so setting about their business.[4] On 20 June, William IV died and in the consequent general election Oastler stood for Huddersfield. His narrow defeat caused a riot and a detachment of cavalry had to be called to restore order. The example spread and in October the Bradford Guardians wavered under public pressure and there were serious riots there in November. Two troops of cavalry were needed to enable the frightened Guardians of Huddersfield to elect a clerk in January 1838 and so to proceed with business.[5]

The success of the anti-Poor Law Movement in Huddersfield and

other northern towns demonstrated the power of the crowd to determine events when combined with a measure of support from
members of the local elite, whether Tories or radicals, opposed to cen-
tralisation and Whig reforming dogma. This experience was carried
over into northern Chartism, though at first some anti-Poor Law agitators considered Chartism a London plot to divide the people from
their Tory supporters. This suspicion was unfounded but it did have
that effect. While the popular movement flowed seamlessly from the
one to the other, the Chartists lost what support the upper classes had
given to their social protest. Oastler was an isolated figure, soon to be
imprisoned by his employer on a charge of debt. John Fielden, the
Todmorden factory master and MP for Oldham since 1832, was one of
the few factory movement and anti-Poor Law leaders to make the
transition to advocacy of Chartist democracy.

Oastler's principal Huddersfield supporter was Lawrence
Pitkethly, a prosperous draper who had achieved the vote in 1832.
Two days before the Poor Law Guardians met to elect their clerk,
Pitkethly addressed a mass meeting in the town on the subject of the
five leaders of the Glasgow cotton spinners' union who had just been
sentenced to transportation for their technical complicity in the death
of blacklegs during a prolonged and bitter strike in the west of
Scotland. His speech is worth considering at length, not only for the
language used, but also for the rhetorical devices employed and the
issues raised. According to the *Northern Star* report,

> Mr Pitkethley said . . . The resolution described tyranny, which
> was disgraceful to any civilised country and barbarity which
> ought not to be submitted to: it was clear that the Whigs were
> resolved to reduce the people to the lowest possible state of exis-
> tence. That this was one of their acts, and in perfect consonance
> with Starvation Law, the Rural Police Law, and the transporting
> of the Dorchester Labourers, and those five virtuous men, the
> coercing of the Irish and the Canadians, left it impossible for us
> to be astonished at any Act which they might perform, and
> exhorted the meeting to place no confidence in them whatever;
> but to unite, be firm, depend upon their own energies, or they
> must remain slaves.

Here Pitkethly was drawing up a general indictment of government
policy, ranging from the Poor Law and the Tolpuddle martyrs to Irish
coercion and the suppression of the Canadian rebels. This illustrates

the degree to which a crowd, presumably motivated by local social and economic grievances, could be led to think nationally and even internationally about political issues related to their own local situation. The report continued:

> He then read some extracts from speeches made at a meeting held at Newcastle-upon-Tyne last Wednesday, on the same subject; which showed that Sir Robert Peel had got his £100,000 from Cotton Spinners, that Brougham had provided Bastiles for them, that they were determined to fight with their tongues, but if that would not do they would use their arms; then one speaker said he would rather than see those men leave Britain's Isles he would lose his life, and added now is the time to plunge your swords into the Whig and Tory faction; those profit-mongers must be consumed in a universal conflagration; and asked if they would permit them to leave Britain's Isle, (and was answered no, no, by the meeting.) and if so sent, then war to the knife; and that another speaker at the same meeting said the time was arrived when the exhortation once given in the land of Judea should be followed in this country, he that hath no sword let him sell his garment and buy one. After stating that rather than see the men leave the country, he would throw a firebrand into the bastile, and see them perish in the flames; that he agreed to petition with reluctance, concluded by asking, what an awful condition they would be placed in if those men were transported, and that a rural police will be established to watch them in their walks, and assassins would be hired to butcher their fellow-creatures; that he objected to revolution but rather than submit to live a slave, he would die. He then moved a resolution pledging the meeting to obtain by every possible means the total omission of the sentence on their five unfortunate brethren of Glasgow.

Pitkethly was here playing a clever game. By quoting from the report of another meeting, he could use seditious language by proxy and achieve his desired effect upon the crowd without serious risk of prosecution. And even in the original speeches, there was a delightful ambiguity in the contrast between 'tongues' and 'arms' which could have been exploited if necessary by a defence counsel in court. The report of Pitkethly's meeting ended: 'Mr P. said he had read those few extracts to show that the men in the north were not less determined than the men of Huddersfield, and concluded by reading the resolution.'[6] This was the well-worn device of using reports of meetings elsewhere to bolster the morale of local groups and convince them that they were but a small part of a much greater movement. In the spring and early summer of 1838, that greater movement became Chartism on a swelling tide of hunger and hatred.

The man who exploited this was Feargus O'Connor, a disaffected former O'Connellite MP and, more importantly, nephew of the United Irishman, Arthur O'Connor, who was still living in exile in Nemours. O'Connor united in his complex personality the aspirations of his revolutionary uncle with the popular journalistic style of Cobbett and the platform appeal and oratory of Henry Hunt. When both Cobbett and Hunt died in 1835, O'Connor stepped into their shoes. His initial political base was Marylebone, a huge urban parish on the north western edge of London, the size of a large provincial town. Here vestry politics were almost democratic. He then extended his influence to the north, where his legal expertise was employed in the anti-Poor Law struggle.[7] He was present at the great West Riding meeting at Whitsuntide 1837, and in November played a leading part in starting in Leeds a radical anti-Poor Law weekly stamped newspaper which was called, like Arthur O'Connor's Ulster paper of the 1790s, the *Northern Star*. This was a very English paper, however, drawing on the style of its publisher Joshua Hobson's own earlier unstamped *Voice of the West Riding* and Cobbett's *Political Register*.

O'Connor never edited this paper, but he wrote many leading articles and controlled its overall direction from behind the scenes. His forte was the platform and the Huntite role of patriotic radical gentleman demagogue. Like Hunt, he stood just on the legal side of illegality, though his passionate language could easily take his followers beyond that point and some later came to believe that he had exhorted them to go where he was not prepared to lead them.

Between the launching of Chartism in May 1838 and the presentation of the National Petition in June 1839, the Chartists concentrated on gathering signatures and electing their delegates to the National Convention. The latter assembled in London on 4 February 1839 and immediately the tensions within the movement became apparent. Aware that the show was being run by the moderates of the LWMA, with William Lovett elected secretary of the Convention, the London Democratic Association provided an alternative focus for more extreme views. One motion, proposed by William Rider of Leeds and seconded by Richard Marsden of Preston,

Resolved that this meeting convey to the General Convention, their opinion that for the due discharge of the duties of the Convention it is essentially necessary that there be no delay, except what may be absolutely necessary, in the presentation of the National Petition, and we hold it to be the duty of the Convention, to impress upon people the necessity of an immediate preparation for ulterior measures.[8]

This last phrase encompassed a wide range of ideas, from traditional legal measures for putting pressure on electors, such as buying goods only from the shops of supporters, and the more unlikely abstinence from excisable goods (drink and tobacco) to wreck government finances; to William Benbow's 'General Strike' as propounded in 1832; to vague threats of arming and drilling such as the *Northern Liberator* was favouring at this time. Already the country was growing impatient. Rioting broke out among the flannel weavers of Llanidloes and Welshpool in the upper Severn Valley at the end of April. Other disturbances were reported in the West Country, the Potteries, Sheffield, Bolton and Newcastle.

The volatility of the situation became clear in early May when the Whig government, which had been remarkably tolerant of the Chartists so far, collapsed and the prospect loomed of a Tory government under Robert Peel, founder of the hated Metropolitan Police in 1829, and of the Irish police before that. Fearful of suppression by the London police, the Convention adjourned to Birmingham. Here the Chartists held nightly meetings in the Bull Ring, much to the alarm of the magistrates who had recently banned meetings there. On 5 July the Home Office sent sixty metropolitan police to restore order. However, they had the reverse effect, and their attempt to disperse the crowd led to a riot which was only ended when the dragoons were called in. This incident raised a number of issues about violence and constitutionality. There was the irony that the magistrates who sent for the police included members of the BPU, some of whom had been delegates to the Convention but had withdrawn over talk of ulterior measures. The government which sent the police was a Whig one, Peel having refused to form a minority administration. The legality of the Home Office employing metropolitan police outside the London police area was not universally accepted: indeed, in a subsequent report on the riots, Joseph Sturge dissented from the views of his middle-class colleagues on this point. For publishing the protest of the

Convention about the 'wanton, flagrant, and unjust outrage . . . made upon the people of Birmingham by a bloodthirsty and unconstitutional force from London, acting under authority of men who, when out of office sanctioned and took part in the meetings of the people', William Lovett and local BPU delegate, John Collins, were prosecuted and imprisoned for a year.[9] Thus two of the mildest and most unrevolutionary of Chartists were punished, leaving Chartists to consider who was constitutional and who was in subversion of the law.

The constitutional niceties of physical force were pondered by the moderate London periodical, the *Chartist*, in May 1839 when news broke of the first riots in Wales.[10]

> That Englishmen have a right, *in extreme cases*, to have recourse to physical force to free themselves from an unendurable tyranny, is a truth so important and so undisputed that it forms the very foundation of our system of government. It is not only admitted, but it is even asserted, reiterated, defended, and justified, by the most zealous of the Tory writers upon, the Constitution of the country.

Sir William Blackstone, the eighteenth-century jurist, was the authority being appealed to. In true Whig fashion, the argument for physical force could be justified, but only in the last resort:

> But although this is upon all sides admitted, it is also upon all sides agreed that this is a fearful remedy, which, like hazardous, extreme, and painful operations in surgery, is only to be brought into action in very extreme cases, when all ordinary courses of treatment have failed. Physical force is a thing not to be lightly had recourse to; it is the last remedy known to the Constitution.

The paper then went on to assess the likelihood of physical force being employed and the conditions which might lead to its use. The very possession of weapons, taken with loose talk about their use, could lead to the kind of outburst which governments since the 1790s had feared:

> We have said long ago that all this light and meaningless talk about physical force is calculated to produce isolated and unsupported ebullitions of men, who, having arms in their hands, and being taught that they should use them, do so upon the impulse of passion. They are fierce and destructive in proportion to their weakness.

This is an instructive caution against the assumption that, just because the likelihood of success was small, a revolutionary outburst was unlikely. The reverse was true but would be self-defeating:

> Brother Chartists, this must not – this shall not be. We are as you know, with you arm and heart; but a noble cause shall not be thus foully lost. We will not see you throw away your lives only that your blood may stiffen the bonds that bind your brethren.

However, this did not mean that in the right conditions physical force should not be appealed to. Those conditions, hoped for in 1794, 1798, 1802, 1812, 1817, 1819, and 1832, were that: 'Nothing but a simultaneous rising at the same hour all over the kingdom could give you a *chance* of success by arms – even that would give you but a slender chance, and that you cannot effect.' This realisation of the weakness and likely failure of the only physical force strategy likely to be effective was a sobering thought and restrained the hands of all but the most headstrong. However, this was not to say that Chartists should not arm and drill. Again, in an argument common since the 1790s and almost universal since Peterloo, the *Chartist* urged, 'Retain your arms then, for it is possible that you may have to use them in your own defence, with the law and the Constitution upon your side. But use them not until that time comes.' In the mean time there was only one course of action for Chartists: 'Pursue the course of *peaceful* agitation – press forward your great cause under the watchwords of "Peace, Law, Order". It may be delayed, but it must prevail. Continue these acts of buccaneering folly, *and you and your children are slaves for ever*.' This appeal was in May. On 12 July the House of Commons rejected the Petition. The Convention, which had returned to London two days earlier, had to consider what to do next. The members were divided, but half-heartedly called for a sacred month – that is a general strike. Support across the country was limited. On 6 August the strike was called off and the Convention prorogued. The problem was what to do next. The hopes and expectations of over a year had led to nothing and all ulterior measures had failed, except the last which was yet to be tried. Many in crushed bewilderment went back to their homes. Some Chartists, armed, angry, frustrated, and filled with heady words of Old Testament prophetic fire, were ready for revolution.

The Monmouthshire and Yorkshire risings

In February 1839, John Frost, Newport draper and magistrate and Monmouthshire delegate to the Convention in London, reported twenty working men's associations in his area with a membership of 15,000 to 20,000. Throughout the spring of 1839, tension grew in south Wales as the Chartist movement expanded rapidly and began to appeal beyond its original artisan membership to workers in the coal fields and ironworks of the valleys north of Newport where it capitalised on industrial disputes between employers and workers over truck payments, low wages and harsh terms of employment. In March, Frost, who was on the 'physical force' wing of the Convention, was relieved of his commission of the peace. In the valleys of Scotch Cattle violence, magistrates grew nervous. As David Jones observed in his history of the Newport rising, 'the working class of Blaina and Ebbw Vale, of Clydach and Pontypool, and of Blackwood and Risca were not only "rebellious and easily roused", but were also past masters in the art of organization, intimidation, and violence.'[11] Jones estimates that at the height of Chartism over 25,000 people, a fifth of the population, were Chartists. On 19 April, Henry Vincent of the LWMA delivered a characteristically colourful speech in Newport which allegedly concluded with the words: 'When the time for resistance arrives, let your cry be 'To your tents, O Israel!' and then with one heart, one voice, and one blow perish the privileged orders! death to the aristocracy! up with the people, and the government they have established!'[12]

The Newport magistrates took alarm, and on 24 April issued a proclamation declaring all meetings and processions illegal. Vincent immediately challenged this with a parade and meeting. On 27 April, Frost published an open letter describing the magistrates' proclamation as 'a declaration of war against your rights as Citizens, against your liberty, against your property' and warned the magistrates and constables to 'beware how they act'.[13] With magistrates and employers restricting and victimising Chartists, and the latter in open defiance, battle lines were being drawn. An unfortunate clash of policies appeared to encourage this sense of conflict when the government issued a Royal Proclamation nationally on 3 May prohibiting military exercises, and then four days later the Home Secretary, Lord John Russell, wrote to Lord Lieutenants and magistrates offering to provide local associations with arms for the protection of property. Warrants were issued for the arrest of Vincent and three others on 7 May and riots greeted their return to Newport which resulted in several further arrests. Despite the efforts made by Frost at this time to calm popular passions, the situation in south Wales was slowly slipping out of control.

The heightened tension in Birmingham, fears that the Petition might be rejected, and organisation to collect subscriptions for the Chartist prisoners sustained and increased Chartist support in the valleys throughout the early summer of 1839, but by August the authorities believed the worst to be over. At the Monmouth Assizes on 2 August, Vincent was sentenced to a year in gaol and the others received lesser sentences. This attack on a popular leader helped consolidate the Chartist belief that it would be necessary to take up arms in self-defence. As early as April, Frost had argued in speeches in Newport and Glasgow that if members of the Convention were taken prisoner, 'we are determined to lay hold upon some of the leading men in the country as hostages for the Convention' and this was now threatened locally. Others recalled how Vincent himself had observed in March that 'A few thousand armed men on the hills could successfully defend them. Wales would make an excellent republic.'[14] In September, Chartists began manufacturing and hoarding pikes and muskets.

These plans for a rising were rooted in the particular circumstances of life and tradition in the valleys, but they were not isolated from reactions elsewhere to the failure of the petitioning movement. The Convention, which had been reconvened on 26 August, finally dissolved itself on 14 September, and it was later claimed by William Ashton, a Barnsley Chartist, that Frost, Peter Bussey of Bradford and others had then fixed 3 November as the date for a simultaneous rising. There was talk in London of using the services of a Polish army officer, Major Beniowski, who had been involved in the Polish rising of 1831. Whether these details were accurate or not, there were over the next few weeks discussions about a projected rising in several different parts of the country, including the West Riding. As Joseph Crabtree of Barnsley later recalled, 'I heard of the expected rise at Newport and that there was to be a rise elsewhere.'[15] Secret meetings and detailed planning continued in Monmouthshire throughout October, and contacts were maintained with the north of England where preparations were less advanced. As the date approached, the difficulties of co-ordinating a simultaneous rising became apparent. Peter Bussey in Yorkshire asked for a postponement, but it was too late to stop the movement towards revolution in Monmouthshire.

On Friday 1 November a meeting in Blackwood made final arrangements for the rising to begin on the night of Sunday, 3 November. The insurgents were divided into three groups. Those at Pontypool, commanded by William Jones, were to march on Newport from the north, while the rest, led from Blackwood by John Frost and Ebbw Vale by Zephaniah Williams, were to meet up outside Newport and attack the town from the west. This is roughly what happened, but torrential rain and slower progress than expected meant that the 7,000 armed Chartists from the valleys did not reach Newport until after dawn and the attack by Frost and Williams began before Jones was ready. The sixty or so troops garrisoned in the workhouse were alerted and a detachment of thirty-two moved into the town to guard the mayor's headquarters at the Westgate Hotel. The Chartists arrived at 9.20 in the morning. What happened next, and who fired first, is lost in the confusion. Each side naturally blamed the other at the subsequent trials. But the outcome was clear. After no more than twenty-five minutes of fierce fighting outside and inside the hotel, the battle was all over. There were deaths and injuries on both sides, but mainly on the Chartist side. The number of casualties is unknown – probably fifty or more seriously injured and at least twenty-four dead. 'What is definite', wrote the historian David Jones, 'is that on this morning in November 1839 the British authorities inflicted greater casualties on the civilian population than at any other time in the nineteenth and twentieth centuries.'[16]

Even so, the rising was not over, not even in the vicinity of Newport itself. William Jones's force of 2,000 men was still intact until news of the defeat caused them to disperse, and there were other contingents in the valleys ready to proceed the following night against towns on the Usk once Newport had fallen. The area had very few troops: perhaps three or four hundred at Brecon, and only thirty-six in each of Monmouth and Abergavenny. Although a troop of Hussars reached Newport from Bristol on 5 November, a letter dispatched that day by the Home Secretary to Thomas Phillips, mayor of Newport, scarcely conceals its mixture of panic and relief as it detailed the inability of the government to provide major reinforcements immediately:

I hasten to acknowledge the receipt of a letter which I have received from Mr Blewitt of yesterdays date written at your request reporting the attack made upon the Town of Newport by a large body of Chartists from the neighbouring Country & to inform you that I have lost no time in communicating with the military authorities, and an arrangement has been made for the immediate march of eight companies of the 45th Reg[imen]t from Winchester for the district in which the deplorable event has occurred, orders have been already dispatched for their march & They will probably arrive at Bristol on the 10th inst. & can of course if necessary cross over by steamer to Newport the same evening. Two Guns with a proportion of Gunners have also been ordered from Woolwich to Monmouth. They will proceed by the Railroad to Twyford from there by forced marches to Bristol – I regret much that there are no Troops stationed at any nearer points that would be available for this service but I think that the check which these Insurgents have received from the Firmness of the Inhabitants of Newport & the small body of Troops stationed in the Town, together with the active measures taken by the Magistrates will have induced their dispersion for the time & the presence of the large force which will arrive in the course of a few days be sufficient to maintain future Tranquillity.[17]

Gradually over the next few days the initiative was regained by the authorities and Chartist insurgents sank back into their communities: 125 men were arrested, two-thirds of whom were later discharged for want of evidence. Twenty-one, including Frost, Williams and Jones, were charged with high treason. Their cases came before a special commission convened on 10 December.

The two most recent historians of this event, David Jones and Ivor Wilks, both emphasised its insurrectionary nature. It was more than a riot, or a demonstration, or an attempt to rescue Vincent or other Chartist prisoners. It was a serious rising, involving careful planning and large numbers of people with a purpose as much political (however vague and unrealistic) as social and economic. This interpretation rests on an examination of the evidence gathered locally by magistrates at the committal hearings shortly after the event, which bears out the otherwise unsubstantiated 'confession' of Zephaniah Williams made on board his transportation ship to Australia. The later treason trials played down the extent of the rising: the defence for obvious reasons, and the prosecution because the government was reluctant to admit the scale of the challenge or the good fortune by which the damage had been limited. Had the Chartists had better military leadership they would have planned a simultaneous rising in south Wales, rather than leaving the other attacks until after success at Newport was reported. They would not have attempted a full frontal assault on the Westgate hotel, and they would not have fled and dispersed at the first set-back. This is not to argue that in the long run the Newport rising could have achieved anything, at least not without similar risings throughout the rest of Britain, but in the short-run matters could have been far worse for the authorities than they were.

Much of the explanation for the scale and ferocity of the Newport rising is found in the peculiar nature of the society and economy of the Welsh valleys at this time, but that cannot be the whole story. There are too many references to the wider movement for the broader Chartist context to be neglected. Newport was fought in isolation, but it was not planned in isolation from revolutionary schemes in other parts of Britain. In the dark days after the House of Commons had rejected the constitutional approach, the idea of a simultaneous rising throughout areas of Chartist strength appealed increasingly to a hardened and desperate minority of the leadership. These included John Taylor of Ayrshire, a romantic with a strong line in revolutionary rhetoric; William Burns, the Convention delegate for Dundee; William Ashton of Barnsley; and Peter Bussey of Bradford. The latter took a prominent part in organising the plot which centred on the West Riding. He was a former wool comber turned innkeeper who had risen to prominence in Bradford as leader of the local anti-Poor Law movement.

Evidence for what was happening in Bradford and elsewhere between the ending of the Convention in London on 14 September and the risings which occurred in January 1840 is thin and inconclusive, but a story can be stitched together from the fragments. There was clearly evidence of arming but the magistrates found it hard to penetrate the local sections into which the Chartist organisation was now divided, and strangers could not eavesdrop on conversations held in private houses. The magistrates eventually learnt enough through spies to abort the risings when they occurred, but they did not know enough in advance to prevent them. The historian has to rely in part on the stories told subsequently by William Ashton and William Lovett in their arguments with Feargus O'Connor over his alleged part in events.[18] Although polemical in nature, these accounts are sufficiently consistent with each other and the other fragments of evidence to enable the story to be told.[19]

Having agreed on 12 September that a rising should take place, Taylor remained in London while Bussey and Ashton returned to Yorkshire. A meeting attended by about forty delegates was called at Heckmondwike on 30 September, at which Halifax was represented by Thomas Kitchenman, a Grange Moor veteran from 1820.[20] There was nothing in the public business to suggest anything illegal, but a subsequent meeting referred back to an unreported resolution carried at this first meeting which was to be sent on to Robert Blakey at Newcastle. This appears to confirm Lovett's account which he got from one of the delegates, that the secret purpose of the Heckmondwike meeting was to allow Bussey and Ashton to communicate to the Yorkshire delegates the London resolution about a rising. According to Zephaniah Williams, messages were sent out to the north of England and Scotland as soon as the day was fixed in Wales. Frost, who was in Manchester on a lecture tour of Lancashire and Yorkshire, was suddenly called back to Wales some time after 10 October. Burns, who was in Manchester with Frost, took the message to Newcastle on his way back to Dundee. The messenger, probably Charles Jones who was wanted in connection with the Llanidloes riots at the end of April, then brought the news to Yorkshire. Feargus O'Connor was probably not at this stage privy to the plot, though he must have known what was generally being discussed, and he conveniently found business to attend to in Ireland.[21]

Bussey doubted O'Connor's commitment and was getting cold feet; so too was Ashton who hurriedly took the boat from Hull to visit his wife in France. Bussey feigned illness and sent a message back to Frost to say that Yorkshire would not be ready for another ten days. George White, an Irish wool comber and Chartist lecturer, was sent round the West Riding to call off the rising planned for 3 November. Charles Jones returned to Wales from Yorkshire by way of the steamer from Hull to London, where he was to alert Taylor before going back to Wales to warn Frost of the unreadiness of Yorkshire. Unfortunately Jones was shipwrecked and Taylor did not get the message until 29 October. He then hurried to Newcastle where he found Robert

Peddie, an Edinburgh staymaker with a revolutionary temperament to match his own, inciting the Winlaton ironworkers to arms.[22] They waited for the news that Newport had fallen. By the time Jones got back to Wales it was too late to delay the rising.

The news of the defeat of the Welsh Chartists caused alarm in the West Riding. Bussey went into hiding and subsequently emigrated. Taylor's men in Newcastle stood down. But that did not mean that the danger of a rising in the north was now over. Indeed, determination to save Frost added urgency to their plans. Taylor and Peddie lectured across the four northern counties. Sheffield organised a mass meeting in Paradise Square on 11 November, and then elected a delegate to attend a meeting in Newcastle at which plans were made for a Convention in London on 19 December. The Yorkshire leaders chose three delegates at a meeting held on 10 December in Manchester and then returned to Dewsbury which they had selected as the starting point for the rising in the West Riding. After an interchange of messages between London and Dewsbury, the rising was fixed for 12 January. Lovett's account becomes confused at this point, but it was probably here that O'Connor was asked to lead the north. He later denied this and supported his editor's decision to use the *Northern Star* of 11 January to denounce such attempts at physical force.

The Yorkshire rising was a disaster. James Allen, an informer, told the authorities in Rotherham of the rising at eight o'clock on the evening of 11 January. A message reached Sheffield in time for the authorities to arrest the local leader, Samuel Holberry, at midnight. The revolution, due to begin at 2.00 a.m., was aborted and only about fifty men turned out. After a brief skirmish, they fled or were arrested. The Barnsley Chartists waited in vain for the news of Holberry's success in Sheffield, and then went sadly home. The Bradford rising similarly came to nothing, amid a rumour (spread by a spy, James Harrison) that the magistrates had been informed of the plans and, without a signal from Bradford, the men of Dewsbury also went home. Newcastle also waited on events which never happened. The rising turned out to be the kind of hopeless shambles that O'Connor had prophesied it would be, although the demoralising effect of the *Northern Star*'s condemnation should not be underestimated. Ashton later recalled with bitterness how this article in the *Star* 'struck dismay into tens of thousands; the whole affair was blown to atoms by that cursed paper'. But the real reason why the risings fizzled out was that in both south and west Yorkshire the authorities had eventually found local Chartists willing to inform on what was being planned.

However, Bradford was not yet finished, for on Saturday 25 January, Robert Peddie arrived in town to address a meeting in support of Frost. Here he met up with Harrison and William Brook, a revolutionary joiner who felt thwarted by the failure of 12 January, a sentiment shared by Peddie. Arrangements, orchestrated by Harrison, were made for a new rising on 26 January. Cannon were to be taken from the Low Moor iron works, the Green Market and centre of Bradford were to be seized, and the Bradford men would then march on Dewsbury. Peddie was appointed leader. The story of the confused happenings on the night of 26 January can be told by one of the participants, Emanuel Hutton, a wool comber sentenced to eighteen months' hard labour in Wakefield House of Correction following his trial at York for riot:

> I was called up at night and when I came down a gun was put in my hands. I don't know who gave it to me. I wish I had. If I had known it at York it would have been told. I went down stairs and saw a man who told me to follow him – I did so for about 200 yards and there I saw a lot of men who bade me go into the market place with them – one gave me a gun. I asked several questions – there seemed no one appointed to lead. We went into the market place and as soon as I saw the Constables I set off – but I was caught. I had been at the Meetings. I was a Chartist only by reading the Star newspaper. I had heard my neighbours talk of a rising – they had fixed many a day.[23]

Others did not live to tell their story. John Clayton, one of the Sheffield insurgents, died in Northallerton House of Correction, and the Sheffield leader, Samuel Holberry, died in York Castle.

The risings were real but futile in the opinion of many at the time and of historians since. They neither removed the government nor won the Charter, but they appeared to succeed in one of their aims – to rescue John Frost. Frost, Williams and Jones were found guilty before Christmas and received the death sentence for high treason on 13 January. On 1 February this was commuted to transportation for life. The petitions for a reprieve contained more signatures than the first Chartist Petition, rejected in July 1839, and they were generated in an atmosphere more angry and desperate than had prevailed in the summer. Though the commutation was actually owing to the recommendation of the Lord Chief Justice, its effect was to defuse what might otherwise have become a very dangerous situation.[24] A firmly effective but not savage sentencing policy in this and in the hundreds of lesser cases brought before the courts in the winter of 1839–40, avoided the danger of provocation and brought the first Chartist crisis to a sullen but peaceful end.

The second Chartist crisis, 1842

The Chartist movement which imprisoned Chartists rejoined on their release from gaol during 1840 and 1841 was superficially the same as in 1838 and 1839 but in important respects was quite different. It still supported the strategy of a National Petition for the People's Charter, but the broad alliance of reforming movements and leaders which had come together in 1838 was now shattered. Some early leaders, like Oastler and Stephens, had never been Chartists as such. The same could be said of Thomas Attwood and the Birmingham Political Union contingent who had left the Convention over physical force and then imprisoned one of their own members, John Collins. Moderates, like Collins and William Lovett, now followed their own 'moral force' route away from the mainstream. They were joined by former extremists, such as Robert Lowery and Henry Vincent. Others, such as John Frost, were safely in Australia, while yet others, such as Bussey, were in voluntary exile in the United States. Mainstream Chartism was more closely than ever identified with Feargus O'Connor and the *Northern Star*. As such it was likely to be demagogic but peaceful, appealing to the moral force of peaceful mass support, constitutional methods and, if armed, then constitutionally armed. It was also better organised, with the National Charter Association (NCA) being formed in Manchester in July 1840. Henceforward Chartism was to be more like a modern mass political party, with a membership, a bureaucracy, and a certain amount of discipline. Meetings were more like party rallies and the annual Convention was a regulated party conference at which policy could be developed and dissidents expelled. If the lesson of 1839–40 had been the futility of physical force, that lesson had been learned.

The release of prisoners and a general election in 1841 stimulated a new and better-organised drive for a second National Petition. As in

1838–39, signatures were gathered against a background of gloomy economic conditions with increasing unemployment and rising bread prices. Again all hopes were pinned on the Charter to resolve these problems, though middle-class radicals offered the alternative of a repeal of the Corn Laws. Again, as in 1839, the National Convention met in London, and on 2 May again the House of Commons rejected the Petition although it claimed the support of 3,317,752 signatures compared with 'only' 1,280,000 in 1839. The coming summer was a troubled one, with widespread strikes and rioting on a scale greater than in 1839. The question which has troubled historians is how far was this activity connected with Chartism? Were the strikes political as well as economic?

Phrases to describe the events of the summer of 1842 have been loaded with meaning, both at the time and since: the 'Plug Plot' suggests conspiracy while 'General Strike' describes widespread industrial action with, following Benbow's pamphlet on the *Grand National Holiday* of 1832, perhaps also a political purpose. 'Riot' suggests localised and undirected violence, while to one contemporary in Accrington, the disturbances of August 1842 seemed 'more like a revolution than anything else'.[25] One can understand why. The strike came closer to the ideal of a simultaneous rising than any other disturbances in the period covered by this book, with the possible exception of the 'Swing' riots of 1830: within a space of a few weeks, fifteen English and Welsh counties were affected, as well as eight Scottish. London experienced disturbances at the same time as the major provincial industrial districts. Local forces for maintaining order were unable to cope and the deployment of troops was stretched by the geographical scale of the disturbances. In the balanced view of one historian

> the disturbances of 1842 were the most intense of any that occurred in Britain from the time of the French Revolution to the Chartist *détente* of 1848. They covered a wider geographical area than Luddism, embraced more trades than the Agricultural Labourers' Rising of 1830, and broke with more concentrated force than the Chartist unrest of 1839 and 1848.[26]

Initially both the Chartist leadership and the Home Secretary, Sir James Graham, believed that the strikes were an Anti-Corn Law League plot, consistent with the way middle-class reformers had used the threat of working-class violence to further their own ends in 1832. Superficially this was plausible. Most factories in the textile districts at the heart of the strike were working short-time anyway, and there would have been little to lose economically by a shut-down. John Bright of Rochdale did in fact suggest using lock-outs to provoke a challenge to the Corn Laws. The strikes began in the Manchester area following a 25 per cent cut in wages at Bayley's factory in Stalybridge – the Bayleys were supporters of the Anti-Corn Law League.[27] The manufacturers and the newspapers that supported them, however, thought the strikes a Chartist plot. The *Leeds Mercury* in the same report on 20 August referred to events as both 'The Holiday–Insurrection' and 'The Chartist Insurrection'.[28] Yet the Chartist leadership, meeting in Manchester in the middle of the strikes to commemorate Henry Hunt and the 'Peterloo' massacre on 16 August, appeared surprised by events which they then followed rather than led. The evidence is, as usual, contradictory, but what has become clear is that local Chartists were closely involved in the strikes, that there was some co-ordinated leadership, and that there was a groundswell of local Chartism which used its position within striking communities to turn industrial action into a strike for the Charter. Just as some Chartists leaders, such as O'Brien, argued that Corn Law repeal would not be to the workers' advantage unless guaranteed by the Charter, so Chartist strike leaders argued that good wages could only be guaranteed by a government elected under the Charter.

The strikes began in early July in the Staffordshire coalfield where the issues were wage cuts, a system of employment known as 'buildas' (work without pay) and the truck system but the resolutions setting out the demands of the south Staffordshire miners on 1 August were proposed by two Chartists, Joseph Linney and Arthur O'Neill.[29] This set the pattern. The Chartists did not create the grievances, or the economic depression which caused employers to demand wage reductions, but they did organise the workers' reaction and turned local strikes and an inclination to riot into a concerted challenge to the authority of employers, the forces of law and order and ultimately the government itself. And they did so all the more effectively because they were not outside agitators with an abstract political programme but members of their own local communities caught up in their own and their neighbours' grievances.

At the end of July, factory masters south-east of Manchester, in

Ashton, Stalybridge, Dukinfield and Hyde, announced a 25 per cent reduction in wages. On 26 July a large public meeting chaired by William Woodruffe, an Ashton Chartist delegate, resolved to stop work 'until we obtain a fair day's wage for a fair day's work'.[30] The two main speakers, William Aitken and Richard Pilling, were both Chartists. This was followed by a further meeting at Stalybridge on 29 July, also addressed by known Chartists. Both meetings were primarily about the wages issue but they also supported the Charter and called for arms to be raised to protect the working classes. Further meetings were held in Hyde and Dukinfield over the next few days with the same and similar speakers to the same effect. As a result most employers withdrew the cuts, but at Bayleys' factory there was some confusion. The employers claimed that Bayleys' offer was rejected and the workers struck work; the workers claimed they were locked out. On Sunday, 7 August a large meeting was held on Mottram Moor where the main speakers were, again, Chartists. Resolutions were carried in support of a strike for a fair day's wage and the Charter, and it was announced that there would be a general turn-out throughout Lancashire and Cheshire on the following morning.

The success of the turn-out in the Ashton–Stalybridge area, straddling the county boundary between Lancashire and Cheshire, points to something more than spontaneity in the strike. It had clearly been organised by that group of Chartist speakers who had led the preliminary meetings.[31] Their leader was Richard Pilling, a weaver from Ashton with a long history of active participation in Chartism, and radicalism before that. O'Connor, quoting a witness against Pilling at his trial at the Lancaster Assizes, subsequently referred to him as 'the father of the movement' and in 1848 Pilling himself boasted that he 'was the sole cause of the turn-out in Lancashire, the originator of the whole proceeding'.[32] But at Lancaster, Pilling had argued more politically, 'I say it is not *me* that is the father of this movement; but that house. Our addresses have been laid before that house, and they have not redressed our grievances; and from there, and from there alone, the cause comes.'[33]

Pilling was clearly unrepentant that this was a politically-inspired strike. On the afternoon of 8 August he led a party from Ashton to Oldham to spread the strike. Then on 9 August the strikers were ready to march on Manchester. Sir Charles Shaw, the commissioner of police in Manchester, wanted to keep them out, but Daniel

Maude, the stipendiary magistrate, who had ultimate authority, saw the women in the procession and the generally peaceful demeanour of 'the mob' and thought it better to allow their passage. Although troops did in fact block several streets, the strikers were allowed to hold a peaceful rally addressed by Pilling. Most of the factories turned out with little or no violence until the crowd reached Birley Mills in Oxford Street. Here a battle began which dragged on into the next day and was ended only by soldiers with fixed bayonets. The senior member of the Birley family, Hugh Hornby Birley, had commanded the yeomanry at Peterloo. By the Saturday 13 August, Birley's too was forced to close.

The turn-outs now spread northwards and eastwards to Rochdale and Bolton, then to Blackburn, Todmorden and over the Pennines to Halifax as the strike went into its second week. Everywhere the pattern was repeated. A party of strikers asked the workers to leave their employment; most did so readily. The factory was then immobilised by driving in the boiler plugs, releasing the water and extinguishing the fire, thus cutting off the motor power and bringing the whole works to a standstill. This prevented the workers from being coerced back to work. Very little damage was done; the plugs on the boilers of high pressure steam engines were not driven in, for fear of causing an explosion. There was little indiscriminate looting, excepting demands for bread. Where there were clashes with the police or troops, the principal weapons were stones. Intimidation came from superior numbers. Outright violence was the exception. In Preston, where a policeman had been killed in an election riot the year before, a stone-throwing crowd ran up against a small detachment of troops who opening fire, killing four rioters and seriously wounding several more. Beyond the Manchester area, there was a serious riot in the Potteries. As in south Staffordshire, the strike began in the north Staffordshire collieries in early July in protest at wage cuts. By mid July, colliers were roaming the coal field halting other pits and stopping their steam engines by driving in the boiler plugs. The shortage of coal then stopped the potteries, creating greater distress and unemployment. On 6 August three miners were arrested for begging. This provoked an attack on the town hall to release them. The local newspaper was in no doubt that, 'The perpetrators of these wanton outrages are believed to consist principally of the more disaffected turn-out colliers, instigated, there is but little doubt, by the

Chartists.'[34] The role of Chartists, as in Lancashire and Cheshire, was as organisers of meetings, providing leadership and oratory.

Thomas Cooper, the Leicester Chartist, addressed one such meeting on Sunday 14 August at Hanley. Next morning, he delivered an ambiguously worded address to a crowd of several thousands, after which a resolution was adopted in favour of the strike. The crowd then dispersed and turned into a mob, raking out the fires and removing the plugs at Shelton colliery, attacking the police station and releasing the prisoners, looting the pawnbrokers' shops, and destroying the poor law records and the court room – all symbols of the oppression of the poor. They then went on to other towns in the Potteries. In Longton they attacked the town hall, the police station and the parish office, and fired the house of the rector, Dr Vale, who was a poor law guardian. Cooper addressed another meeting that night, urging (by his own account) 'Peace, Law and Order!', but the crowd did not disperse and held sway all night. Cooper fled to Macclesfield on his way to Manchester. Next day, troops confronted the rioters in Burslem but were able to reassert control only by firing into the crowd. At least three rioters were killed and several injured. Gradually order was restored in all Five Towns.[35]

As the movement spilled over the Pennines from Lancashire into Yorkshire, the *Leeds Mercury*, the paper read by most Whig mill-owners, reported events in terrifying detail. Despite the obvious bias in the reporting, it conveys a sense of the power and terror of the plug-drawing mob:

> The concourse of people, which has been computed at not less than from 15,000 to 20,000, came from the neighbourhood of Bradford, Hebden Bridge, Todmorden, and there were some women who had even walked from Oldham, and appeared quite hearty in their novel undertaking. There were at least 5,000 from Hebden Bridge, and they entered the town singing the hundredth psalm, the women forming the middle portion of the procession. On the arrival of the procession from the neighbourhood of Bradford, at about eleven o'clock, the riot act was read by George Pollock, Esq., and it was read again on the arrival of the Todmorden men.
>
> The mob, some of them ferocious looking, directed their malice first at the mill of Messrs. Jon. Akroyd and Son, the Shade mill, at Haley Hill.

The number of men and women who marched up to Mr. Akroyd's mill could not be less than 10,000, covering, as they did, the whole line of road from the North Bridge to Haley Hill. They arrived at this mill shortly after twelve, and the work-people being at dinner, the turn-outs were saved the trouble of clearing the premises, but two of their number demanded an interview with Mr. Akroyd, at which they insisted that the plugs should be drawn out of the boilers. Mr. Akroyd, thinking probably that opposition would be unavailing, not only agreed to this *modest* request, but also permitted one of his workmen to assist the deputation in their labour of mischief. The mob outside, however, would not rest satisfied until they had full confirmation that the work had been done effectually, and in a few minutes afterwards a deputation of six presented themselves to see that all was *right*. Having all doubts removed respecting the plugging of the boilers, they then not only requested, but insisted, that the reservoir should be let off. On this point they were met on the part of Mr. Akroyd with a decided negative, which only tended to increase the eagerness of the turn-outs, to effect their object. In order to prevent so disastrous a calamity, (for, by turning off the reservoir, which is merely supplied by rain and other smaller reservoirs, the works would have been stopped for several weeks) a present of a £5 note was tendered to the men to induce them to go quietly about their business. This temptation not having the desired effect, the military were hastily sent for, and in a few minutes they were at the scene of action, and arrived just at the moment to prevent incalculable mischief; . . .

The soldiers secured six young men near to Mr. Akroyd's mill, for riotous conduct, – apparently about the ages of from 18 to 23, – and they were taken from Mr. Akroyd's grounds to the Magistrates' office, under an escort of about a dozen foot soldiers, with loaded muskets.

On their way through the streets an attempt was made to rescue them, and stones were frequently thrown at the soldiers, one or two of whom, it is said, but we cannot vouch for the fact, in a moment of excitement, fired upon the people, wounding one young man in the legs.

Another man, in the course of the afternoon, was taken into custody and placed in the prison, for breach of the peace – thus making seven in all; and no doubt numbers more might have been taken up, but for the leniency of the military and the special constables.[36]

Akroyd had been one of the first manufacturers in the area to reduce wages.

The magistrates decided next day it would be best to move the prisoners to Wakefield. The railway had not yet reached Halifax, and so the prisoners had to be transported by coach with a military escort down the steep hill at Salterhebble to the station at Elland in the Calder Valley. The crowd decided to ambush the coach and release the prisoners. They failed to do so, but were able to take their revenge on the returning troops as they made their way slowly up the hill back to Halifax.

> But, on a sudden a cry was raised that the soldiers were advancing, and as suddenly the apparent calm was succeeded by an overwhelming tempest, for, in a moment as it were, a shower of large stones were hurled from all parts of the eminence among the soldiers, who then came up at full gallop, and on to the heads of the devoted and innocent passengers, who thus suffered severely from the accidental circumstances of being compelled, though only for a few moments, to be apparently under the protection of the soldiery. With such direct aim were these missiles hurled, that scarcely a soldier escaped unhurt – some of them received severe cuts – three of them were fairly felled from their horses, the animals setting off and leaving their late riders to the mercy of the mob. . . . Of course there was a scene of very great confusion; an express was sent to Halifax for the infantry, and the gallant Hussars, after charging with ball, returned, headed by Mr Briggs, to the rescue of their companions, which they effected. During the affray, Mr Briggs received a wound on the arm from a stone, which disabled him, and he went home: the soldiers had previously received orders to fire, and these orders were carried into effect, we are afraid with a fatal result, but of this we cannot speak with certainty; the soldiers' horses were retaken at Elland.[37]

The final irony was that one of the passengers wounded on the coach was a reporter for the *Northern Star*.

The above account illustrates both the methods by which the strikers proceeded, with a very orderly negotiation over stopping Akroyd's mill and a quite proper rejection of his bribe while he played for time; and the suddenness with which violence could flare up, demonstrating the vulnerability of both sides but ultimately the superiority of the force available to magistrates like the gallant William Briggs.

Despite such occurrences, most of the strike was conducted with an ominous restraint, indicating a more sophisticated approach than would have been expected of a mere hunger riot. Back in Manchester, the extent of this organisation was apparent and it was this aspect of the strike that worried the Home Secretary most.

The form that central leadership of the strikes took was the Great Delegate Conference meeting in Manchester under the chairmanship of Alexander Hutchinson, an Owenite Socialist and Chartist who was secretary of the Manchester smiths and a member of the National Charter Association (NCA) executive. On 11 August at a meeting in the Carpenters' Hall, a delegate conference of mechanics, engineers, millwrights, moulders and smiths met to agree a common programme of action. The following morning a delegate conference of the mill trades met at the Sherwood Inn to do the same. Both conferences carried almost identical motions in favour of the Charter.[38] The two conferences then made arrangements for the Great Delegate Conference at the Sherwood Inn on Monday, 15 August. This was adjourned to the Carpenters' Hall to better accommodate the 143 delegates who attended. The following day, 16 August, 141 delegates representing eighty-five trades met in the largest hall available in Manchester, the Owenite Hall of Science – the Carpenters' Hall had already been booked by the Chartists. Here the trades delegates voted by a large majority to cease work until the Charter became the law of the land.[39] As the conference was coming to the end of its business for the day, the hall was surrounded by police and troops and the chief constable ordered the meeting to disperse. When Hutchinson refused on the grounds that the meeting was legal, the magistrates were sent for to pronounce it illegal. The delegates then complied, but defiantly issued a placard announcing the resolution of the meeting:

> that the delegates in public meeting assembled, do recommend to the various constituencies we represent, to adopt all legal means to carry into effect the People's Charter; and further we recommend that delegates be sent through the whole country to endeavour to obtain the co-operation of the middle and working classes in carrying out the resolution of ceasing labour until the Charter becomes the law of the land.[40]

Their ranks thinned by arrests and hurried departures out of Manchester, a rump of delegates reconvened the following day at the Sherwood Inn where they formed a central committee and urged the formation of local committees to direct the strike.

Meanwhile, the NCA executive had arranged to meet in Manchester on 16 August to commemorate Peterloo, with O'Connor unveiling a statue of Henry Hunt at James Scholefield's chapel in Ancoats. A placard had been issued on 1 August, announcing a procession from Stevenson Square to the Ancoats chapel, and then back to the Carpenters' Hall for a tea party and ball. Scholefield called off the procession on the morning of 16 August and in the evening, instead of attending the ball, O'Connor stayed behind at the chapel 'with other Chartists, engaged in considering what measures were best to be adopted in the present crisis'.[41] He was probably considering the reversal of Chartist policy towards the strike which emerged at the NCA executive conference the following day. Hitherto, O'Connor had agreed with William Hill, editor of the *Northern Star*, that the strike was probably an Anti-Corn Law League plot or a trap designed to discredit the Chartists, but on 17 August he supported Peter Murray McDouall's ringing endorsement of the strikes:

> That whilst the Chartist body did not originate the present cessation from labour, this conference of delegates from various parts of England, express their deep sympathy with their constituents, the working men now on strike, and that we strongly approve the extension and continuance of their present struggle till the People's Charter becomes legislative enactment, and decide forthwith to issue an address to that effect, and pledge ourselves, on our return to our respective localities, to give proper direction to the people's efforts.[42]

Only six delegates votes against this resolution, including Hill and, remarkably, the 'Marat' of the revolution, George Julian Harney.[43]

This resolution and two addresses that accompanied it committed Chartism to the strikes.[44] This fact was used against O'Connor and other leaders when they were brought before the Lancaster Assizes in April 1843 on a charge of seditious conspiracy. Although the strikes were to continue well into September, hunger, the arrest of leaders and a tightening of control by the police and military were already beginning to turn the tide against the workers. By October, around

1500 arrests had been made: about half were tried before magistrates' courts and half before special commissions held in Carlisle, York, Chester, Lancaster, Liverpool and Stafford. Fifty-nine of those arrested, including O'Connor and the rest of the Chartist leadership, were reserved for the Assizes at Lancaster. In the end, these were the lucky ones for, despite being found guilty, a fault in the indictment meant they were never called up for sentence.

In this interpretation of events, the strikes of 1842 were more than industrial actions, and the riots were not spontaneous outbursts of popular anger or anguish – though doubtless they were for some participants. There was a seditious conspiracy in that local Chartist leaders provided organisation and co-ordination and directed the strikes to a political end. The degree of co-ordination and organisation with its controlled use of violence seemed a real threat to the authorities. The government was particularly alarmed at the prospect of the strikes spreading to London where a large open-air meeting was held on 16 August on Stepney Green. It was addressed by a speaker from Ashton, and passed a resolution in favour of the Charter. Further meetings followed on Clerkenwell Green, Bethnal Green, Lincoln's Inn Fields and other open spaces throughout the city. The Duke of Wellington pressed for the Grenadier Guards, who had just been sent to Manchester, to be brought back to the capital. Further meetings on Kennington Common and Paddington Green on 22 August were dispersed by large numbers of police supported by troops.

The danger passed but it had seemed real enough while it lasted. Although in retrospect one can see that the authorities could hold out longer than the strikers, so that a strike until the Charter was enacted was simply not realistic, the threat to public order in the summer of 1842 was considerable. Yet, the very act of striking for the Charter was a constitutional one. It was not revolutionary in the conspiratorial sense of the United Irishmen or the Thistlewood group. The paradox of the Holiday–Insurrection of 1842, as the *Leeds Mercury* pointed out in its editorial for 20 August, was that the cause of their success was also the reason for their failure:

> Their entire want of cohesion, their going without weapons, and their abstinence from all but one act of violence at each mill, enable them often to *elude* the soldiery and the police, and to get into towns and into mills unawares: they also prevent the masters from having any great apparent interest in resisting them

and further, they blind the workmen to the real danger of this lawless movement. But that same want of cohesion, that want of any tangible and visible form of insurrection, render their operations as evanescent as they were surprising.

However, 'if the turn-outs were to change their character, and to form a rebel army, no sooner would they be thus brought to a head than they would be utterly demolished'. for 'the masters who submit quietly to the driving in of a boiler plug, would act in a very different manner if their property was threatened with serious and extensive mischief'. There may have been an air of complacency here, or the editor was trying to allay the fears of his readers, but he was right to note in the events of the summer of 1842 the unusually peaceful nature of the 'insurrection'. The Chartists had learned how to turn an 'ebullition' into an organised mass protest. That made it more, not less, of a challenge to the established order and an important development in the character of working-class politics.

The third Chartist crisis, 1848

As the economic depression lifted and bread prices fell after 1842, mass Chartist support declined and the constitutional mainstream prevailed, but with the downturn in the European economy in 1847, revolution returned to Europe and with it the possibility of renewed violence in Britain and Ireland. The revolutionary upheavals of 'the springtime of the peoples' which swept the continent in the wake of the fall of the French monarchy in February 1848 seemed to promise as never before the realisation of the dream that, 'For a nation to love liberty, it is sufficient that she knows it; and to be free, it is sufficient that she wills it.' As the world was to rediscover again in 1989, the impossible could sometimes happen; immovable regimes could collapse before the power of the people; even constitutional revolution might be possible.

Chartism had already begun to revive before the news from France gave new heart to the movement. At the general election in 1847, Feargus O'Connor had been elected to the House of Commons for Nottingham and fear that his victory would be challenged reinvigorated the NCA in his support. As one old Chartist later recalled, perhaps with some exaggeration for the entertainment of his readers:

In this year flour was very dear, reaching the price of 5s. per stone, whilst trade was also very bad. This was the time to make politicians, as the easiest way to get to an Englishman's brains is through his stomach. It was said by its enemies that Chartism was dead and buried and would never rise again, but they were doomed to disappointment. . . . We were only waiting for the time to come again.[45]

The NCA launched a new National Petition in favour of the Charter and arranged mass meetings to whip up support. This time, though, the centre of the movement was London where the *Northern Star* and NCA were now based. The first wave of rioting began in early March, but little of this was specifically 'Chartist'. On 6 March a demonstration in Trafalgar Square against a proposed rise in the income tax (hardly a cause of immediate concern to Chartists) was banned and resulted in rioting and a rush towards Buckingham Palace that caught the police by surprise. A few lamps and windows were broken on the way but it was three days before the metropolitan police were fully in control. Of the 127 rioters arrested, two-thirds were aged between 16 and 22.[46] Worse news was received from elsewhere in the country. In Glasgow, a crowd of several thousand unemployed, reported to be mainly Irish, complained about the quality of the food provided by the Relief Committee and resorted to looting local shops including gunsmiths. A barricade was erected and cries of 'Bread or Revolution' and '*Vive la République*' were heard. The Riot Act was read and troops were called out. Three people were killed as soldiers fired to clear the threatening crowds. The knowledge of recent events in Paris gave this occasion greater significance than it might otherwise have had.

On 8 and 9 March a similar though lesser riot took place in Edinburgh. In Manchester the unemployed rioted at the imposition of oakum picking by the poor law authorities, but they were dealt with by the police. On 17 March (St Patrick's Day) the Chartists held a demonstration on Kennington Common in south London, which was followed by some looting in Camberwell. The authorities nervously enrolled special constables. On the same day in Salford a Chartist meeting outside the town hall voted a congratulatory address to the French people and a Chartist–Irish Confederate alliance was cemented.[47] Again, nervous magistrates enrolled special constables. As the day for the presentation of the Petition drew near, there was heightened expectation on both sides throughout the country and, anticipating its rejection by the House of Commons, Chartists were reported to be arming and drilling on the moors as in 1839.[48] In the *Northern Star*, the editor, Harney, outdid even his usual revolutionary rhetoric as he proclaimed:

> The work goes bravely on. Germany is revolutionised from end to end. Princes are flying, thrones are perishing. Everywhere the oppressors of nations yield, or are overthrown. 'Reform or Revolution' is now the order of the day. How long, Men of Great Britain and Ireland, how long will you carry the damning stigma of being the only people in Europe who dare not will their freedom?
>
> Patience! the hour is nigh! From the hill-tops of Lancashire, from the voices of hundreds of thousands has ascended to Heaven the oath of union, and the rallying cry of conflict. Englishmen and Irishmen have sworn to have THE CHARTER AND REPEAL, or VIVE LA REPUBLIQUE![49]

The Chartist Convention met in London on 4 April and arranged to present the Petition on 10 April. The plan was to convene a large demonstration on Kennington Common, with parallel meetings elsewhere in the country (and, indeed elsewhere in London), after which the Petition would be taken in procession to the House of Commons. The very idea was intimidating and the government was concerned that London should not slide into revolution as had happened in Paris and Berlin. Accordingly, massive steps were taken to ensure that the meeting would not get out of hand. Initially the government would have banned the meeting, but then realised that this would be more likely to cause trouble than allowing it to proceed on a peaceful basis. But they banned the procession, closed the bridges across the Thames to confine the Chartists to the south of the river, and organised their own massive counter-demonstration of physical force throughout the capital: 85,000 special constables, many of them workmen enrolled to defend their own places of work and possibly to prevent them attending the meeting; 4,000 police, mainly on the bridges and in the vicinity of Parliament; and 8,000 troops in reserve. Estimates of Chartist numbers range from the official 15,000 to O'Connor's 'rather under than over 400,000'. The latest scholarly guess suggests somewhere around 150,000.[50]

Much of the mythology about the great Kennington Common

meeting on 10 April is based on hindsight. Within a few days, everyone knew that the meeting had dispersed as peacefully as the Chartists had always intended, that the Petition had been taken to the House of Commons in six cabs, and that the number of signatures was not the 5,706,000 claimed but 'only' an estimated 1,975,496. London could afford to relax and laugh at the Chartist 'fiasco'. This view needs revising in three respects: most people were not laughing at the time; the 'fiasco' effect was in part planned by the government to discredit Chartism; and from the point of view of revolutionary threat, the worst was still to come.

Most people were not laughing until it was all over. This is clear from diaries kept at the time by prominent figures. John Cam Hobhouse, one-time Radical but now deeply conservative and anti-Chartist Whig minister, recorded 10 April apprehensively:

> There was an appearance of the expectation of some struggle or disastrous event. When I got to the Indian Board I found some clerks rather annoyed at there being no arms nor any military force there. I cannot say I felt quite easy, separated as I was from my children, and recollecting that my door had been chalked, as also had Lord Grey's and Labouchere's. Lord J. Russell had a force of constables in his house.
>
> I sat down to office business, not expecting, but thinking it by no means improbable that I should hear discharges of musketry or cannon from the other side of the river. Indeed, the slamming of doors made me start once or twice, and I looked at Westminster Bridge to see whether it was crowded. I heard cheers, and, going to the window, saw a boat with soldiers going under the bridge, and a crowd on the bridge, with men on horseback waving hats; and shortly after the bridge was completely empty, and a few mounted police were guarding it. Shortly after, Mr. Plowden came into the room full of glee, and said, 'It is all over.' He had been to the Home Office and learned that Feargus O'Connor had just been with Sir George Grey to announce that the meeting had broken up, that the procession was abandoned, and that he was about to take the monster petition to the House of Commons in six cabs.
>
> I went to the House of Commons at half past four, and saw the petition in two great rolls on the floor of the outward lobby.[51]

Charles Greville, secretary to the Privy Council, noted on 9 April the extensive preparations being made for the following day, uncertain

whether they were 'very sublime or very ridiculous'.[52] However, all
doubt had been removed as to which when he wrote his next diary
entry, at Newmarket races on 13 April:

> Monday passed off with surprising quiet, and it was considered
> a most satisfactory demonstration on the part of the Government,
> and the peaceable and loyal part of the community. Enormous
> preparations were made, and a host of military, police, and
> special constables were ready if wanted; every gentleman in
> London was sworn, and during a great part of the day, while the
> police were reposing, they did duty. The Chartist movement was
> contemptible; but everybody rejoices that the demonstration
> was made, for it has given a great and memorable lesson which
> will not be thrown away, either on the disaffected and mischie-
> vous, or the loyal and peaceful; and it will produce a vast effect
> in all foreign countries, and show how solid is the foundation on
> which we are resting. We have displayed a great resolution and
> a great strength, and given unmistakeable [sic] proofs, that if
> sedition and rebellion hold up their heads in this country, they
> will be instantly met with the most vigorous resistance, and be
> put down by the hand of authority, and by the zealous co-oper-
> ation of all classes of the people. The whole of the Chartist move-
> ment was to the last degree contemptible from first to last.

Here he gives not only the typical reaction of those whose fears had
not been realised, but also suggests that the build up on 10 April had
been government policy, partly to overawe and discredit the Chartists
once and for all, and partly to impress foreign governments which
had shown themselves unable to cope with their own revolutionary
crowds. There is a coincidence between the sentiments expressed in
this diary entry and words used by the prime minister, Lord John
Russell, writing to the Queen on the afternoon of 10 April: 'A quiet
termination of the present ferment will greatly raise us in foreign
countries.'[53]

One of the advantages of the defeat of Chartism was, in Greville's
opinion, its effect on the Irish. Hobhouse too had the Irish on his mind
and the major event in the House of Commons on 13 April was not
the discrediting of the People's Charter but the debate on the bill 'for
the more effectual repression of seditious and treasonable proceedings' in Ireland. This Treason–Felony Act was followed on 22 July by
the suspension of *Habeas Corpus* in Ireland where the situation had

deteriorated since 1847, partly as a result of nationalist anger over the famine and partly an outcome of the realignment in Irish politics that was accelerated by Daniel O'Connell's death in 1847. A group of romantic nationalists, including Charles Gavan Duffy, had started a paper, the *Nation*, in October 1842. They did not favour violence and were opposed to the Chartists. This moderation was carried over, even after the miseries of the famine had begun, by Duffy and William Smith O'Brien in a secession in early 1847 from O'Connell's Repeal Association, known as the Irish Confederation. A minority of Confederates, however, took up the cause of tenant right and in early 1848 two of this group, John Mitchel and Thomas Devin Reilly, set up their own paper, the *United Irishman* in rivalry to the *Nation*. The news from France then brought the two groups closer together again. O'Brien called for the formation of a National Guard, for which he was charged with sedition but acquitted when the jury was unable to agree a verdict. The Confederates also struck a working relationship with the Chartists in Britain. This had always been Feargus O'Connor's dream, but he had been thwarted while O'Connell lived.

The old fear of an Franco-Irish alliance in revolution revived. Russell was under no illusions about what the Irish might do. As he wrote to Lord Clarendon, the Lord Lieutenant, on 1 March 1848, 'The Irish are not the French but they have a knack of imitation.'[54] Indeed the very next day the Duke of Wellington, as Commander in Chief, sent a memorandum to his opposite in Dublin warning that 'the Irish Revolutionary or Repeal leaders had sent over to Paris persons to enquire respecting the mode of constructing the Barricades in the streets which have been used there and have been considered so formidable'.[55] The government acted swiftly. By the time Smith O'Brien (on bail for sedition) got to Paris with a congratulatory address at the end of March, Britain had already agreed with the French Provisional Government a pact of mutual non-interference in each other's internal affairs. If the Irish were to rise successfully they would have to rely on their own resources, which meant looking to the Irish in Britain to cause a diversion and in North America for military support.

By 1848 London, Manchester, Liverpool, Bradford, Glasgow and smaller British towns such as Barnsley and Ashton had considerable Irish minorities. In Bradford and Ashton, even in 1841, some 10 per cent of the population was Irish.[56] The threat of a Chartist–Confederate alliance was considerable. In Manchester just such an alliance had been formed on St Patrick's Day, and in his letter to the Queen on 10 April, Lord John Russell had noted amid his pleasure over the London débâcle, 'At Manchester, however, the Chartists are armed, and have bad designs.' In London, Confederate clubs had been spreading since the autumn of 1847 and on 4 April 1848 they came together with the Chartists at a meeting arranged by the Fraternal Democrats. There was a separate Irish contingent at Kennington Common on 10 April. Thereafter, some joint associations were formed.[57] Thomas Frost later recalled, 'Communications passed at this time between the plotters of revolution on both sides of St George's Channel.'[58] In Glasgow, where pikes were being manufactured at Anderston, Thomas D'Arcy McGee tried to persuade the Glasgow Irish to seize the Clyde steamers and sail for Ireland, presumably with weapons. As another Irish speaker informed his audience: 'prayer and petitions were the weapons of slaves and cowards; arms were the weapons used by the free and the brave. They would best help Ireland by keeping the army in Scotland'.[59] These were brave words, but a proposed National Guard materialised only in Aberdeen, Dundee and Edinburgh, and not on the scale of the 6,000 at Aberdeen that Ernest Jones later claimed. In Liverpool, ships from North America were searched on entering British waters, and the police in Dublin were instructed to arrest all returning Irish emigrants and search them for treasonable papers.[60] In Bradford throughout April and May there were reports of drilling and pikes being manufactured. Desperate, unemployed wool combers, many of them Irish, attended meetings at which inflammatory language was used. One informer reported, apparently without exaggeration, 'that there is reason to apprehend that the Chartists here would rise if there should be an outbreak in Ireland or anywhere in England'.[61]

The background to mounting unrest in the early summer of 1848 was the impending trial of John Mitchel under the new Treason–Felony Act, following his arrest on 22 March for publishing seditious articles in the *United Irishman*.[62] There was widespread fear of a rising should he be convicted. In London, where the Chartist Convention had been succeeded by a National Assembly on 1 May, a New Plan of Organisation was agreed, similar to that employed by the United Irishmen in the late 1790s, with a basic unit of ten men to a class and ten classes to a ward. This structure was both flexible and opaque, lending itself to conspiratorial organisations which in individual localities easily merged with local Irish Confederate clubs. At the same time, regular outdoor meetings were held, particularly in East London. Chartism at this level was more active than ever. Mitchel was tried on 25 and 26 May and sentenced to death, later commuted to transportation for fourteen years. Meetings in his support were held on Clerkenwell Green during the trial, and on 28 May perhaps 10,000 to 12,000 people gathered on the Green. The following evening several thousand gathered again and hear a rousing speech from John Fussell in which he said 'If John Mitchell [sic] is sent to Spike island then it is quite evident that you may use spikes for the government. I have five sons and I would disown them if they were not ready to assassinate men who sent me out of the Country for such a crime as that of which John Mitchell is said to be guilty.'[63]

The crowd then marched towards Trafalgar Square. They were joined en route by another 3,000 who had been listening to speeches from Ernest Jones and other Chartist leaders on Stepney Green. They marched through the West End and then back east in a formidable display of strength. At its height the crowd was estimated to be between 50,000 and 60,000 strong. Although the main procession was peaceful, there was some marginal rioting and next morning the police banned all assemblages and processions in the capital. Meetings nevertheless continued: on Clerkenwell Green on 31 May where troops stood by as the police cleared the Green; and in Bonner's Fields on 4 June, where Ernest Jones was the main speaker. These and smaller, simultaneous meetings, often unannounced so no reporter could be present to collect evidence for a prosecution, were gradually wearing down the police and demoralising property owners in the vicinity of the meetings. On 4 June the police snapped and rioted against the crowd.[64] The tone of Charles Greville's diary was very different from that of 13 April. The mood of the people had changed for the worse and

> many who on 10th of April went out as special constables declare that they would not do so again if another manifestation required it. The speeches which are made at the different meetings are remarkable for the coarse language and savage spirit they display. It is quite new to hear any Englishman coolly recommend assassination and the other day a Police Superintendent was wounded in the leg by some sharp instrument. These are new and very bad symptoms, and it is impossible not to feel

alarm when we consider the vast amount of the population as compared with any repressive power we possess.[65]

Finally, warrants were issued for the arrest of the leading speakers, including Jones and Fussell.

The culmination of these meetings came on Whit Monday, 12 June, on Bonner's Fields. This was a re-run of 10 April but in far less auspicious circumstances. The government banned all meetings and called up over 5,000 troops and 4,000 police; only a few special constables re-enlisted, and they did the duties of the ordinary police who were on riot duty.[66] David Goodway has offered the conclusion that 'The Chartist leadership would probably have welcomed the Bonner's Fields demonstration developing into a rising.'[67] In fact the only member of the Chartist Executive left in London was Peter Murray McDouall. He sized up the situation, and called the meeting off. A heavy thunderstorm did the rest.

That evening, at the Albion beershop in Bethnal Green Road, McDouall sat down to plan an insurrection, but two days later called it off on the instructions of the Chartist Executive: spies had been detected. Nothing further happened until 10 July when the conspirators resumed their meetings, this time independently of the Chartist Executive, although the latter came to know of the plot. On 20 July a secret committee was formed to plan for the day of insurrection which was to be 16 August. Then, on 27 July news came that Smith O'Brien had attempted a rising in Ireland which had been a complete failure and the leaders had all been arrested. Neither this, nor a realistic (and justified) fear of spies, deterred the conspirators who were now in deadly earnest.[68]

The conspiracy was not just a London one, for events in London since April had been repeated elsewhere.[69] The main centres of concern to the authorities were Manchester, Liverpool and Bradford where the situation was especially dangerous. Bradford, which had grown rapidly over the past two decades and become the centre of the worsted trade, had been incorporated as a borough and acquired its own police force only in 1847. This numbered sixty-nine men, or one to every 1,343 inhabitants. With such an inadequate force, the mayor was powerless to stop Chartist activities. As one correspondent complained to the Home Office:

Nothing can induce him to put a stop to illegal meetings, drillings and secret armings of the tumultuous mob who even hold their meetings and perambulate the streets on the Sabbath day, marching in military style with their captains in red and green caps and divided into sections and companies, keeping the step with true military precision, carrying tricolour flags and others bearing abominable inscriptions such as 'more pigs and less parsons', 'down with the aristocracy', 'England free or a desert' etc., etc. A ferocious looking Blacksmith named the Wat Tyler of Bradford and who openly makes pikes and other deadly weapons for the Chartists is allowed to carry on his nefarious traffic without ever being molested. He is not going to shave his beard until the Charter becomes the law of the land. I enclose you a Bill that they force upon the shopkeepers to put in their windows – those who refuse are told they will not support them nor will they let others. I will give you one case that came under my own notice. They called upon a shopkeeper to beg something for to purchase Flags etc, and he refusing, on the market night they surrounded his shop and would not let a single customer enter; so that he was compelled to apologize and give them 5s and promise to become one of them.[70]

'Wat Tyler' was Isaac Jefferson, a huge man whose wrists were too thick for the police to handcuff. But they had to catch him first. The centre of his power was Adelaide Street off Manchester Road, an area densely packed with unemployed wool combers. This was an area the authorities entered at their peril. On 13 May, the police attempted to make an arrest during a military-style parade and had been beaten up by the inhabitants who successfully retrieved their leader. The reluctance of the mayor to intervene was understandable. Then, on 23 May, a mass meeting was addressed by Peter Murray McDouall who made a seditious speech with impunity. The Home Office decided that action would have to be taken. With such a large Irish population – half the Chartists were estimated to be Irish – the Mitchel verdict was clearly going to be very important and the magistrates were informed that the intention, as in Scotland, was to tie troops up to prevent them being sent to Ireland. On 27 May, extra troops arrived bringing their numbers up to 800, and 1,500 special constables were sworn in. On Sunday 28 May the magistrates finally decided to act and next morning they sent the police into Adelaide Street to arrest Jefferson and conduct a house-to-house search for arms. The police and specials had got as far as the corner of Manchester Road and Adelaide Street when the inhabitants surged out of the back streets, armed with whatever came to hand, and drove the police back to the court house. They then marched triumphantly through the streets singing Chartist songs. Troops were sent for. The police armed with cutlasses, 1,000 special constables, 200 infantry with fixed bayonets, and two troops of Dragoons then advanced and drove the mob back to their homes. Nineteen arrests were made but the leaders escaped. The Chartists subsided, down but not out. They resumed their meetings. Jefferson was finally arrested on 16 July but the mob rescued him. On 15 August the magistrates reported that pikes were still being manufactured, as the Chartists waited for news from Manchester of the general rising. When the signal came, they had at least 4,000 men ready to take the town. The history of the past few months makes this informer's estimate credible.[71]

In Liverpool, things were quiet until after Mitchel's conviction when the number of Irish clubs began to grow under the direction of a central Club Council. As with the New Plan of Organisation in London, this arrangement provided a highly co-ordinated, secret organisation from which an insurrection could easily spring. The intention, as elsewhere, was to detain troops in England. With an estimated quarter of the population Irish, Liverpool clearly presented a considerable problem for the authorities. The situation was made worse by reports from the United States where the Irish Republican Union had been formed to extend to Ireland the republican freedom enjoyed in the United States. This involved raising an Irish Brigade which would return home under the guise of disillusioned emigrants to fight the Irish cause.[72]

Mitchel's conviction hardened their determination to assist a rising in Ireland with arms, men and money, which would take place by way of Liverpool. More troops were sent to the city; more police were appointed to what was already the largest police force outside London; and there were gunboats in the Mersey. Unlike in Bradford, however, there was very little Chartist involvement. The unrest in Liverpool was an extension of the Irish problem. On 25 July, the day that *Habeas Corpus* was suspended in Ireland, a 1,000-signature petition from Liverpool asked for the Suspension Act to apply to their city also. Towards the end of July, with the corporation unable to pay for any more troops to be billeted, decisive action was taken by the police. The arrests which followed, the departure of the leader, Terence Bellew McManus, for Ireland to join the rebellion there, and then news of the failure of the Irish rising, enabled the magistrates to take control of what had been a potentially dangerous situation.[73]

In Manchester, the Irish adopted the club system as in Liverpool, and again the rhythm of protest followed the history of the Mitchel case, with a mass meeting in Stevenson Square planned for 31 May and a call for a one-day strike. The magistrates banned the meeting, and police and soldiers turned back contingents from Oldham and Ashton as they marched down the turnpikes to Manchester. There was some disturbance in the town but no serious rioting, and the police did not need to call on troops to restore order. On 6 June, Ernest Jones arrived to repeat the speech he had made in London on 4 June. Next morning he was arrested. On Whit Monday, 12 June, in common with other towns Manchester held a meeting to protest at Mitchel's sentence and in support of the Charter, but again there were no serious disturbances. The magistrates now began to arrest leaders throughout the country, but the more they arrested the more they drove the rest to desperation.

As in London, it was now that secret plotting for a rising began, and on 18 July a delegate meeting on Blackstone Edge, high in the Pennines between Halifax and Rochdale, resolved that the moral approach had failed and the time had come for physical force. The plan was for Lancashire to rise on 15 August, followed by Bradford the day after – the same day as the London rising. The government was made aware of all this through its informers. On the night of 14 August, seventy armed Chartists left Oldham for Manchester and at Ashton-under-Lyne the Chartists paraded with their arms just before midnight and one policeman was killed before the military could be called out. In Hyde, a mob began drawing the boiler plugs and the local constable was greeted with cries of, 'They're now all out, all over England, Ireland and Scotland, and before this time tomorrow night we'll either make it better or worse.'[74] The following evening, 15 August, 300 police simultaneously arrested the Chartist and Confederate leaders in Manchester. The rising was aborted so the signal was never sent to Bradford.[75] On the next night, the metropolitan police raided the taverns where the London rising was about to begin. The revolutionaries had been betrayed by a spy named Thomas Powell. The revolution was over and the gaols were filled.[76] On 14 September, Isaac Jefferson was found in his bed in a remote inn at Illingworth, near Halifax. At the York assizes he was sentenced to four months in gaol.[77] The danger was past.

Conclusion

'The conspiracy of 1848', writes David Goodway, 'was the last of the revolutionary attempts which originated in the 1790s.'[78] The violence was less widespread than in 1842, and nothing so spectacular occurred as the Newport Rising of 1839, but as a conspiracy it was the most serious since 1817 or 1819, if not 1802. With its French and Irish dimensions – the latter more than the former – it was comparable to the revolutionary plotting of the 1790s, but this time the French were not interested and the Irish were too debilitated by famine to provide the lead that their compatriots in exile looked for. So the scale of the subversive activity, all of which came to nothing, could be erased from historical memory. Chartism in 1848 came to mean only the 'fiasco' of 10 April. The idea that working people in Victorian Britain could threaten revolution became inconceivable and dropped out of the historical reckoning. Only by recovering that contemporary fear, and the reality behind that fear, can the historian come to address the question of how political stability was created and why there was no revolution in Britain.

Notes

1   *Bronterre's National Reformer*, 15 January 1837, extract reprinted in Cole, *British Working Class Movements* pp. 351–2.
2   See M. Taylor, 'The Six Points: Chartism and the Reform of Parliament', in O. Ashton, R. Fyson and S. Roberts (eds), *The Chartist Legacy* (Rendlesham, Merlin, 1999), pp. 1–23.
3   J. Hugman, 'A Small Drop of Ink': Tyneside Chartism and the *Northern Liberator*', in Ashton, Fyson and Roberts (eds), *Chartist Legacy*, pp. 24–47.
4   N. C. Edsall, *The Anti-Poor Law Movement, 1834–1844* (Manchester, Manchester University Press, 1971), pp. 94–6.
5   Edsall, *The Anti-Poor Law Movement*, pp. 100–15.
6   *Northern Star*, 27 January 1838.
7   J. A. Epstein, *The Lion of Freedom: Feargus O'Connor and the Chartist Movement, 1832–1842* (London, Croom Helm, 1982), pp. 7–59, 90–101.
8   BL, Add MSS. 34,245, Letter Book of the General Convention, 1839, letter from the London Democratic Association to William Lovett, secretary to the Convention.
9   *Northern Star*, 13 July 1839.
10   'The First Essay in Physical Force', *Chartist*, 12 May 1839.
11   D. J. V. Jones, *The Last Rising: The Newport Insurrection of 1839* (Oxford, Clarendon Press, 1985), p. 45.

12   PRO, HO 40/45, Deposition of S. R. Jeffreys, 26 April 1839, as quoted in Jones, *Last Rising*, p. 71.

13   J. Frost, *A Letter to the Working Men's Association of Newport and Pillgwenlly* (Newport, Partridge, 1839), pp. 3–7, quoted in Jones, *Last Rising*, p. 76.

14   *Western Vindicator*, 6 April 1839, quoted in I. Wilks, *South Wales and the Rising of 1839: Class Struggle as Armed Struggle* (London, Croom Helm, 1984), p. 145, and Jones, *Last Rising*, p. 94.

15   PRO, HO 20/10, Report of Inspector of Prisons, W. J. Williams, on an interview with Joseph Crabtree, 23 December 1840, facsimile printed in *Bulletin of the Society for the Study of Labour History* no. 34 (Spring 1977), pp. 33–4.

16   Jones, *Last Rising*, p. 156.

17   PRO, HO 41/15, Lord Normanby to Thomas Phillips, Mayor of Newport, 5 November 1839.

18   Ashton's account is in a letter of 30 March 1845, reprinted in *Northern Star*, 3 May 1845; and Lovett's appears in his *Life and Struggles of William Lovett* (London, 1876, new edition, MacGibbon & Key, 1967), pp. 196–9.

19   See Wilks, *South Wales*, pp. 166–75; A. J. Peacock, *Bradford Chartism, 1838–1840* (York, St Anthony's Press, 1969), J. L. Baxter, 'Early Chartism and Labour Struggle in South Yorkshire, 1837–40' in Pollard and Holmes (eds), *Essays*, pp. 146–50. See also his 'Armed Resistance and Insurrection: the early Chartist experience', *Our History* 16 (July 1984).

20   Baxter, 'Armed Resistance', p. 22.

21   *Northern Star*, 3 May 1845.

22   S. Roberts, *Radical Politicians and Poets in Early Victorian Britain* (Lampeter, Edwin Mellen Press, 1993), pp. 60–1.

23   PRO, HO 20/10, Report of Inspector of Prisons, W. J. Williams, on an interview with Emanuel Hutton, 23 December 1840.

24   Thompson, *Chartists*, pp. 80–5.

25   PRO, HO 45/249, W. Hutchinson of Accrington to W. L. Mabberley, 17 August 1842.

26   F. C. Mather, 'The General Strike of 1842', p. 116 in J. Stevenson and R. Quinault (eds), *Popular Protest and Public Order* (London, George Allen & Unwin), 1974, pp. 115–40.

27   *The Trial of Feargus O'Connor and Fifty-Eight Others on a Charge of Sedition, Conspiracy, Tumult & Riot* [1843], reprinted (New York, Kelley, 1970), p. v; N. McCord, *The Anti-Corn Law League* 1958, second edition (London, Unwin, 1968), pp. 123–31.

28   *Leeds Mercury*, 20 August 1842.

29   G. J. Barnsby, *Chartism in the Black Country* (Wolverhampton, Integrated Publishing Services, n.d.), p. 26.

30   Placard entitled 'Behold the Reckoning Day is Nigh', as quoted in M. Jenkins, *The General Strike of 1842* (London, Lawrence & Wishart, 1980), p. 64.

31   Jenkins, *General Strike*, pp. 242–3.

32   *Northern Star*, 27 December 1845, 13 May 1848, quoted in Jenkins, *General Strike*, pp. 117, 119.

33   *Trial of Feargus O'Connor*, p. 249.

34   *Staffordshire Advertiser*, 13 August 1842, as quoted in R. Anderson, *The Potteries Martyrs* (Newcastle, Military Heritage Books, 1992), chapter 1 (no page).

35 T. Cooper, *The Life of Thomas Cooper* [1872], reprinted (Leicester, Leicester University Press, 1971), pp. 186–96.

36 *Leeds Mercury*, 20 August 1842.

37 *Leeds Mercury*, 20 August 1842.

38 See the documents reproduced in Jenkins, *General Strike*, pp. 263–4.

39 The voting was 58 for the Charter, 7 against, 19 delegated to follow the majority and 1 with no instruction: see Jenkins, *General Strike*, p. 154.

40 As quoted in Jenkins, *General Strike*, p. 267.

41 *Leeds Mercury*, 20 August 1842; *Trial of Feargus O'Connor*, pp. 107–8, 309–10.

42 Text in Jenkins, *General Strike*, p. 275.

43 A. R. Schoyen, *The Chartist Challenge* (London, Heinemann, 1958), pp. 115–16.

44 For the full texts, see Jenkins, *General Strike*, pp. 270–4.

45 B. Wilson, *Struggles of an Old Chartist* (1887), p. 206, reprinted in D. Vincent (ed.), *Testaments of Radicalism* (London, Europa, 1977), pp. 195–242; K. Tiller, 'Late Chartism. Halifax, 1847–58', pp. 314–16 in Epstein and Thompson (eds), *Chartist Experience*, pp. 311–44.

46 D. Goodway, *London Chartism* (Cambridge, Cambridge University Press, 1982), pp. 111–15.

47 P. A. Pickering, *Chartism and the Chartists in Manchester and Salford* (London, Macmillan, 1995), p. 176.

48 Thompson, *Chartists*, p. 313.

49 *Northern Star*, 25 March 1848.

50 Goodway, *London Chartism*, pp. 129–42.

51 J. C. Hobhouse, Baron Broughton, *Recollections of a Long Life*, edited by his daughter, Lady Dorchester, 6 vols (London, Murray, 1910–11), vol. 6, pp. 214–15, diary entry for 10 April 1848.

52 C. C. F. Greville, *The Greville Memoirs*, edited by H. Reeve, new edition, 8 vols (London, Longman, 1888), vol. 6, p. 168, journal entry for 13 April 1848.

53 A. C. Benson and Viscount Esher (eds), *The Letters of Queen Victoria*, 3 vols. (London, Murray, 1908), vol. 2, p. 169.

54 Bodleian Library, Oxford, Clarendon Papers, Box 43, Russell to Clarendon, 1 March 1848, as quoted in J Saville, *1848* (Cambridge, Cambridge University Press, 1987), p. 81.

55 PRO, HO 45/2368, Irish Disaffection, 1848, as quoted in Saville, *1848*, p. 81.

56 D. Thompson, *Outsiders* (London, Verso, 1993), pp. 106–7.

57 Goodway, *London Chartism*, pp. 64–7, 80–5.

58 T Frost, *Forty Years' Recollections* (London, Sampson Low, Searle, and Rivington, 1880), p. 148.

59 L. C. Wright, *Scottish Chartism* (Edinburgh, Oliver & Boyd, 1953), pp. 194–5.

60 J. Belchem, 'Britishness, the United Kingdom and the Revolutions of 1848', p. 147 in *Labour History Review* 64:2 (Summer 1999), pp. 143–58. For further detail, see his 'Liverpool in the Year of Revolution: The political and associational culture of the Irish immigrant community in 1848', pp. 80–97 in J. Belchem (ed.), *Popular Politics, Riot and Labour. Essays in Liverpool History, 1790–1940* ((Liverpool, Liverpool University Press, 1992), pp. 68–97; and 'Nationalism, Republicanism and Exile: Irish emigrants and the revolutions of 1848', *Past & Present*, 146 (February 1995), pp. 103–35.

61 D. G. Wright, *The Chartist Risings in Bradford* (Bradford, Bradford Libraries, 1977), pp. 37–50.

62 What follows draws on Goodway, *London Chartism*, pp. 79–96; and Saville, *1848*, pp. 130–65.

63 TS 11/389, fo 70, transcript from shorthand reporter, Henry James Potter, 29 May 1848.

64 Goodway, *London Chartism*, pp. 81–4.

65 Greville, *Memoirs*, vol. 6, p. 193, journal entry for 3 June 1848.

66 Goodway, *London Chartism*, pp. 142–5.

67 Goodway, *London Chartism*, p. 86.

68 Goodway, *London Chartism*, pp. 87–93 gives full details of the development of the plot.

69 For a large but peaceful meeting in Edinburgh, see Wright, *Scottish Chartism*, pp. 197–201.

70 As quoted in Wright, *Chartist Risings in Bradford*, p. 49 [source not given].

71 Wright, *Chartist Risings in Bradford*, pp. 37–58; Saville, *1848*, pp. 144–50.

72 PRO, FO 5/488, fo 269, cutting from *New York Herald*, 7 May 1848, enclosed in Arthur Barclay to Lord Palmerston, 25 March 1848; see also Belchem, 'Nationalism, Republicanism and Exile', pp. 114–16.

73 Saville, *1848*, pp. 151–6; Belchem, 'Liverpool in the Year of Revolution' pp. 80–97; and 'Nationalism, Republicanism and Exile', pp. 114–31.

74 PRO, HO 48/40, Deposition of Thomas Brown, as quoted in F C. Mather, *Public Order in the Age of the Chartists* (Manchester, Manchester University Press, 1959), pp. 24–5.

75 Pickering, *Chartism and the Chartists in Manchester*, pp. 176–7; Saville, *1848*, pp. 142–4; Wright, *Chartist Risings in Bradford*, pp. 57–8.

76 Goodway, *London Chartism*, pp. 93–4. For lists of prisoners, see R. G. Gammage, *History of the Chartist Movement, 1837–1854*, second edition [1894], reprinted (New York, Kelley, 1969), pp. 336–44.

77 Wright, *Chartist Risings in Bradford*, p. 58.

78 Goodway, *London Chartism*, p. 94.

4

Why was there no revolution?

The absence of revolution in Britain becomes a historical problem in the light of what happened elsewhere. In the age of revolutions, Britain was largely unaffected by the challenges that shook and in some cases overthrew governments on the continent of Europe and beyond. Yet much of the story of social conflict in Britain between 1789 and 1850 suggests that the potential for revolution existed, so why was Britain different?

A theoretical approach to revolution risks imposing an unrealistic expectation of what a 'true' revolution is and how it should come about. The historical process is more complicated and much depends on how contemporaries understood the many shades of meaning behind such words as revolution, revolt, rebellion, insurgency and uprising in relation to the less serious challenge implied by the more widely used disturbance and riot. As was suggested in the Introduction, the word revolution is difficult and ambiguous, partly because of the way different parties used it in their propaganda, and partly because the word itself was acquiring a new meaning during the 1790s.[1]

There was a significant shift in the idea of revolution following developments in France after 1789. Before that, 'the Revolution' in British history referred to what had occurred in 1688: it was a corrective, conservative event, a turning of the wheel of fortune to right a wrong state of affairs. When Edmund Burke wrote his *Reflections on the Revolution in France* in 1790 he was using the word in this sense, only with irony since his argument was against those who thought that France was simply experiencing a corrective measure to the excesses of Bourbon absolutism, analogous to the events of 1688. His point was that France was *not* experiencing this kind of revolution.[2] The Foxite Whigs and, to begin with, the United Irishmen continued to be supporters of revolution in the old sense until events and new definitions overtook them. By the late 1790s, the Whigs had substituted Reform for Revolution, and the United Irishmen had espoused revolution in its modern sense of 'a complete overthrow of the established government in any country or state by those who were previously subject to it; a forcible substitution of a new ruler or form of government'.[3] This modern definition, which assumes the use of force of some kind, will be the usual sense in which the word is used in the rest of this chapter. As one liberal member of the German National Assembly in 1848 asserted, 'We all know: revolution is constitutional change taking place against the will of the ruling power whereas reform means change taking place with the assent of that power.'[4] This is an important distinction.

Revolutionary change granted by a government of its own free will is not a revolution. But there is ambiguity if a government implements revolutionary change as a result of pressure put upon it from outside the normal political process. That *might* be called a revolution. If so, then even within the modern usage of the word there are two concepts of revolution to consider: the revolution which overthrows existing institutions by direct force; and the revolution which forces existing institutions to change themselves. From the point of view of the government under pressure, insurgents pressing for change might properly be called revolutionaries even if the historian doubts whether they could ever have overturned the existing government by force. The threat of revolution might therefore lie either in the intentions of the would-be revolutionaries, or in the perceptions of the government being pressed to change, or both. Thus in the language of the governing classes which dominates the historical record, genuine revolutionaries intent on using force to bring about political change might be dismissed as mere rioters without political understanding or aims; while constitutionally-minded protesters unwilling to appeal to force might be condemned as wicked revolutionaries.

Although governments in Britain carried many reforms in the period 1789–1850, only three concerned what might be called 'the constitution'. In 1801 the Act of Union with Ireland came into effect as a result of government policy and so can properly be called a reform. In 1829 the Catholic Relief Act was granted by a reluctant Parliament in the face of widespread unrest in Ireland, so that would seem to make it revolutionary. In 1832, the first Reform Act was carried as government policy, but popular pressure played a part in events. It was a major constitutional reform or a constitutional revolution, depending on the emphasis given to the reasons why the measure was carried. On none of these occasions was the government forcibly overthrown.

To the Whigs the 1832 Reform Act was a revolution in the old sense – a conservative, corrective adjustment – and a reform in the new sense, conducted along traditional English lines of change through continuity, avoiding the French way of change through violent rupture. This perception of the superiority of reform over revolution was widely accepted by all classes in Britain by 1850, but this outcome was not at all obvious to the two generations who lived through the events between 1790 and 1850. Revolutionaries in those years were seeking change, either by putting pressure on governments or by looking to some undefined way of overthrowing them. Contrary to later Victorian liberal ideology, governments did not always grant reasonable reforms ungrudgingly and without resistance, and they constantly feared insurgencies from below. The equilibrium of the mid-nineteenth century was a compromise achieved through the experience of disequilibrium in the preceding sixty years.

Overshadowing all events during this period was the French revolution: not the neatly packaged event of historical theory but a messy, incoherent process, the direction and outcome of which were neither intended nor foreseen. This left contemporaries all too aware that an uprising might create its own revolutionary situation, as arguably happened again in Paris in 1830 or in several European capitals in 1848. Revolution in this period was an accident waiting to be caused – or prevented. So, how close did Britain come to revolution and how did the country avoid it? The rest of this chapter attempts to consider this question thematically by looking at the balance of conservative and revolutionary forces in the structures and institutions of British society, the outlook of the people whose leadership and support would have been necessary to turn a rising into a revolution, and the ideological and physical means available to those who wished to prevent them.

The nature of the popular movement

In a strikingly powerful metaphor, Edmund Burke sought to belittle the supporters of revolution in 1790:

Because half a dozen grasshoppers under a fern make the field ring with their importunate chink, while thousands of great cattle, repose beneath the shadow of the British oak, chew the cud and are silent, pray do not imagine that those who make the noise are the only inhabitants of the field; that, of course, they are many in number; or that, after all, they are other than the little, shrivelled, meagre, hopping, though loud and troublesome, insects of the hour.[5]

If Burke's polemic were as true as it was effective, then the revolutionary threat was an illusion, and historians who think otherwise have followed magistrates and politicians of the time in confusing noise with numbers. In this view, the political insurgents were small, untypical groups of troublemakers. Though they sometimes attracted wider support, this was unreliable and dependent on a downturn in the trade cycle or a rise in the price of bread. The popular movement throughout was largely peaceful. It was therefore caught in the paradox of seeking a revolutionary end by non-revolutionary means. At most it could appear revolutionary in order the frighten the government into concessions, but it had no response if the government refused to be frightened or was frightened only into suppressing rather than yielding to those who threatened it.

If true, this is a powerful argument, though it begs the questions of why the majority was constitutional and why the revolutionaries were not popular. It also implies a passive relationship between minorities and majorities rather than a dynamic interrelationship, and it assumes that revolutions must be made by majorities.

One theory of revolution in the nineteenth century, which can be traced back to Babeuf's 'Conspiracy of the Equals' in 1797, accepted that revolutions are the work of minorities. Governments no less than revolutionaries are minorities and so vulnerable to conspiratorial plots. English radicals were made aware of this when Bronterre O'Brien's translation of Buonarotti's *History of Babeuf's Conspiracy for Equality* (1828) was published in 1836. Although Marx's purpose in writing the *Communist Manifesto* was to reject this model of revolution in favour of raising the consciousness of the mass of the people – which is what he thought was happening in Chartism – the Marxist-Leninist approach has reinforced the idea that revolutions are created by a small revolutionary leadership. On this definition, revolutions do not have to be the work of majorities to be threatening or even successful.

The reports produced by informers overwhelmingly referred to dangerous minorities. This evidence exposed a series of revolutionary conspiracies, from Robert Watt's plot in Edinburgh in 1794, which so alarmed the Committee of Secrecy, through Thistlewood's repeated schemes between 1817 and 1820 to the Chartist revolutionaries of 1848 with a new French revolution to emulate. The expectation of these conspirators was that there was a wide body of support in the country which would rise once they had commenced the deed. The government, from a more fearful perspective, shared this view. In their reports on individuals the informers were probably not wildly inaccurate, providing the detail which enabled the authorities to pick off the leaders and so extinguished their plots. Where they were not so reliable was in their estimates of wider support and here they drew on their own imaginations and, more importantly, the optimism of the revolutionary leaders. In this way spies and revolutionaries deluded themselves, each other and sometimes the government.

However, this lack of realism was its most dangerous aspect. It was recalled, with some unfair exaggeration, in the memoirs of a one-time Chartist, Benjamin Brierley. His context was a group of hand-loom weavers meeting to read the *Northern Star* in the village of Failsworth near Manchester on the eve of the 1842 strikes:

> Every Sunday morning these subscribers met at our house to hear what prospect there was of the expected 'smash-up' taking place. It was my task to read aloud so that all could hear at the same time; . . . A Republic was to take the place of the 'base, bloody, and brutal Whigs,' and the usurpers of all civil rights, the Lords. The Queen was to be dethroned, and the president of a Republic take her place. This would be a very easy task.[6]

Brierley's irony in the final sentence indicates, at least in retrospect, his scepticism on this point. Few men who rationally contemplated the odds of a successful revolution would ever start one. Those who thought seriously about the prospects for change – Thomas Hardy and Francis Place of the LCS; Henry Hunt on the edge of the Spencean post-war conspiracies; Feargus O'Connor in Chartism – knew the limits of their powers and worked within them. Those who did not were either *agents provocateurs* or fanatics, driven by frustration or desperation or filled with the millenarian hope of a new dawn that did not rely on numbers or rational human agency.

Much depended on how popular this minority of revolutionaries was: that is, how they related to 'the people', not in the Whig sense of those having or deserving the franchise but in its increasingly common meaning of those who were excluded from it, the 'masses' as opposed to the 'classes'.[7] Though there is little evidence to support the idea of a mass rising to start a revolution, there were certainly large numbers of discontented people who could have responded if the minority had been united and able to create and exploit a revolutionary situation. Magistrates and ministers alike were always alert to the potential dangers of the 'mobility', the inverse of the 'nobility', 'the disorderly and riotous part of the population'.[8] The word 'mob' conjures up the view of a crowd seen from the hustings, or from horseback, or the town-square balcony before the Riot Act was read: a dark, secret and seething anonymous sea of heads, ever in motion and liable to break out from time to time in tempestuous fury, lashing itself against the defences of law and order until its force was spent. The people, on the contrary, were good-hearted and deferential, loyal subjects of the King. But there was always the possibility, especially in times of high food prices and unemployment, that the high winds of 'trading agitators' might whip them up into a furious rabble, a mob. Those responsible for law and order could never be complacent about the reliability of 'the people'.

The aim of government propaganda was to maintain the idea that there was an identifiable minority of revolutionaries who were separate from the larger body of 'the people'. This distinction was emphasised, for example, by speakers from both parliamentary sides in the debate in the House of Commons on the Charter in 1839. As Lord John Russell, the Whig Home Secretary, stated in a rather convoluted speech,

> My own opinion is, that these are the exhortations of persons, several of them, no doubt, conscientious persons, but others very designing and insidious persons, wishing not the prosperity of the people, but exhorting the people, by those means most injurious to themselves, to produce a degree of discord – to produce a degree of confusion – to produce a degree of misery, the consequence of which would be to create a great alarm, that would be fatal, not only to the constitution as it now exists, not only to those rights which are now said to be monopolised by a particular class, but fatal to any established government.[9]

Here Russell was attempting to divide the naively idealistic from the malevolent, and both from the people, who needed protection from those who would agitate them for their own nefarious purposes.

The problem for the leaders, though, was not that they were unrepresentative of a great many of the people, but that they were divided among themselves and this severely limited their effectiveness in harnessing the discontents of the majority in a consistent and coherent way. Lack of leadership or clear political aims, rather than lack of potential numbers, meant that for most of the time the challenge presented to the government by the revolutionaries was to be one of law and order rather than political survival.

A major theoretical division existed between those who sought to amend the constitution to purge it of aristocratic corruption and make it more accountable to 'the people'; and those who wished to establish 'a republic', sometimes (like the Failsworth Chartists in Brierley's recollections) without any clear idea of what that might mean beyond forming a democratic government which would give 'the people' the laws they wanted. As James Epstein has argued, although Paine and many of his radical contemporaries, filled with enthusiasm for events in France in 1789 and imbued with the language of the Enlightenment, advocated a break with the past and a recognition of the natural rights of the people with the formation of a republic, others appreciated the strategic merits of adopting the conservative view of revolution as a restoration of traditional, historic rights, using the language of Burke to subvert his conclusions and argue for radical change. Thus constitutionalism became the language of revolution in a linguistic struggle with the propertied and enfranchised. The object was to present the latter not as defenders of the constitution but its enemies, subverting the usual argument employed against radical reformers.[10] Such a strategy depended upon a peaceful agitation, at least until the political classes could be shown to have violated the peace.

Feargus O'Connor's phrase, 'Peaceably if we may; forcibly if we must', may look like a rhetorical device for staying within the law while at the same time uttering a threat, but in fact the mainstream of radical reformers in Britain did prefer the peaceable and constitutional way not only through necessity but also as their chosen strategy. Even in the 1790s, advocates of Paine's thorough-going republicanism did not command the entire argument and in the nineteenth century they were in the minority. The petitions of the LCS against the Two Acts in 1795, written by John Thelwall and thoroughly approved by Francis Place, appealed to the House of Commons as 'the constitutional guardian of the people's liberties, and the champion of its rights and privileges', referring back to the reign of Edward III and, inevitably, 1688.[11] While such phrases addressed to the ideal Parliament may have revealed a desire to expose the shortcomings of the actual one, the constitutional language of the radicals should be taken seriously. The device of petitioning Parliament was urged by Major Cartwright and William Cobbett, and was central to Chartist strategy. The image which the majority of radicals wished to convey was that of a body defending the traditional rights of the people against the dangers of arbitrary government. In this respect they were at one with the Foxite Whigs in the 1790s and with Grey in 1831. The Whig 'betrayal' after 1832 was felt all the more bitterly because the Whigs had promoted themselves as defenders of the liberties of the people – until they themselves got power. Then with Irish coercion and the Poor Law Amendment Act, they legislated like Tories.

The determination of the majority of reformers to act peacefully pushed the revolutionaries to the margins of radical protest but it did not entirely isolate them. When the House of Commons rejected petitions, when *Habeas Corpus* was suspended or new Acts were rushed through Parliament to limit the people's liberties, the peaceful approach could become discredited and larger numbers were then persuaded that, to preserve the constitution, it was necessary to cross the narrow line between peaceful pressure and insurrection. As William Stevens reasoned, perhaps rather disingenuously, in 1818:

> until after the passing of the Suspension and other violent Acts, in the month of March 1817, he never heard any person propose, or hint at, any measure of resistance in arms on the part of the people; but, that, after those acts had been passed, he himself, as well as many hundreds of others, and, as he believes, many Thousands, said, that, as the Laws of the land were now destroyed, as there was now no safety for any man, and as the people were not allowed even to petition, it was time to *resist*, or, if not, to make up our minds to die slaves.[12]

Though leaders like Cobbett, Hunt and Feargus O'Connor usually preached peace, they could not always contain the logic of their own arguments or the forces they were unleashing. Other radicals, from John Baines, Thomas Bacon, James Wilson and Joseph Mitchell to John Frost and Peter Murray McDouall, could become convinced that the enfranchised classes had stepped beyond the limits of the constitution and that the peaceful approach was no longer adequate: then they were drawn into support for insurrection. The right to bear arms, enshrined in Magna Carta and the Common Law, was legal for defensive purposes. So the division between minority revolutionists and majority constitutionalists was never hard or fast. It was the moderate William Lovett who seconded the motion in the Chartist Convention in 1839 advising the people to arm because the government was putting down meetings by Proclamation which he held to be illegal.[13] A great deal of activity which the government feared might be revolutionary and which alarmed magistrates was, strictly speaking, perfectly legitimate. England was not under an arbitrary government and the legal powers available for the suppression, even of arming and drilling, were uncertain. The neat division into 'moral' and 'physical' force, like the division between agitators and people, was an oversimplification.

More significant in weakening the popular movement for reform were the differences between social classes. In George Rudé's opinion, middle-class leadership was needed for a revolution to be successful. As he observed, there was no revolution in 1831–32 because 'nobody *of importance* wanted one' [my italics]. In the Marxist model of revolution, the proletariat does not rise spontaneously but is led by a fragment of the *bourgeoisie*. This may have been possible in Ireland, with support from the United Irishmen and later the Confederates, but it did not happen in Britain, unless people such as Muir, Palmer, Cobbett, Hunt and O'Connor are made to fill the role.

As was pointed out in Chapter 2, there was an imprecise relationship between the language of class relating to socio-economic groupings and that referring to political positions.[14] The phrases 'middle class' and 'working class' were widely used by the 1830s, but more by leaders to project an image of themselves for polemical purposes than to offer social analysis of use to the historian. Those who were thought of as the middle class in Britain were a relatively small group, internally divided. The radical middle class was even smaller and dependent upon working-class support to make an impact – what Richard Cobden of the Anti-Corn Law League called 'something in our *rear* to frighten the Aristocracy'[15] – but middle-class radicals were prepared to lead the masses only on their own, non-revolutionary terms.[16] Probably before, and certainly after, 1832 most leaders of working-class opinion did not trust the middle classes. In 1832 and again in 1839, whatever Thomas Attwood might have threatened and Francis Place recorded for posterity, the middle-class political unions drew back from actual violence. The concession made by the Whigs to their supporters in 1832, extending the political nation to include moderates (the 'middle class') while isolating democrats (the 'working class'), removed any possibility of revolutionary leadership coming from the middle classes in Britain. The Anti-Corn Law League peered into the abyss in 1842, and hastily drew back.[17] By extending the property base of politics in 1832, stability was reinforced. Whereas in 1848 across Europe, revolutionary leadership was provided by liberals turning popular discontents against existing regimes, in England the same sort of people joined the special constabulary and turned out in Lord John Russell's massive counter-demonstration against what was portrayed as revolution.

Geography and the problem of London

A further division which weakened the revolutionary movement was not of its own making. In July 1849 the Owenite and latter-day Chartist lecturer, George Jacob Holyoake, delivered a lecture in London on the question, 'Why have we had no revolution in England?' His answer was excessive individualism, by which he meant no common objects, no united organisation and no accepted leadership. Since he had spend the past few years trying to destroy all three, this may have been true of Chartism after 1848. But in offering his analysis he considered firstly three other reasons, which will be considered later in this chapter. His second was

> We have equality of towns. When Paris is conquered, France submits; but when London shall be possessed, there will be Birmingham, Liverpool, Manchester, Glasgow, Edinburgh to subdue. A revolution here could only be effected by a protracted civil war. A provisional government in London would be useless without a Cromwell.[18]

This is worth considering. Forgetting, as Holyoake apparently did, the role of the French provinces in 1789 and the revolutionary part played by the major textile centre of Lyon in the 1830s, from the standpoint of 1848 it did seem that French revolutions were actually political revolutions made in Paris. A comparison and contrast between London and Paris can be instructive.

London was much bigger than Paris and contained a larger percentage of the country's population: around a million inhabitants in 1801 and over two and a half million in 1851 – more than 10 per cent of the population of England. Paris was half this size in 1801 but held only about 2 per cent of the population of France and with a population of a million in 1851 held about 3 per cent at that date. Both were major manufacturing centres and both were centres of government. London ought to have been more important in England and in Britain as a whole but Holyoake was right that London could not speak for Britain in the way that Paris had come to speak for France. Whereas in 1801, Lyon was still larger than any provincial British town, in 1851 it was much smaller than Liverpool, Glasgow, Manchester, Birmingham or Leeds. Indeed, these provincial British cities were in the same league as many European capitals.[19] London was huge and yet only first among equals. Though it could be argued that this made life difficult for governments, they were able to overcome the problem of the dispersed nature of the British urban and industrial population more effectively than the would-be revolutionaries.

London best fitted the role of a European revolutionary capital in the 1790s, but with only the Foxite Whigs to play Jacobins to the LCS's sansculottes, there were many reasons why no revolutionary situation matured in the capital in these years: no bankrupt administration, no significant divisions within the political elite, no attempt to re-write the constitution in a way that encouraged every political opportunist to have his say, no actual military defeat and threatening foreign armies by land, no manipulation of the crowd in support of political faction. If London had been placed under these intolerable strains, the story might have been very different.

Holyoake's remarks about London in 1848 arose from the unusual situation of the capital taking the lead in serious revolutionary planning, but for much of the first half of the nineteenth century the reverse was true. The mobilisation of the discontented masses to exert pressure on the government was achieved not in London but 100–200 miles away. As the Blanketeers discovered in 1817, putting pressure on London at that distance was not easy. The Vice-Lieutenant and magistrates of the West Riding felt frustrated in 1812 that Lord Sidmouth in London did not truly appreciate the difficulty of maintaining law and order in the industrial districts as he did not have their first hand experience of the Luddites.[20] Had there been Luddites in the capital, they might have had more effect. This was appreciated by the London-based *Chartist* newspaper in 1839:

> Chartists, what are you now about? We hear, we see nothing of you – the metropolis scarcely knows of the existence of such a class of people. They are found only at our police-offices, and there they appear in twos and threes, without causing any more excitement than the arrest of an equal number of pickpockets. How is this? Is it that the Charter was a mere popular phantasy, which has been cried up and deserted with all the customary fickleness of a crowd? or is it that the people do not feel the evils of which they were accustomed to complain? It never can be the case that there are five hundred thousand workmen in London and its suburbs ardent to obtain a suffrage which will enable them to better their condition, and yet that a party of a few thousands cannot be got up to make a demonstration, or, what is still better, to smash a Whig or Tory meeting.
>
> That there is this number of workmen in the metropolis is certain enough. But are these men Chartists? If they are, why do they not show themselves so? . . . The fact is, that, be it from listlessness, ignorance, want of thought, incapacity to reason as to political causes and effects, or satisfaction with things as they are, the great majority of the working men of the metropolis are altogether indifferent as to representation. They feel certain evils, and they complain of them, but they do not apply themselves to consider whence they proceed.
>
> In the country, we believe it is far otherwise. The men of Birmingham are as one man – the hardy spirits of the north know no difference – the acute and reasoning Scotchmen have satisfied themselves where the evil lies. Throughout the provinces all is unanimity. We are sorry to have to report that in the metropolis, where the lead should have been taken, there is nothing doing; and unless the metropolis be set working, all agitation elsewhere is useless. It is here that the seat of government is. A demonstration in the streets of London comes before the very eyes of those who make the laws. An atmosphere of agitation here does not dissipate without first involving the two houses of legislation in

> its influence. A hundred demonstrations in the country are only
> heard of through the newspapers of the factions, which invari-
> ably describe them as contemptible, diminish the numbers, and
> caricature the speeches.[21]

In this extract, there is a combination of frank admission of the failure of
early Chartism in London, a perhaps exaggerated view of the provincial
movement, and a proper appreciation of the centrality of London to any
effective political pressure group. One major reason why early Chartism
failed, both as a pressure group and as a revolutionary threat, was that
the source of its energy was not in the capital. London Chartism did not
really become well-established until after 1840. The failure of London
and the provinces to exert maximum pressure at the same time was one
reason for the failure of Chartism. The hope of attaining simultaneous
action across the country was never to be realised, yet this was the only
chance for a planned revolution to be effective.

Loyalism and the silent majority

The assumption so far has been that structural weaknesses and divisions prevented the minority of revolutionaries from realising the
potential support of the masses of the people and using it to bring
pressure to bear on, or to overthrow, the existing institutions of
society. This is to ignore the efforts made by the governing classes to
secure or maintain the loyalty of the people – Burke's cattle content-
edly chewing the cud, rather than his more celebrated 'swinish multitude' of revolutionaries. Revolutions may be made by minorities but
they need the willing acquiescence of majorities, and this they failed
to win, not for want of trying but because the governing classes
proved themselves better at winning it.

In achieving this they were aided by several characteristics of the
popular mind. The first, detected by the *Chartist* in 1839, was indiffer-
ence. Many people were committed to the daily task of survival. Any
further commitment to political action depended upon a conviction that
this was relevant to survival. The task of the radicals was to persuade
them of this. Cobbett's achievement, according to Samuel Bamford, was
that, 'He directed his readers to the true cause of their sufferings – mis-
government; and to its proper corrective – parliamentary reform.'[22]

Although riots aimed at an unpopular local personality (even the

King in London), might have an immediate political motivation, those who turned seriously to revolutionary activity did so only in reaction to the failure of parliamentary reform. They had to pass through quite a sophisticated process in order to reach the serious decision to use physical force against the existing political order. From his Conservative perspective, Benjamin Disraeli was highly sceptical about the probability of this, even in 1839. In his speech in the House of Commons on the Petition, he argued that 'Political rights had so much of an abstract character, their consequences acted so slightly on the multitude, that he did not believe they could ever be the origin of any great popular movement.'[23] Although this point was made in the context of an argument to show how the Whig attack on the civil rights of the people had changed this situation in the 1830s, the point about the minority appeal of abstract rights remains a valid one. Though the popularity of Paine's *Rights of Man* is more often asserted than demonstrated, such popularity as it enjoyed has to be put in context. Much of the evidence, including the alleged sale of 200,000 copies of Part 1 by 1793, comes from loyalist propaganda with a vested interest in tarring radicals with Paineite and French brushes.

The constitutionalist alternative to Paine to which many radicals turned, if only in self-defence, was open to a loyalist counter-attack because it employed the same language, images and concepts and was more effectively organised without hindrance from the law. As H. T. Dickinson has reminded us, 'The variety, the sheer volume and the social and geographical distribution of conservative propaganda was certainly much greater than that disseminated by the radicals in the years from 1789 to 1815.'[24]

Popular wrath was often directed against those seen to be locally responsible for the hardships of the people: the baker, the miller, the farmer, the hoarder, the profiteer, the factory owner or farmer who created unemployment by introducing new machinery, or the employer who reduced wages. As Edward Thompson argued, such direct actions were in themselves highly rational, aimed at redressing the market and re-establishing traditional practices, but they had a relevance which was easily understood.[25] When Cobbett urged the journeymen and labourers of Norfolk in 1816 to meet and petition for the redress of their grievances, 'and let it not enter into your minds, that Bakers, Butchers, Millers and Farmers are the cause of your sufferings', he was asking them to understand something much harder.[26] Tradition and history were a sounder basis for popular propaganda than abstract rights. Major Cartwright's language of 'Saxon liberties' remained more appealing than Paine's newer abstractions even though Paine presented them in graphic and at times humorous language which clearly made some impact. However, as we have seen, the defence of tradition could feed revolution and it could equally well open the popular mind to the arguments of conservatives.

The plural 'liberties' is important. Unlike the abstract 'liberty' to which the American Thomas Jefferson had appealed in the language of the Enlightenment and in which the French had followed him, liberties meant privileges or exemptions. The liberties of 'the freeborn Englishman' had concrete meaning: a patriot rejoiced in the liberties of the English, not granted to foreigners: roast beef, white bread and no wooden shoes at the most basic; Magna Carta and trial by jury at a more elevated level. But the word 'liberties', frequently coupled with 'patriotism', was ambiguous. To love one's country could mean both defending it against its traditional enemies – the Pope, Spain, France – and defending it against corruption and despotism, the enemies of freedom at home.[27] This view was developed in anti-Jacobite propaganda in the 1740s and in anti-French propaganda throughout the century, especially during the Seven Years' War. David Garrick's celebration of British military victories in 1759, 'Heart of Oak', may read like a recruiting song for the navy, but its contrast of free men and slaves was telling:

> Come cheer up, my lads, 'tis to glory we steer,
> To add something more to this wonderful year;
> To honour we call you, not press you like slaves,
> For who are so free as the sons of the waves?

Freedom and patriotism were also the themes of James Thomson's verses, set to music by Thomas Arne in 1740 in what was to become one of the most popular of patriotic songs:

> When Britain, first at Heaven's command,
> Arose from out the azure main,
> This was the charter, the charter of the land,
> And guardian angels sung this strain,
> Rule Britannia! Britannia rule the waves,
> Britons never will be slaves.

This charter of freedom, redolent of Magna Carta, preceded the People's Charter by a hundred years. Conservatives, loyalists, radicals and Chartists used a common vocabulary to compete for the hearts and minds of the people. A later verse from 'Rule Britannia' drew the image of the firmly rooted 'native oak' withstanding the storms of 'each foreign stroke'. This exploited a fruitful line in propaganda appealing to traditional xenophobic anti-French feeling. Propagandists readily returned to this on the outbreak of war with France in 1793, in loyalist tracts which scoffed at the French, and in didactic or amusing cartoons such as Thomas Rowlandson's 'The Contrast' and James Gillray's 'Fashion before Ease; or, A good Constitution sacrificed, for a fantastic Form', both of 1793.[28]

In the Rowlandson the viewer is offered a contrast between British Liberty and French Liberty': on the one hand, 'Religion, Morality, Loyalty, Obedience to the Laws, Independance [sic], Personal Security, Justice, Inheritance, Protection of Property, Industry, National Prosperity, and Happiness'; on the other hand, 'Atheism, Perjury, Rebelion [sic], Treason, Anarchy, Murder, Equality, Madness, Cruelty, Injustice, Treachery, Ingratitude, Idleness, Famine, National & Private Ruin, and Misery'. The print concludes by asking the unnecessary question 'Which is Best?'

In the Gillray, Britannia is being forced into a pair of stays made by Thomas Paine (who had been a stay-maker), while she clutches a British oak. This was a potent and widely used symbol, for the oak was not only the material out of which the navy's ships were built, but referred also to the symbol of the Stuart Restoration, recalling that Charles Stuart had hidden in an oak tree after his defeat at the battle of Worcester in October 1651. His birthday and the anniversary of his re-entry into London on 29 May 1660 was commemorated annually from 1664 with the wearing of sprigs of oak and special services in church. Burke was playing on this image in 1790 when his cattle lay in the shade of the British oak.

A third patriotic song, which eclipsed 'Rule Britannia' in the 1790s and attained the religious status of national 'anthem' was an anti-Jacobite song made popular in 1745. Although the words of the opening verse were much older, and had been sung (in French!) for Louis XIV in 1686, the words of a later verse were explicitly loyalist:

> O Lord our God, arise,
> Scatter his enemies,
> And make them fall;
> Confound their politics;
> Frustrate their knavish tricks;

On him our hopes are fix'd;
O save us all.[29]

When Benjamin Brierley came to reconstruct in fiction the political life of Failsworth in the 1840s, his symbol of loyalism was a character called Nokin, who scrawled 'Damn Tom Paine' and 'Honour the King' on the loom-house wall; and who went around singing 'Confound their politics, frustrate their knavish tricks'. Even so, Nokin became a Chartist, but only for the duration of the depression.[30]

When faced with the growth of popular societies and the circulation of seditious literature, the government cultivated these images and appealed to 'public opinion' for support.[31] In response to the Royal Proclamation of 1 May 1792, some 382 loyal addresses were sent in during the next three months, and with the first invasion scare towards the end of 1792, the governing classes again turned to this well of potential loyalism for support against those who favoured French innovation to home-spun liberties.[32] Pitt himself was wary of encouraging popular politics, even of a loyalist kind, but on 20 November 1792 with semi-official government support, John Reeves, who held the government post of Receiver of the Public Offices, started the Association for the Preservation of Liberty and Property against Republicans and Levellers to rally public opinion against the radicals. Over the next three months between 1,200 and 1,500 associations were founded to sign loyal addresses. Sheffield was one of the few places where the loyalists did not outnumber the radicals. It is true that the lead was taken by a rather higher social class – mayors, aldermen, councillors, clergymen and other local leaders – and that pressure could be exerted on people to sign, but for the most part the number of signatures gathered and the attendance at meetings suggests widespread support from the lesser ranks of society. In only eight places was the loyal address taken round every house so that non-signers (like William Blake in Lambeth) would become marked men.[33]

The loyalists proceeded by a combination of persuasion and bullying, with personal threats against known radicals, pressure on landlords not to permit radical meetings on pain of losing their licences, and intimidating processions and burnings of Paine in effigy.[34] This upsurge in loyalist activity was accompanied by the production of tracts to counter the 'seditious' literature of the radicals. These included simple but effective chap-books, such as *One Pennyworth of Truth from Thomas Bull to his Brother John*, and Hannah More's *Village Politics; a dialogue between Jack Anvil the Blacksmith and Tom Hod the Mason; Addressed to All the Mechanics, Journeymen, and Day Labourers, in Great Britain*. Here the loyalist argument was simple and straightforward; the radical case was over-simplified and distorted – all radicals were levellers and thieves, idlers who wished to live by other people's industry – and naturally plain common sense was triumphant. Other literature appealed to straightforward class interest. A manifesto issued by the Loyal Associations of Manchester and Salford against the Unitarian radicals in 1795 described the latter as

> Hypocrites whose ears are *always shut* to the cry of *distress* – who oppress their servants – who exact with the GREATEST SEVERITY EXORBITANT RENTS FROM THEIR POOR TENANTS – who endeavour to compel the labouring poor to maintain the necessitous poor, and remove the burden from themselves, TO THEIR BOSOMS, the soft impulse of philanthropy is a stranger. – They who are continually seeking their own aggrandisement – incessantly panting after supremacy, and to acquire it, would see, with unconcern, their native soil DELUGED *with the Blood of their Countrymen*, know nothing of the animating glow of true Patriotism.[35]

This was dangerous talk, the violence of the language and demonstrations summoned up by the loyalists not only matching that of the radicals, but also setting them a precedent.

The function of this propaganda was partly to keep the mass of the people loyal, partly to boost the confidence and morale of the lesser property-owning classes, and partly to isolate and demoralise the radicals. By 1794 this last objective had been achieved with the radicals reduced to a beleaguered minority, but how far any permanent impact was made on the mass of the people – by either radicals or loyalists – is hard to tell. It may be that the most effective work was done in bolstering the middling group in society, who could identify with John Bull and his prejudices, and whose support was necessary to the traditional governing classes.

The initial impact made by the Reeves' Association was over by the spring of 1793 and, although the loyalists remained in the ascendancy until the Treason Trials of 1794, thereafter the trend seems to have been reversed. With the rise in food prices in 1795 and the growing unpopularity of the war, much popular opinion was now turning against the government. The Volunteer force, raised from March 1794 to provide additional local defence forces, drew on the loyalism of the middling and upper classes to produce cavalry units in the counties and urban infantry, but its recruiting owed its appeal to many factors, including its local base, its attractive uniform and opportunity for display, and also the fact that volunteering exempted a man from the militia ballot. Even so, local enthusiasm and voluntary subscriptions to pay for the force proved difficult to maintain in the longer term and in 1798 government funds had to be used to supplement local subscriptions. Anti-French feeling may have remained powerful, but so did opposition to a war that was blamed for high taxes and economic hardship.[36] John Bull may have been a patriotic figure, but he was one often portrayed as the victim of an unreasonable tax burden.[37] With the next grain crisis and even higher prices in 1799–1801 as the government sought unsuccessfully to end the war, popular loyalism were tested to the limit. Food rioting and industrial unrest on a major scale were the background to the suppression of the popular societies and the widespread political unrest that surfaced in the Despard plot. In these years it was by no means certain that the soundness of the people could be depended upon.[38]

This was to set the pattern for the early nineteenth century. There was undoubtedly some popular loyalism, but it was fickle and spasmodic: anti-French but also at times anti-ministerial. During times of hardship and in depressed sectors of the economy, revolutionary support was bred among men who felt they had little to lose. In 1812, the magistrates of the West Riding felt the situation so slipping out of control that they asked the government to introduce General Warrants and impose military law.[39] In 1812, 1817 and 1820 the widespread accumulation of arms in the population at large was greater than the right of 'constitutional self-defence' could warrant. In the industrial districts this amounted to far more than a minority-based London *coup d'état*. The same pattern was repeated in the Chartist years. Though it would be hard to claim at any time that the insurgents commanded the support of the majority, what ministers feared was that the government did not either and that events might therefore be decided by whichever side looked like winning. At this point, security became a practical and not an ideological matter.

The ambiguities of loyalism are illustrated in the 1830s by the loyalist crowd called out in 1832 to demonstrate against the Leeds Whigs and factory-owners as personified by Edward Baines of the *Leeds Mercury*. In the middle of the debate over the Reform Bill, the Leeds Tories took up the issue of factory reform in a bid to outflank the parliamentary reformers. This produced a working alliance between the radical *Leeds Patriot* and the Tory *Leeds Intelligencer*, building on the Tory–Radical compact forged by Richard Oastler and Michael Thomas Sadler. The occasion was the great 'Pilgrimage to York' by supporters of the factory movement at Easter 1832, a march attended by the sympathetic editor of the *Intelligencer* but vilified by the hostile Baines in the *Mercury*. His account appeared on the streets of Leeds on Saturday 28 April. Immediately, a crowd gathered and a copy of the *Mercury* was tied to a pole with a piece of black crepe and borne aloft as the crowd marched on the *Mercury* office where they burned the offending paper to the accompaniment of hisses, booings and groans.

That evening a far larger crowd assembled, bearing an effigy of Baines draped with banners proclaiming the words which William Cobbett had recently applied to the *Mercury* and its editor – 'The great Liar of the North'. Preceded by a brass band, the crowd marched past the *Mercury* office to the accompaniment of the 'Rogues March', then to the *Leeds Patriot* office where they gave three cheers, and then to the *Intelligencer* office where they gave three cheers and made the effigy bow down. They then marched to the homes of prominent supporters, including Sadler, where the band played 'God Save the King' and 'Rule Britannia' before returning to the *Mercury* office where they set fire to the effigy amid deafening shouts.[40] This immediately preceded the 'days of May' when Baines and the Leeds Political Union were supposed to be in the forefront of the revolution against the Duke of Wellington. Yet this same anger of a 'Rule Britannia' marching crowd – Britons never will be (factory) slaves – was a few years later to be turned against Poor Law guardians, and it led to Chartists marching and drilling on the moors in 1839, drawing boiler plugs in 1842 and defeating the incompetent and outnumbered Bradford police in 1848.

The cohesion of social welfare

In his influential Ford lectures of 1983–84, Ian Christie offered an explanation of the avoidance of revolution in terms of social cohesion.[41] Undoubtedly the factors he pointed to were important, although at times he idealised social relationships and appeared to admit that what may have been true of the 1790s was not necessarily applicable in the nineteenth century. This was a society of ranks and orders, of deference and paternalism. Although such a society, as appealed to by Disraeli in his attack on the Whigs for causing Chartism in 1839, was always something of a fiction, there was some reality behind the myth, particularly in rural communities where the economic interests of landlords, farmers and labourers could be bound together in a social network of charity and paternalism. There was often much to be gained and little to be lost by deference to the squire and the parson, either through habit or rational calculation. A great deal of charity was dispensed to the lower orders in times of personal or national hardship, whether through Christian benevolence or self-interest is not really relevant. Much of society was maintained in equilibrium by a recognition of what the rich and influential owed to the poor and of what the poor deserved from the rich.

On 19 October 1831, a deputation waited upon the Duke of Newcastle with the following address, signed by 313 of his tenants on his Clumber estates in Nottinghamshire:

> We, the undersigned inhabitants . . . deeply regretting the attempts that have been made to destroy your grace's property, cannot find terms sufficiently strong to express our detestation of proceedings so revolting to every good feeling. Living, as we do, in the neighbourhood of your grace's residence, where your character and virtues are felt and appreciated, and sensible as we are of the comforts and advantages derived from so kind and liberal a landlord, we feel a real pleasure in coming forward to declare our respect for, and attachment to, your grace; and to offer our united services to protect your person, and that of every individual member of your family; and at the same time to assure your grace, that it is our unanimous determination to exert every energy in our power to prevent the destruction and plunder of your grace's property, and a repetition of outrages so flagrant and disgraceful to the county.[42]

Admittedly this was from the tenantry, not the peasantry, and it was not written with the unlettered hand of an agricultural labourer, but it nevertheless probably contains sentiments not wholly forced or false.

Similarly, in 1843, in the Yorkshire township of Slaithwaite which had been a regular centre of industrial unrest since William Horsfall was murdered by the Luddites in 1812, the landlord and lord of the manor, the fourth Earl of Dartmouth, visited his people in order to celebrate the coming of age of his eldest son by laying the foundation stone of a new Church of England Sunday School high on the moors to serve the scattered communities of weaver/farmers on land he had given the previous year. Two years later he was back to open it, and in 1852 he was expressing concern for handloom weavers who 'do not partake in the general prosperity of factory labour'. In 1840 his wife had become patron of a maternal society for lying-in women started by the vicar's wife. 'He responded promptly and liberally, though with much discrimination, to every appeal made to him, for the spiritual and educational improvement of the tenants of his estates.' For over a century of industrialisation, successive earls from the second to the fifth bestowed this kind of personal patronage on the people of the village.[43] Whatever the motives of the Earls of Dartmouth – and they were men who took their religious faith seriously – this kind of personal benevolence could only add a warmth to the economic relationship which tied tenants to their landlord and villagers to the lord of the manor.

In 1795, Henry Yarbrugh of Heslington near York rebuilt the ancient almshouses and gave land for a village school. The same year soup kitchens were started, funded by private subscriptions or subsidised from the poor rates. Enormous amounts of private charity went into the relief of distress and more was contributed through the poor rates. One estimate is that in the first half of 1795, the first crisis of the war years, some 15–40 per cent of the population received relief from private and public charity.[44]

Against this background the system of poor relief was modified, following the emergency decision of the Speenhamland magistrates in 1795 to pay relief in proportion to need and the price of bread. The crisis of 1799–1801 was even worse, and need outstripped the ability of rate payers to find adequate funds. In London the government had to make loans to the poorest parishes to prevent starvation. Parishes further from the seat of government were dealt with less promptly but the need was unavoidable.[45] Christie concludes that had the poor law 'not been in operation, then the degree of desperation can only be guessed'. Wells argues that the poor law was breaking under the strain, and that the degree of desperation was a real threat to social stability. The same could be said of the third great wartime crisis in 1811–12, when harvest failure coincided with trade depression. Whereas Poor Law expenditure in 1801 had been £4,017,871, in 1811 it rose 65 per cent to £6,665,105. Private charity amounted to at least as much again. A fifth of the population in most Lancashire towns was estimated to be in receipt of relief.[46] Though Poor Law expenditure then declined a little, it was back up to the 1811–13 level again in 1817 and peaked at £7,517,000 in 1818. The 1820s saw a decline to under £6 million, but this was still above the level of the first crisis in 1795, and in 1832 the total was back to over £7 million.[47]

Without this huge transfer of funds from rate payers to the poor, the social fabric might well have crumbled. But such enormous calls on taxation led to a reconsideration of the basis on which relief was awarded. New philosophical ideas challenged older religious notions of the duty of the rich to feed the poor by suggesting that hand-outs produced dependency and encouraged both idleness and low wages. This thinking led to the Poor Law Amendment Act of 1834. It looked like punishment in the countryside for the collapse of social deference in 1830.

To conservative thinkers, the spirit of *laissez-faire* that lay behind the new Poor Law was, in Thomas Carlyle's memorable phrase, 'an *abdication* on the part of the governors'.[48] Disraeli had used the same idea a few months earlier in the debate on the 1839 Petition in his argument that there was a 'sentiment on the part of the people of England, that their civil rights had been invaded' and that this was what had made Chartism a mass movement. By civil rights he meant the right of the destitute to look to their neighbours for relief in the expectation that those in authority would recognise their social duties. Disraeli may have been constructing a golden age under the pre-1832 constitution and the old poor law in order to criticise the Whig reformers, but the values embodied in that myth were ones widely shared and to that extent he was right. The obverse of the argument that the system of poor relief saved Britain from revolution in the period 1790–1820 is that the change in the system brought Britain close to revolution after 1837. The word 'Britain' is used deliberately because, although the poor law applied only to England and Wales, the less adequate systems in Scotland and Ireland offered the safety net of emigration to England. Even so, the widespread agrarian discontent in Ireland, exported to both Britain and the United States, did owe something to the lack of a resident aristocracy and structure of public welfare underpinning private charity.

In practice, the anger against the new Poor Law was directed against its threat rather than what actually happened. Whatever Disraeli might say and although it is true that poor law expenditure was cut back from the 1830s, so that even in the period 1839–42 it was lower than in any previous crisis since 1799–1801 despite a near doubling of the population, much of the old system of private charity and public relief outside the workhouse continued as before. In Nottingham, for example, the mayor, William Roworth, led the opposition to the building of a new workhouse, and when the Guardians applied for land on which to built one, the corporation refused permission.[49] Major-General Napier, in charge of the troops garrisoned in the north to keep the Chartists in control, observed in his journal in December 1839: 'Spoke to the mayor about a subscription: – the excellent mayor, Mr Roworth. He joins me in all my opinions as to the thrice-accursed new poor law, its bastiles, and its guardians. Lying title! They guard nothing, not even their own carcases, for they so outrage misery that if a civil war comes they will immediately be sacrificed.'[50]

Another voice, sympathetic to the poor though hostile to Chartism, came from the Domestic Missionary to the Poor in Manchester at the time of the Plug Riots in 1842. This was John Layhe, reporting from his journal entry for July 1842 to the Manchester middle class at the Cross Street Unitarian chapel:

> The demand for soup tickets continues unabated, and the very early hour at which many persons are accustomed to resort to the kitchen in Bale-street proves the extremity of their destitution. I was lately conversing with a poor man, who has a wife, three sons and a daughter, all of whom except the woman were then out of work, and he informed me that being unable to sleep or rest, he went for soup one morning so early as half-past one o'clock, and even then found 50 or 60 persons before him. At the time referred to in the above statement, though the more skilled of the hand-loom weavers and out-door labourers had pretty regular employment, yet many other classes were suffering unusual depression. Such was the case with factory operatives and mechanics, and there were numbers of dyers and spinners,

and the more common descriptions of weavers, who had long had nothing to do. I was myself acquainted with many individuals connected with these branches of industry, who had been almost without any work for periods varying from a few weeks to twelve months. When to all this is added the long-continued depreciation of wages, we shall be convinced that the measure of human endurance was filled to the brim.[51]

He added, 'At length this measure was exceeded, and the waters of civil strife and commotion threatened to overflow the land, and sweep away the institutions of society.' The strike and lock-out, though, made things worse, for the few who had work were now deprived of it. 'Yet these poor people are of remarkably peaceable habits,' he reassured his subscribers, 'and would have been glad to have worked if they had been allowed. In these circumstances, I rendered them some assistance, which they received with great thankfulness.' In all this one small charity distributed 3,000 soup tickets, as well as bedding and clothing.

Layhe's report shows why the idea of strikers holding out until the Charter was the law of the land was impracticable. It also shows how the view that unrest was the work of a minority exploiting the grievances of the majority could be used to win charitable sympathy for the majority. Though Layhe may have been aware that some of his subscribers might have wished to starve the strikers back to work, his emphasis was on the need to relieve those whose distress was no fault of their own. Motives are always hard to disentangle, and contemporaries probably could not do it even for themselves, but in Layhe's report – as in the novel which the wife of the secretary to the Mission, Elizabeth Gaskell, based on his report – compassion appears more important than social control.[52] Compassion had the effect of blunting those edges of class hostility which fed the anger and despair of Chartism. Similarly, the grateful recipient's motives are hard to isolate. The donor naturally heard or wanted to hear gratitude, but we cannot now tell whether sullen resentment was also present.

Layhe also observed how many working people were too proud to accept charity, and turned first to 'incurring debts, and withdrawing funds from benefit societies'. The friendly society was seen by Professor Christie as another of those institutions which helped bind society together,[53] but it also gave working men independence and lessons in organisation. In 1793 Rose's Act help separate these societies from trade societies by giving them a legal existence but the trade societies also continued to offer financial support to their members parallel to that offered by the friendly societies. They undoubtedly helped take the edge of distress and, if one regards distress as a major cause of revolutions, they may have correspondingly reduced the risk. But in so far as they encouraged the capacity for independence and organisation they did not – unlike the poor law – promote those ties of paternalism and deference which Tory thinkers regarded as essential to social stability.

Religion

In 1913 the French historian, Elie Halévy, sought to explain 'the extraordinary stability which English society was destined to enjoy throughout a period of revolutions and crises'. His answer was that 'the *elite* of the working class, the hard-working and capable bourgeoisie, had been imbued by the evangelical movement with a spirit from which the established order had nothing to fear.'[54] Since then historians have both rejected and been attracted by this theory. It was given a twist by Edward Thompson for whom Methodism was a conservative force which indoctrinated the workers, gave them an alternative sense of community and belonging, and offered them a spiritual safety valve on Sundays and during periods of religious revival.[55] Halévy himself meant by 'Methodism' the whole evangelical movement in Church and Dissent; other historians have extended the theory to apply to other religious emphases as well. William Jones, curate at Nayland in Suffolk and author of the *John Bull* loyalist tracts, was a high churchman and a millenarian.[56] Hannah More, who followed up her *Village Politics* (1793) with the monthly *Cheap Repository Tracts*, issued from 1795 to 1797, was an Evangelical.[57]

Religion provided a powerful language and exerted a greater impact on the way people thought than the secular language of political debate. It dominated cultural life and the media of communication: the sermon and homily, Sunday and weekday schools, charities and popular reading matter. The Bible and *Pilgrim's Progress* were central to the self-awareness of many a working-class autodidact. This meant that religion often provided the ideological ground on which revolution and stability were contested. For the followers of Richard

Brothers in 1795, Robert Wedderburn in 1819, John Thoms in 1838 or Joseph Rayner Stephens in 1839, religion could release revolutionary language, remove mundane inhibitions and promote revolt. A favoured text, used by United Britons in 1801 and by Luddites in 1812,[58] was taken from Ezekiel 21, verses 25–7:

> And thou, profane wicked prince of Israel, whose day is come, when iniquity shall have an end, Thus saith the Lord God; Remove the diadem, and take off the crown: this shall not be the same: exalt him that is low, and abase him that is high. I will overturn, overturn, overturn it: and it shall be no more, until he comes whose right it is: and I will give it him.

This was the spirit, with its vision of the revolutionary wheel of fortune, which inspired Luddites and anti-Poor Law protesters, incited Spenceans in Wedderburn's chapel, and made political preachers so dangerous in south Wales.

Counter-revolutionaries appreciated the importance of religion in maintaining the social and political order and reinforcing the legitimacy of 'the powers that be'. When Thoms found that a gang of men working in a gravel pit near Sittingbourne would not join his band of disciples in 1838, his response was to dismiss them as 'a set of Methodists'.[59] John Wesley had been a Tory, opposed even to American independence, and after his death in 1791 Methodism continued to stress its loyalty. In 1792 the Conference resolved that

1   None of us shall, either in writing or in conversation, speak lightly or irreverently of the Government under which he lives.
2   We are to observe, that the oracles of God command us to be subject to the higher powers; and that honour to the king is there connected with the fear of God.[60]

This continued to be the official policy throughout the period, but as a developing party outside the established Church, employing itinerant preachers and spreading its message by unorthodox means, Methodism was not always seen in this light by the authorities. In 1811, Lord Sidmouth proposed a Bill which, among other things, would have prohibited itinerant preaching. The Methodists demonstrated their loyalty as a matter of survival and then gratitude.[61] The Reverend John Stephens, Wesleyan Methodist superintendent minister in Manchester in 1819, expelled 400 Manchester Methodists suspected of radicalism after the Peterloo massacre and published a sermon in defence of the magistrates.[62] The fact that there were so many Methodists whom he felt he had to expel indicates the ambiguity of the Methodist contribution to stability and conflict no less than the politics of Stephens's sixth child, Joseph Rayner Stephens. Samuel Bamford's father and uncle were the sons of a leading local Methodist in Middleton. They found Wesley's theology perfectly compatible with reading Paine's *Rights of Man* and joining a reading society to support parliamentary reform.[63]

The established Church was more reliable, and here the Evangelicals did make an important contribution. Their deeply pessimistic view of human sinfulness caused them to see the French Revolution both as a manifestation of evil and as a divine punishment for the sins of everyone, including the ruling classes of Britain. Their moral mission, therefore, should not be seen as a simple instrument of repressive politics, though it had that effect. Their mood is caught in a memoir of one of their number, the Reverend William Richardson of York:

> Though Mr Richardson avoided mixing with politics and parties, he was a true lover of his country, and omitted no suitable opportunity of enforcing the duties of loyalty and subordination, and of denouncing the too frequent disposition to 'murmur and complain,' as equally contrary to the express precepts and to the spirit of the Gospel.
>
> During the twenty years' wars of the French Revolution, he suffered great distress and anxiety of mind, on account of the spirit of revolt and blasphemy which extended over Europe.[64]

Following the de-Christianisation campaign in France and the publication of Paine's *The Age of Reason* (1795), the debate in Britain switched emphasis from the constitution to religion. Atheism was the bugbear. Religion underpinned the law and morality; without it, all that was sacred would count for nothing. Repentance and divine mercy were needed if Britain were to resist France. The Evangelicals were unusual in identifying the high-born as well as the low as needing this message, and in this they had the support of the pious King George III, if not of his rather lax and sceptical prime minister, William Pitt. Religion was not a front for repression, but a vital necessity if Britain were to be saved from revolution and the wrath to come.

It was in this mood that the leading Yorkshire Evangelical clergy-men of the Elland Clerical Society (founded 1767) received and approved in 1797 a resolution from a kindred spirit in Sheffield, sol-emnly declaring 'that the revolutionary spirit of these Καιροι Χαλεποι [Perilous Times] calls for new and extraordinary exertions & methods of grace to oppose it' and agreed to form a committee 'for the purpose of conducting the Circulation of cheap Tracts & pamphlets in order to counteract the pernicious principles that have been diffused amongst the lower orders of people'.[65]

Over the next few years tracts and sermons urged repentance, loyalty and subordination on the West Riding which was sinking ever deeper into that revolutionary abyss that culminated in Luddism. One of their number was Hammond Roberson, curate in the parish of Dewsbury. Remembered as the model for Mr Helstone in Charlotte Brontë's *Shirley* and his apparently callous attitude to the dying Luddites after the attack on Rawfolds mill in 1812, he was not only an energetic opponent of the Luddites but also a founder of Sunday schools, the builder at his own expense of Christ Church, Liversedge, of which he became incumbent in 1816, and 'a devoted and highly conscientious man whose motives were pure and elevated'.[66] Yet Roberson's character was all of a piece. His sermons, tracts, Sunday schools, churches and anti-Luddite activities were all aimed at the ele-vation of the people, the promulgation of morality and an end to that spirit of disloyalty and insubordination that brought Europe so close to tragedy between 1789 and 1815.

Through militant and conscientiously pious pastors like Roberson in the parishes, and politically appointed bishops in the House of Lords, the Church and its message were woven into the fabric of unreformed society in defence of religion and against rev-olution. As much by their support of charities and Sunday schools as by their ideological underpinning of the existing system of pol-itics, they helped create a society capable of weathering the storms of radicalism. Their impact was probably greatest on the morale and sense of purpose of the governing classes, nationally and locally; but it may be that their non-commissioned officers in the reserve armies of Methodism and Nonconformity made a greater impact on the middling sections of society. However they operated, the combined forces of religious revival may have called people's minds to higher things, softened the edges of social conflict and, where they did contribute to radical organisation and consciousness, turned that into constitutional and non-revolutionary channels.

The strength of the state

Modern revolutions are often described as overthrowing 'the state' but this view usually assumes a Germanic model of what constitutes 'the state', as found in the philosophies of Hegel and Marx. This abstract concept is hardly appropriate in a discussion of revolution in late eighteenth-century Britain. The word 'state' is a derivative of 'estate' and originally had territorial implications. Then, by extension, it referred to the legal and administrative machinery by which the territory was governed. The 'state' was therefore a legal abstraction, and the word was used in this sense in the 1790s in contexts such as 'State prisoners' and 'State Trials'. The machinery which made up the state included the courts of law, the established church, the privy council, the king's ministers and the supreme legislature – the king-in-parliament. The exact concept was vague, for Britain possessed no defining constitution, which Edmund Burke regarded as a virtue and Thomas Paine as a vice. A programme of reform which sought fundamental change to any of these aspects of the state could be thought revolutionary. In fact, the word 'state' was rarely used: Paine preferred to discuss 'systems of government' or 'constitutions'. What usually appears to have been meant was the nature of the administration. The personnel of the legal system might be swept away, Parliament might be reformed, but apart from the church there was little hostility to the institutions of the state as such.

The main object of hostility was the administration: the government; the king and his ministers. Revolution to overthrow 'the state' could therefore mean little more than a violent alternative to a general election for a people excluded from the normal political processes, in order to destroy that corruption whereby the propertied classes were parasitic upon the over-taxed poor. The king, his ministers, or even the whole of Parliament were tangible symbols of government, and as such objects of radical attack, but beyond them Britain was actually governed not by a centralised bureaucracy such as modern revolutions are directed against, but by a diffuse, amateur, local, part-time and numerous body of men who collectively substituted for what a later age would call 'the state'. At the start of the French Revolutionary War, the Treasury employed only seventeen clerks; the Home and Foreign Offices each had an establishment of nineteen, including the secretaries of state.[67] What central administration there was concerned internal and external security – although much of this was also local and amateur – and collecting the money to pay for it and the interest on loans raised to pay for past wars: what has been called 'the fiscal-military state'.[68]

The paradox of a small and apparently weak state that was actually strong and resilient has been explored by John Brewer. The British state was strong because it was militarily effective and relatively efficient at raising tax revenues. France was, by eighteenth-century criteria, a much wealthier country than Britain, yet the long series of wars with Britain bankrupted the Bourbons not the Hanoverians. Even the crisis of 1797, which Paine had anticipated in his *Decline and Fall of the English System of Finance* (1796) and expected to lead to rapid collapse, was surmounted with surprisingly little difficulty. Whatever Cobbett might say about paper money, it worked for Britain because of the underlying financial strength of the country. The diffuse nature of the largely amateur administration also meant that it was not as vulnerable as a centralised bureaucracy to the *coup d'état* approach to revolution. Local self-government may have weakened the central state but in so doing actually strengthened the capacity of the state to survive a crisis at the centre.

Another apparent weakness but actual strength lay in the rule of law. State power and authority were exercised in England through the law, which was made in the courts as well as in Parliament and was administered locally as well as nationally.[69] The 'rule of law' was widely accepted as the foundation of English liberties, and the different Scottish system held a similar position north of the border. Only in Ireland was there dissent about the legitimacy of the law, which always made Ireland a special case. In Britain, it was the law which restricted Parliament and prevented despotism. This weakened the theoretical powers of the executive but strengthened their legitimacy. Revolutionaries in Britain did not seek to overthrow the rule of law. They objected to specific laws, or the absence of them, and to those who administered the law in what was seen to be an 'unjust' way, but such conflict as occurred was within the framework of the law. The justification for bearing arms by appeal to Blackstone is a good example of this. Constitutionalism and respect for the law was reinforced when the jury system, which could be notoriously independent of government, led to the acquittals of Hardy and the rest in 1794, O'Connor in 1798, and Thistlewood and the Folly Hall insurgents in 1817. The safeguard of *Habeas Corpus* was seldom suspended, and then mainly in time of war; its suspension in 1817 was unusual. The innate constitutionalism of British radical protest blunted its revolutionary edge. Conversely, this meant that when the constitutional approach was frustrated, when particular laws were seen to be so unjust as to be unacceptable, when ministers made laws by Proclamation and not by Act of Parliament, or when the normal paths of legitimate protest were stopped by the suspension of *Habeas Corpus*, the moral and indeed constitutional justification for revolution was all the greater. It could be sanctioned by an appeal to 1688 or even 1642 which few conservatives could gainsay.[70]

The diffuse and amateur British state was also strong because of the people who administered it. The British aristocracy, like the British state, was the opposite of its public image. Apparently an open elite, cascading its younger sons down into the gentry and drawing its daughters-in-law and their money up from wealthy merchant families, in fact the mobility of the upper reaches of the social order was more a matter of recycling through the same small number of titled families than a genuine openness of access. The occasional lawyer or churchman might ease his way upwards from the professions to the House of Lords, and a career might be made in politics or a position bought with money made in India or finance and commerce (and, even more rarely, industry) but these were the exceptions. The result was that Britain was administered by an elite of families from the peerage and titled gentry who dominated positions in every aspect of national and local government at every significant level.

Furthermore, by socialisation in a common education dominated by Eton or Westminster and then Christ Church, Oxford, or Trinity or St John's, Cambridge, followed by marriage into one another's families, the peerage and its relations formed a homogenised elite.[71] They provided around a fifth of the membership of the House of Commons but their connections reached beyond politics to other significant institutions, notably the higher ranks of the armed forces. The key figure in the administration of law and order locally was the Lord

Lieutenant, who almost invariably in England was a peer or the son of a peer. He was at the apex of county society and wielded important patronage, nominating local magistrates and officers in the militia.[72] Though the numbers of peers increased dramatically after 1784, rising from 189 in 1780 to 267 in 1800, most of these new creations came from old peerage families.[73] Beyond the peerage families, among the titled aristocracy at large and down the social scale to the baronets, much of the argument remains true. At the county level the gentry supplied the Deputy Lieutenants and Sheriffs, they dominated the magistracy and filled the lesser commissioned ranks in the armed forces. Many of them through intermarriage were also more or less distantly related to peerage families.[74] In 1818 four-fifths of MPs were elected from the landed elite of gentry or aristocracy.[75]

The economic interests of this elite were as broad as their social base was narrow. Aristocratic landlords exploited, directly or indirectly, the mineral wealth of their estates; wealthy commercial and industrial families bought estates and merged into the gentry at the lower levels, and then by further well-placed marriages their links to the greater county families were established. In this way the governing elite could both remain relatively small and closed, and yet at the same time be part of the mainstream of wider gentry and commercial society. They were part of the single, seamless fabric of society. Below them they controlled a network of patronage which reached down through their tenants and employees to tradesmen dependent on the local 'big house' for custom. Though Cobbett might dismiss this as part of 'Old Corruption' it was much more and remained an important characteristic of British society well into the nineteenth century. It faltered but recovered in 1832, having shed its less acceptable characteristics. When Robert Peel judged that the Corn Laws were bringing the system into disrepute, he repealed them – aided by the most aristocratic section of the legislature, the Whigs. From the 1820s onwards the British elite showed a remarkable ability to reform its institutions and move from a fiscal–military state to an administrative state capable of meeting the needs of an increasingly complex commercial and industrial society.[76] The third reason given by the Chartist, G. J. Holyoake, for the lack of revolution in England in 1848 was, 'The mixed interest of our commercial nobility and the people.'[77]

The significance of this elite is the unity of direction and purpose it gave to British society. If revolutions are caused when the elite is divided, the opportunities in Britain were few. If there were a hint of weakness or dissent, that was quickly disposed of. When the Duke of Norfolk unwisely toasted 'Our Sovereign, the Majesty of the People' at Fox's birthday celebration in 1798, Pitt dismissed him from the lord lieutenancy of the West Riding.[78] When his successor, Earl Fitzwilliam, supported a county meeting in 1819 to protest at the Peterloo massacre, he too was dismissed.[79] Both men were Whigs who saw themselves as defenders of English liberties and the rule of law. If there was to be a revolution, it would be one to protect liberty as in 1688, and they would lead it. When they bid to do so in 1832, Wellington drew back rather than risk civil conflict.

Revolutions are also made when the army rebels. Revolutionaries need troops, which must come from within the existing armed forces or from abroad. The British army was not divided vertically by region or tribe, but horizontally by social class. Because the same elite which controlled the army controlled everything else, there was unlikely to be a military *coup*, or a revolution led by disgruntled regiments. As John Cannon has reasonably asked, 'What in the eighteenth century, could army officers have rebelled against and, if they had taken over, how could they have constructed a society more congenial to their own aristocratic views and interests?'[80]

The authority of the law

The legal hand of the British system of justice was deceptively light. Acceptance of the rule of law and the independence of the jury system meant that arbitrary justice was thought neither desirable nor possible. There were relatively few political trials, and many of these ended in an acquittal including, spectacularly, the trial of Hardy and others in 1794. Fox's Libel Act of 1792 gave a measure of protection in seditious libel cases. The Two Acts of 1795, despite their potential, were rarely used. The government did not usually interfere in the work of local magistrates who were on the front line of administering justice, and frequently left them to their own devices and complaining at the lack of support they received from the centre.[81] Nevertheless, the law was effective. Exemplary punishments, some of them harsh, were exacted. The outcomes of the Scottish treason trials of 1793 and 1794 under the different Scottish legal system, contrast with those in

England at this time, but even in Scotland Lord Braxfield's use of transportation against Muir, Palmer, Skirving, Gerrald and Margarot was dubious but legal.[82]

The device of proceeding by *ex-officio* information circumvented unreliable grand juries. Under an *ex-officio* information filed by the Attorney General, there was no Grand Jury to give a case a preliminary hearing; the accused need not be informed of the charges against him (or, very rarely, her); there was no need to bring the accused to trial, and if they could not afford bail they might be imprisoned without charge and without trial. Even if a case did come to trial, and even if normal procedures were followed or the case were dropped, a poor bookseller could be ruined and thus silenced without any need to prove guilt. The very threat of such proceedings was often enough.

The Attorney General could also call for a special jury to be appointed. These were not chosen at random and could be vetted by the prosecution in advance. In Scotland, juries were selected by the court and the presiding judge, no challenges were allowed, and majority verdicts were accepted. As a result of these limitations on the jury system in both parts of Britain, in the 1790s the majority of trials for politically-related offences, other than the treason trials, resulted in convictions.[83] Clive Emsley's estimate of 200 prosecutions for treason and sedition in the 1790s has been challenged as an underestimate, but his overall point remains: that Pitt's 'Terror' was based not so much on the new legislation introduced in the 1790s as on the regular processes of law available to the authorities at any time they cared to use them. Despite spectacular failures, repeated in William Hone's trial for libel in 1817 when the jury refused to convict, this remained true and the law was used to punish rioters, demonstrators, libellers, publishers and insurgents throughout the period of this book. But even an important case like the trial of Smith O'Brien for sedition in May 1848 could fail when Catholics on the jury refused to produce a unanimous verdict of guilty, unlike the case of John Mitchel who was convicted by a carefully packed jury.[84]

Not all prosecutions were initiated by the law officers of the crown or local magistrates. One feature of the loyalist reaction against the radicals was the creation of private prosecution societies. In response to a Royal Proclamation in June 1787 for the encouragement of piety and virtue, and for preventing and punishing vice, profaneness and immorality, William Wilberforce set up what was known as the Proclamation Society. One of its tasks was, in the words of the Proclamation, the suppression 'all loose and licentious prints, books and publications, dispersing poison to the minds of the young and unwary; and to punish the publishers and vendors thereof'.[85] Among its successes was the prosecution of Paine's *The Age of Reason* in 1797. This society later merged with a parallel society, created in 1802, entitled the 'Society for the Suppression of Vice and the encouragement of religion and virtue, throughout the United Kingdom, to consist of members of the Established Church' – known to radicals as the 'Vice Society'. By the end of 1803 it had over eight hundred members and nearly seven hundred convictions. These were for 'moral' offences, but since in the evangelical view of the world morality underpinned the civil order, these could include 'political' offences. As the secretary explained in the disturbed year of 1817, 'The influences of religious obligation seem much on the decline among the lower orders of society, to which is probably attributable much of that impatience under civil restraint which is the characteristic feature of the times.'[86] This purpose was taken over more explicitly in 1820 by the 'Constitutional Association for Opposing the Progress of Disloyal and Seditious Principles', founded with offices in Bridge Street, Blackfriars (hence its alternative name, 'the Bridge Street Gang') by 20 peers, 40 MPs, 9 bishops and 97 clergy. The Bridge Street Gang operated by prosecuting booksellers in order to disrupt their businesses and land them with heavy costs irrespective of whether a conviction was secured. During 1820–22 they obtained only four convictions, one of which resulted in a sentence – on Mary Ann Carlile, wife of the republican publisher, Richard Carlile who was already in gaol for republishing Paine's *The Age of Reason* as a result of a Vice Society prosecution.[87]

The government found these private prosecutions convenient, for they distanced ministers from measures of which they could approve privately but did not wish to endorse officially. The impartiality of the rule of law was important and ministers had to balance the need for security with reforms to improve the way the law worked and how it was perceived. Lord Sidmouth, in his earlier days as Henry Addington, Speaker of the House of Commons, had consoled himself following the acquittal of Hardy in 1794 with the thought that 'It is of more consequence to maintain the credit of a mild and unprejudiced administration of justice than ever to convict a Jacobin.'[88]

In 1812, as Home Secretary in the middle of the Luddite panic, he refused the urgent demands of the Vice-Lieutenant and magistrates of the West Riding for the issue of General Warrants so they could raid homes for arms because he did not see 'under present circumstances, cause for adopting the strong measure of a forcible seizure, nor for resorting to any measure, that does not derive its effect from the Law as it now stands'.[89] Subsequent reforms at the Home Office under Robert Peel extended this policy of emphasising the impartiality of the rule of law. An important change introduced by his ministry in 1842 removed from the justices in Quarter Sessions to the Assizes a number of cases, including those involving punishment by transportation, unlawful oaths, blasphemous and seditious libel, arson and most unlawful combinations and conspiracies, which had figured large in prosecutions against those involved in disturbances and worse over the previous half century.[90]

The determination of governments to maintain the impartiality of the law illustrates the extent to which most conservatives and many revolutionaries had consciously elected to confine their operations within constitutional limits until such time as the other side should break them. The threat of revolution on constitutionalist grounds might therefore be seen as one reason why restraints were observed by successive British governments; but equally the fact of such constitutionalism on the part of the authorities is one reason why the revolutionaries were themselves constrained in the main to constitutional methods. Both sides accepted, as it were, the rules of the game, written in a common language of constitutional liberties.[91]

In practice, however, there were players on both sides who did not appear to accept the rules. A minority of revolutionaries, like Paine, rejected the language of historical rights and by the 1830s were beginning to be attracted by the alternative language of socio-economic conflict; and a minority of magistrates and armed civilians in the yeomanry were impatient with the blatant exploitation of constitutionalist language by subversive troublemakers intent only on seizing property which they did not own. Either of these could upset the delicate balance which helped prevent outbreaks of revolution.

The law was still subject to the vagaries of individual judges. Those tried in 1842 before Special Commissions presided over by Baron Abinger were dealt with by a judge who appeared to think that supporting the Charter was itself a political offence; but then, as plain

Mr James Scarlett, he had led the prosecution of Henry Hunt after Peterloo.[92] In contrast is Lord Chief Justice Tindal who recommended the commutation of the life sentences on Frost, Williams and Jones in 1840.[93] By the 1840s, the government and its law officers, if not all judges and magistrates, had realised the strength of justice tempered with mercy. In the wake of the Chartist disturbances of 1848, most sentences passed were for periods of between six months and two years. That avoided making martyrs, but took troublemakers out of circulation for long enough to ensure that the forces of law and order would prevail. Moderation and restraint by the authorities deprived would-be revolutionaries of their moral case for rebellion.

The forces of order

Under the Lord Lieutenant of the county, the next effective person responsible for the maintenance of law and order was the Justice of the Peace in England and Wales, and the Sheriff in Scotland where the Sheriff Principal was usually the Lord Lieutenant, while the Sheriff Depute and his Sheriff Substitutes exercised the law and order role left to magistrates south of the border.[94] The role of the magistrate, according to an Act of the reign of Edward III, was 'to restrain offenders, rioters and all other barrators, and to pursue, arrest, take and chastise them according to their trespass and offence, and then cause them to be imprisoned and duly punished'.[95] When necessary in his judgement, he could suspend civil law and hand over to the military by reading the Riot Act of 1715.

> Our Sovereign Lord the King chargeth and commandeth all Persons, being assembled, immediately to disperse themselves, and peaceably to depart to their Habitations, or to their lawful Business, upon the Pains contained in the Act made in the first year of King George, for preventing Tumults and riotous Assemblies. God Save the King.[96]

This Act could be applied whenever twelve or more persons were 'unlawfully, riotously and tumultuously assembled', and following this proclamation, anyone remaining after one hour, whatever his or her intentions or actions, was guilty of an offence.

The Duke of Wellington felt that the magistrates were much

maligned but in fact made the difference between England and France in 1830:

> We have mobs; we have riots; we have broken windows and broken heads; and much injury done to, and destruction of, property. But we never fail to find the Justice of the Peace faithful to his trust, making the most energetic, the most moderate that circumstances will permit, but at the same time the most effectual and successful exertions to put an end to the mischief.[97]

On the other hand, Francis Lindley Wood feared in 1812 that magistrates were, as in Ireland, reaching the end of their tether and might refuse to serve;[98] and in 1839, Major-General Napier grumbled at magistrates who chose to go grouse-shooting in August 1839 in the middle of the Chartist crisis.[99]

In the eighteenth century, the forces available to the magistrates were limited. Parish constables were part-time officials concerned only with collecting local taxes and dealing with petty crimes and perhaps the odd instance of drunken disorder. Magistrates might pay informers to supply information useful for maintaining the peace and this role was performed by the police employed by stipendiary magistrates appointed in London under the 1792 Middlesex Justices' Act, but in cases of major unrest they had to resort to the military. Their powers included issuing search warrants, forbidding meetings, and calling upon the militia, yeomanry or regular army for support.

The most ancient auxiliary force on which the magistrates could call was the *posse comitatus* or *levée en masse*, the whole body of adult males in the county called out by the sheriff in the event of a riot. This was both impractical and largely inoperative by the end of the eighteenth century, despite its resurrection with the Levée en Masse Act of 1803.[100] Theoretically, under the provisions for Watch and Ward every citizen could be called upon to assist the authorities, and an attempt was made to revive this in 1811–12, but it was preferable to swear in 'the most respectable members of the community' as special constables and in an emergency this was usually the first line of defence.[101]

The other ancient resource available to magistrates was the county militia, reformed in 1757. This provided for a levy on every parish, chosen by lot if insufficient numbers volunteered, to produce a corps of men who were to be trained (hence they were sometimes called 'train bands') and serve for three years in county regiments which could be called out in the event of 'actual or imminent danger'. Militiamen were to be paid.[102] Under pressure of the French Revolutionary and Napoleonic Wars, several changes were made to the militia: in 1796, the Supplementary Militia and the Provisional cavalry were created. The former increased the levy beyond what many local men found sustainable and it was very unpopular. The latter was not a success, and gave way to the Volunteers. In 1808 the Local Militia was formed to serve only in their own areas and release the Regular Militia for wider service. After the war, the militia sank into relative insignificance.[103]

This was not true of the Volunteers, first formed during the invasion scare of 1794 to rally loyalist opinion to the government and marginalise the Foxite opposition. As such it was always something of a political force, employed to maintain order at home as well as providing a defence against foreign invasion. In the absence of the latter, the only action they saw was as domestic police. Although the Volunteer Infantry were important during the war, it was the Volunteer Cavalry, or Yeomanry, who were to continue important in peace time. Possession of a horse determined the social rank and status of the Yeomanry, described by one military historian as 'full of life and vigour, less as complete regiments than as troops and squadrons of tenant farmers and their sons, acting under command of their landlords and their landlords' sons for the preservation of internal order'.[104] As the Vice-Lieutenant of the West Riding wrote in June 1812, 'no force seems to me so much to be depended upon as the yeomanry cavalry'.[105] When magistrates felt the need, beyond these auxiliary part-time forces were the Fencibles – full-time troops on garrison duty in Britain – and the regular army.

The numbers of troops of various kinds were formidable, but their efficiency was variable. Recruiting for the militia could itself cause riots, especially in 1796 following the Supplementary Militia Act. Yorkshire was the worst county affected, but there were anti-recruitment riots also in Lincolnshire, Bedfordshire, Cambridgeshire, Hertfordshire and Northamptonshire. Regular troops had to be used to restore order.[106] Such was the reaction in Scotland in 1797, when the militia was introduced for the first time, that the commander-in-chief felt that his forces were inadequate to deal with widespread simultaneous disturbances. In East and West Lothian, Stirlingshire, Ayrshire,

Lanarkshire and indeed right across south, central and eastern Scotland from Dumfries to Inverness, riots broke out.[107] At Dalry in Ayrshire, the Liberty Tree was planted. At Tranent in East Lothian, the Riot Act was read on 29 August 1797 and the troops opened fire, killing twelve people. As a result of these riots across Scotland, eighty people were subsequently charged with riot, two of them also being charged with sedition: eight men were transported.

These disturbances were happening only a few weeks after the navy mutinied in England and, as in that case, there was a suspicion of Jacobin involvement. The minister at Campsie, Mr Leslie, was doubtless right to 'perceive some of the old Jacobin Societies using every effort to alarm the farmers and the Country people with mis-representations about the wording of the Militia Act'. The Duke of Montrose suspected that those behind the disturbances were 'the set of men who were active with Muir &c'.[108] A closer examination of the militia riots does suggest some truth in this, linking the disturbances to the formation of the United Scotsmen societies in the same places.[109] To set against this were the loyal addresses by men protest-ing against the principle of the militia but offering to volunteer for military service. The reason no militia had been created for Scotland in 1757 had been fear of arming Jacobites. Forty years later, there was a danger of arming Jacobins. For this reason Pitt's government was wary of loyalists who were armed, throughout Britain, unless they also had a stake in the property they were called upon to defend.

The reaction of militiamen to food riots again shows the unreli-ability of drawing men from the same social class as those whom they were to control. With a fixed food allowance of fivepence a day, mili-tiamen were vulnerable to rises in the price of food such as happened in 1795. Riots occurred across the south coast. In Lewes, the Oxfordshire militia marched on Seaford and Newhaven with fixed bayonets to seize provisions which they sold at reduced prices: as a result, four of them were executed and several more flogged. At Canterbury, the Volunteers had to be called out to control the South Hampshire Militia.[110] In the worse crisis of 1800–01, Volunteers and Regulars were used to guard grain stocks and disperse riots, but as with the militia the Volunteer Infantry proved less than reliable.[111] In Dartmouth, the Volunteers mutinied, telling their officers: 'that Gover[nmen]t had been applied to long & nothing done for them, therefore it was high time they should do something for themselves to prevent their Families from starving.'[112] For this reason, magistrates came to rely heavily on the Volunteer Cavalry, backed up by the Regular Army.

The extent of this dependency became clear during the Luddite disturbances of 1811–12. The magistrates began by swearing in special constables by the hundred: 600 in Nottingham at the end of 1811; 1,500 in the Salford Hundred of Lancashire – 10 per cent of all adult males – in April 1812, and another 400 in Bolton. An attempt was made to revive Watch and Ward, but this was largely unsuccessful and voluntary associations were felt to be a more appropriate way for property owners to protect their own property. This proved insufficient in the winter of 1811–12, and so the authorities had to turn to the militia, the yeomanry and regular troops. In May 1812, arrangements were made to garrison 3,000 infantry and 500 cavalry near Nottingham, and in Lancashire and Cheshire, General Maitland had at his command 79 companies of infantry, 18 troops of horse and two detachments of artillery – amounting to 5,500 infantry and 1,400 cavalry. In the West Riding, General Grey had 1,000 infantry and 800 cavalry. But even with so large a number of troops, the army could not be everywhere at once or guard every factory. All they could hope to do was to supplement local self-defence, and hope to surprise or overawe Luddite gangs by garrisoning the towns and scouring the countryside with highly mobile troops.[113]

Military cut-backs after the war meant that by 1817, when social tension had again reached wartime heights, the entire British army available for effective service in Britain and Ireland probably amounted to only 16,000 soldiers. The yeomanry, with 17,818 was to be the mainstay of public order, supplemented by the 11,000 pensioners called up in the emergency of 1819.[114] The disastrously undisciplined performance of the yeomanry at St Peter's Field, Manchester, on 16 August 1819 exposed the weakness of relying upon a part-time, armed civilian force to maintain order, particularly in large towns. Thereafter when dealing with localised disturbances, magistrates looked to regular troops to support their special constables. Even in 1831, it was the Hussars who were called on in Derby and Nottingham (as they had been, along with the yeomanry, at Peterloo), and the Dragoons and Dragoon Guards in Bristol. In south Wales in 1831, detachments of the East Glamorgan Yeomanry, the 93rd Highlanders and the 3rd Dragoon Guards were all involved. In April

1839, when General Napier wished to put the yeomanry on permanent duty, the Whig Prime Minister and Home Secretary, Melbourne and Russell, declined to do so. Napier noted in his Journal on 15 August – Napoleon's birthday as well as the eve of Peterloo – 'If the Chartists want a fight, they can be indulged without yeomen, who are over-zealous for cutting and slashing.'[115]

For the Tories, Sir James Graham continued this preference for regular troops. His reasons were partly financial – the yeomanry were paid only when they were called out but regular troops had to be paid anyway; partly political – he appreciated the need not to call out farmers at harvest time; and partly tactical – he knew that the yeomanry was hated and its appearance would be as likely to cause a riot as prevent one.[116] But where disturbances were widespread, as in the 'Swing' counties in 1830, and again in the industrial districts in 1839, 1842 and 1848, traditional forces had to be employed, including the yeomanry and voluntary associations. The military, though, was always intended to be the second line of defence. Magistrates were supposed to maintain order by calling on civilians – in voluntary associations, as special constables and, increasingly in the nineteenth century, as regular policemen.

In London the double issue of crime and the maintenance of order led the Home Office under Robert Peel to introduce the Metropolitan Police in 1829. This did not at first supersede existing police arrangements; nor was it necessarily better. William Popay, a police sergeant, was accused in 1833 of having infiltrated the National Union of the Working Classes as an *agent provocateur*; and at Copenhagen Fields in the same year a baton charge against the crowd resulted in the death of a constable. At the subsequent inquest, the coroner's jury returned a verdict of 'justifiable homicide'. Though quasi-military in organisation and discipline, the new London police was a civilian force, its constables were usually armed only with batons and, unlike the yeomanry and regular soldiers with their colourful uniforms, they dressed to look like civilians.[117] With an average strength of 3,389 during 1834–38,[118] the new police only slowly made an impact on the metropolis and, by example, on ideas about policing elsewhere. In 1835, the Municipal Corporations Act required corporate boroughs to establish police forces, but Birmingham and Manchester were incorporated only in 1838 and Bradford in 1847. When Birmingham needed police in 1839, controversially the Home Office sent down a force of metropolitan policemen on the train.

Outside the corporate boroughs, county magistrates were given the option of appointing a police force by the Rural Police Acts of 1839 and 1840. On grounds of cost, not all did so and there was no clear correlation with areas of Chartist strength: Lancashire adopted the Act; the West Riding did not. Their reasoning in Yorkshire was clear: 'for common times and purposes they conceive the present force sufficient, and that upon occasions of Outbreak or riot, such as we have unfortunately seen, no addition to the Police force, which can be contemplated, would be sufficient for their protection'.[119]

This meant that magistrates preferred to rely on the army. The Northern District, based on Nottingham, was put under the charge of Major-General Charles Napier in April 1839. He was a cousin of Charles James Fox and politically a radical, whose condemnation of Feargus O'Connor's brand of Chartism was matched only by his contempt for local magistrates. His fear was not revolution, but widespread disturbances. He sought to prevent these by concentrating his forces and overawing his opponents, on the grounds that prevention was better than cure. If large-scale disturbances broke out, there would be deaths among the rioters and this he wished to avoid. His approach probably suited Whig Home Secretaries, Lord John Russell and Lord Normanby, whose Liberalism was fortified by their paying insufficient attention to detail, but the Tory Sir James Graham was different: Napier was sent to India in September 1841. During the summer of 1842 both the Northern and Midland Districts were put under the overall control of Lieutenant-General Sir Thomas Arbuthnot, based in Manchester. He worked closely with the Home Secretary and the Commander-in-Chief, the Duke of Wellington. The Home Office remained in overall control however, even in 1848 when the Duke advanced his own schemes for the defence of London, parallel to those of the government.[120]

The effectiveness of the army was important in the maintenance of order. In retrospect, we know that on each occasion when an armed rising was planned or actually occurred it was suppressed, even though the number of would-be insurgents outnumbered those available to defeat them. This was partly because of the efficiency of the government's intelligence systems. The structure and effectiveness of the informer system built up in the 1790s has already been discussed in Chapter 1.[121] Despite some decline in efficiency in the nineteenth century and the reluctance of peacetime governments to spend money on informers, and despite the exaggeration contained in many of the informers' reports, they, nevertheless, remained essential. At every level the government had to sift the wheat from the chaff for important clues about the plans of 'the disaffected'. During the Luddite disturbances, Earl Fitwilliam was infuriatingly calm most of the time, but capable of resolute action when necessary. The same was true of Napier, who refused to be panicked by the magistrates and preferred to use soldiers to check the information supplied by them. The problems experienced in Yorkshire in 1812 and in south Wales in the autumn of 1839, arose when traditional sources of information dried up.[122] Usually, however, the effectiveness of the government lay not in its superior armed forces but in its superior intelligence sources. Most of the plots from 1794 to 1848 were exposed by spies. As the schemes matured, the government knew as much about them as the plotters. Sometimes the government probably over-reacted to the information gathered, but in 1839 Russell at the Home Office almost certainly under-reacted to the clear signs available to him during the summer from south Wales. The Newport rising suggests the wisdom of over-reaction. The policy of forestalling insurrection generally worked.

When there were open conflicts, these were suppressed by small numbers of troops. This was sometimes a matter of luck, particularly with the weather, but the authorities made their own luck through superior organisation and forethought. When Napier took charge of the Northern District in 1839 he did not have enough troops to suppress a Chartist rising. He out-thought the Chartists rather than out-fought them. His policy was to keep his troops together in sufficiently large numbers not to risk conflict. He set out his ideas in a letter to his subordinate in Manchester, Colonel Wemyss, in April 1839:

> With regards to detachments, my mind is made up to have as few as possible. . . . I lay down as an axiom, and our first, greatest principle, that the queen's troops must not be overthrown anywhere, because the effect in the three kingdoms would be fearful. If only a corporal's guard were cut off it would be 'total defeat of the troops' ere it reached London Edinburgh and Dublin; and before the contradiction arrived the disaffected, in moral exaltation of supposed victory, would be in arms. This is more especially to be apprehended in Ireland, where rivers of blood would flow.

Napier here showed his understanding of the importance of play-acting in the maintenance of order, where the control of the majority by the minority was based on a successfully maintained illusion. The fact was that there were never enough troops to enforce order by physical power alone, and by 1839 successive government cut-backs had left the army and yeomanry much reduced in numbers. Napier continued his letter:

> Now let us look at the other side. Suppose from want of soldiers a rising takes place in some town; suppose the worst, and nothing can exceed what happened at Bristol . . . What did Bristol amount to? Only individual loss. The troops were victorious the instant they were put in motion and all the world knew it was a riot; it produced no national evil; it had no public results, though one of the largest towns in the empire was nearly laid in ashes.[123]

Here was another version of Holyoake's 'equality of towns' argument. Napier's overall sense was sound, though his argument was exaggerated. In 1842 at Salterhebble a small detachment of cavalry had been defeated, more because of the terrain than the smallness of their numbers, but this had not led to a rising largely because the Plug Rioters were not seeking one. On the other hand, even a small detachment of thirty-two soldiers in a good defensive position were able to deal with the thousands pitted against them at Newport.

Napier was right. With only about sixty soldiers in Newport, there was no alternative: it was a high risk brought about by neglect of earlier warnings, and if the troops at the Westgate had been defeated, then south Wales in 1839 might have looked very different from Bristol in 1831. If necessary Napier was prepared to sacrifice the police to preserve the army. This was not a point of view shared by the magistrates but, as he pointed out to the magistrates of Halifax in 1839, 'The cavalry at Halifax are quartered in the very worst and most dangerous manner. Forty-two troopers in twenty-one distant billets! Fifty resolute Chartists might disarm and destroy the whole in ten minutes.'[124] This had been the strategy discussed at Folly Hall in 1817. But Halifax was dependent on its soldiers: it was not a corporate borough until 1848 and there was no rural police.

By 1848 the position of the forces of law and order was immeasurably strengthened. Firstly, the small number of troops had been made more effective by the establishment of the railway network.

Already by 1839 Napier was able to move some troops by train, but when the national network was established the logistical situation was transformed. As Sir James Willoughby Gordon, the Quartermaster General, explained to a select committee in 1844:

> you send a battalion of 1,000 men from London to Manchester in nine hours; that same battalion marching would take 17 days; and they arrive at the end of nine hours just as fresh, or nearly so, as when they started. By moving troops to and fro by that mode of conveyance, you do most important service to the public, so much so that without that conveyance, you could not have done one tenth part of the work that it was required of the troops to do, and necessarily to do, in the year 1842.[125]

The second development was the London police. Their handling of crowds in the 1830s had been poor and ineffective, but by 1848 they had learned a great deal about crowd control. Not only were they able to confront the peaceful demonstration on 10 April with firmness and without provocation, but they also survived the much more testing time during the summer evenings of May, June and July.

The short answer about the effectiveness of the troops is to see what happened when they came into conflict with rioters and insurgents when numbers alone would have suggested defeat. At Folly Hall and Pentrich, the insurgent forces ran away at the sight of troops; even at Bonnymuir and Merthyr Tydfil where the insurgents stood their ground and fought, they were easily defeated. At even a suspicion that troops might be coming, as at Grange Moor in 1820, the revolutionaries melted into the night. It is not that they were cowards but, for the most part, they were realists. When they were not, as in Bossenden Wood in 1838, they were overcome.

One reason for this lies not in the strength of the army, the weaknesses of which have been discussed and which were all too obvious to nervous commanding officers, but in the greater weakness of the insurgents. Two aspects of this can be considered here: first, their tactics. One of the few works on military tactics that the would-be revolutionaries used was Colonel Macerone's *Defensive Instructions for the People*. The use of pikes as recommended by him may have been suitable for street fighting against cavalry in the narrow rookeries of London's Seven Dials, and a knowledge of recent revolutionary history in France had taught people about barricades. As Napier observed, in urban warfare 'cavalry can do little better than get out of it with all possible speed', and leave it to the infantrymen with their rifles.[126] But in open warfare the pike was useless. For a start, as Napier explained, a six-foot pike was not long enough.[127] Secondly, he noted in his journal as he prepared to take up his command,

> I expect to have very few soldiers and many enemies: hence, if we deal with pikemen my intent is to put cavalry on their flanks, making my infantry retire as the pikemen advance. If they halt to face the cavalry, the infantry shall resume fire, for if the cavalry charge pikemen in order the cavalry will be defeated; the pike must be opposed by the musquet and bayonet, in which the soldiers must be taught to have confidence: it is the master weapon.[128]

Napier went on to say that he would use buckshot not bullets, in order to wound but not kill. The Chartist tactic, as at Newport, was the headlong charge. The naivety of this was recaptured many years later by Benjamin Brierley as he recalled the rebellious readers of the *Northern Star* in his father's house in Failsworth as he ground their pikes on his father's stone: 'My father did not encourage these "physical forceist" ideas. Having been at Waterloo, he knew what fighting meant, especially on battle fields where they could not run away.'[129]

The lack of military expertise was telling, which is why the insurgents in every decade looked to desertions from the army to swell their cause. The danger with the militia and the volunteer infantry in the 1790s is that they gave men a military training, though not officers or weapons. The period of greatest military threat was therefore likely to come during the war and, especially, after the war when large numbers of soldiers were discharged into civilian society where they suffered unemployment and hunger. One of the most worrying aspects of the Despard plot in 1802 was the involvement of guardsmen. When Alexander Somerville of the Scots Greys wrote to a Birmingham paper in 1832 that, although the soldiers would put down riots and defend property, 'against the liberties of our country we would never, never, never raise an arm', he was court-martialled and flogged.[130] More humanely, when Major-General Napier heard that there were many Chartists among the riflemen, he wanted to send for their leader to reason with him on the grounds that he shared his political opinions but differed only over method.[131] Military men and insurgents alike

understood the critical importance of army loyalty. With few exceptions, the common soldiers, despite their affinity with the protesters
and the repeated hopes of would-be insurgents, remained loyal – or, at
least, obedient – to their officers and their regiments.

Although in the nine months following the Newport Rising, the
45th Regiment of Foot suffered over a hundred desertions, all had
stood firm on 4 November. As one of the Chartist leaders had advised,
'the only way to succeed is to attack and remove those who command
them'.[132] Even this underestimated the loyalty of many soldiers.
Despard was betrayed when a soldier who had been approached to
join the plot reported back to an army agent who 'gave him advice as
to what he was to do' – so he became a spy.[133] Although there was
always a danger of subordination when soldiers drank with civilians
in public houses, Napier turned this to his advantage by encouraging
his men to drink with ex-soldiers and get them to boast of their plans
and then report them back to him.[134]

If the soldiers had been won over, they would have brought not
only their expertise but also their weapons. Despite all the arming and
drilling that went on throughout the half century between the 1790s
and 1840s, the would-be insurgents lacked weapons. They made
pikes by the thousand because they could not get anything else. They
had no response to the rifle but to run away. The first reason that G. J.
Holyoake gave in 1849 for the lack of revolution in England was that
'our populace are unused to arms'.[135] Had he but known it, G. J.
Harney, the Marat of the English revolution, had written to Friedrich
Engels in 1846 along similar lines:

> The English people will not adopt Cooper's slavish notions
> about peace and non-resistance but neither would they act upon
> the opposite doctrine. They applaud it at public meetings, but
> that is all. Notwithstanding all the talk in 1839 about 'arming,'
> the people did not arm, and they will not arm. A long immunity
> from the presence of war in their own country and the long sus-
> pension of the militia has created a general distaste for arms,
> which year by year is becoming more extensive and more
> intense. The *body* of the English people, without becoming a
> slavish people, are becoming an eminently pacific people.

Then, Harney forgot himself for a moment as national pride in the
British army took over.

I do not say that our fighting propensities are gone, on the contrary I believe that the trained English soldiery is the most powerful soldiery in the world, that is, that a given number will, ninety times out of a hundred, vanquish a similar number of the *trained troops* of any nation in the world. (I hope I shall not offend your Prussian nationality.) Wanting, however, military training, the English *people* are the most unmilitary, indeed anti-military people on the face of the earth. To attempt a 'physical-force' agitation at the present time would be productive of no good but on the contrary of some evil – the evil of exciting suspicion against the agitators. I do not suppose that the great changes which will come in this country will come altogether without violence, but organized combats such as we may look for in France, Germany, Italy and Spain, cannot take place in this country. To organize, to conspire a revolution in this country would be a vain and foolish project and the men who with their eyes open could take part in so absurd an attempt would be worse than foolish, would be highly culpable.[136]

Britain did not have a conscript army and, apart from the Yeomanry Cavalry, it did not have a large number of men trained in arms. This state of affairs was not new, despite the temporary impact of enlistment during the French Revolutionary and Napoleonic Wars, and can be traced back to the decision to disarm the general population in the reign of Charles II and to the Game Laws from 1671 onwards which restricted who was to hunt, and empowered gamekeepers to search for and impound guns and other sporting gear that might be used for taking illicit game.[137] Britain was increasingly a de-militarised society, despite all the vaunted 'right to bear arms'. In all the actual risings there was a woeful lack of serious weaponry. Pikes and agricultural implements far outnumbered guns. The first object of an insurrection was to acquire weapons: in Sheffield in 1812, John Blackwell's attack was on the local militia armoury; the Spa Fields rising of 1816 attacked gun shops on the way to the arsenal at the Tower of London. The Luddite strategy in 1812 was to threaten individual property owners into giving up their weapons; so much so that 'well affected people' were refusing to hand their arms over to the authorities because they feared for their property if they had nothing left to hand over to the Luddite gangs.[138] When the authorities wanted to know the extent of arming in the 1790s, they watched the levels of production and sales by arms manufacturers in Birmingham and elsewhere.[139] It is not known how many of the half million or so stands of arms ordered in Birmingham for 'people not connected with government' in the latter part of 1792 were intended for illicit purposes. But the alarmist second Report of the Committee of Secrecy in 1794 thought, 'The number of firelocks actually provided, as far as it has been discovered, may seem inconsiderable for the execution of any design' and then went on to discuss the manufacture and stockpiling of pikes at much greater length.[140]

Two generations later, a return of arms sold in London during the first six months of 1848 shows that 122 guns and 162 pistols went to 'Mechanics, Labourers etc. who are believed to be, and others known to be, Chartists' while three times that number went to the much smaller class of 'Gentlemen, Respectable Tradesmen, Gamekeepers etc.'[141] Though Sheridan was no doubt exercising dramatic licence in 1795 when he described the supposed conspiracy as possessing 'an arsenal furnished with one pike and nine rusty muskets',[142] half a century later Major-General Napier, who took the Chartist threat very seriously, was probably not being over complacent in December 1839 when he wrote

> An anonymous letter come, with a Chartist plan. Poor creatures, their threats of attack are miserable. With half a cartridge, and half a pike, with no money, no discipline, no skilful leaders, they would attack men with leaders money and discipline, well armed, and having sixty rounds a man. Poor men![143]

Back in August he had confined to his journal:

> The plot thickens. Meetings increase and are so violent, and arms so abound, I know not what to think. . . . Poor people! They will suffer. They have set all England against them and their physical force: – fools! We have the physical force, not they. . . . Poor men! Poor men! How little they know of physical force.[144]

Conclusion

Explanations in history are never certain. As Herbert Butterfield observed, the only safe thing we can say is that the whole of the present has come out of the whole of the complex past.[145] How that happened is for historical speculation and there will never be agreement. The accidental and the contingent, the unique combination of events at a particular time, will determine an outcome in a situation created by many factors, and that situation is never static. The easy contrasts of reform or revolution, physical or moral force, constitutional or illegal behaviour, belong to propaganda not historical analysis. The understanding which people had of their situation at different times was ever changing. How individuals behaved, and whether enough of them were persuaded to behave in the same way, varied according to circumstances. Undoubtedly, for most of the time most of the people were loyal, law abiding, contented, quiescent, subdued, apathetic, sullen. Most popular leaders for most of the time sought constitutional means to improve the political, economic and social position of the people: they believed in historical liberties and accepted the rule of law. There were many reasons for this 'normal' situation: some positive, such as an unquestioning acceptance of prevailing ideology and of things as they are, and a rejection of change and innovation which might threaten what they already enjoyed; some negative, such as an awareness that the dominant ideology was underpinned by political, economic and military power.

Readings of the period 1790–1850 which see a comfortable and natural harmony in society do not seem to me to fit the evidence. When one has allowed for exaggeration, scaremongering, and panic born of ignorance or malice, one is left with sufficient evidence of tension to realise that the idea of revolutionary change in Britain cannot be dismissed out of hand. If the ship of state appears in retrospect to have been sailing like a modern liner smoothly through the seas, stabilised against the storms (though the complacent should remember the *Titanic*), at the time the governing classes felt they were in a small, oak-built ship-of-the-line, buffeted by storms and easily driven off course or prevented from making a safe landing.

The government was composed of neither fools nor knaves – as Samuel Bamford discovered to his surprise when he was hauled before the Privy Council in 1817.[146] Their duty was to maintain the ship of state in defence of liberty and property. Reformers who challenged this view in the name of liberty and individual rights wished to blow it off course. How they were to do this depended on the options open to them. Throughout the period, the option of revolution through insurgency always remained a possibility. Indeed, from Whig politicians to popular demagogues, there were many men who believed that the only way to achieve change was to force ministers to legislate revolution from above by threatening it from below. For most of the time, the forces for stability and change were in balance, but it was an artificial equilibrium maintained with difficulty during years of unprecedented social and economic change.

Occasionally the balance was upset. Revolution from below came closest when popular leaders despaired of peaceful constitutional change. The device of petitioning was discredited when petitions were not heard. The situation was most dangerous when larger numbers of people in one or more parts of the country no longer felt tied by the bonds of conventional loyalty. This could happen for a number of reasons: desperate hunger brought about by high food prices, low wages and unemployment; threats to liberty caused by dubiously legal recruitment practices to the armed forces; novel legislation threatening traditional values; heightened expectations of change induced by violent changes in governments overseas; hopes of the millennium. All these and more could, separately but more usually in combination, produce instability and gave opportunity to those who believed there was no other way to achieve change but by leading the people in revolution.

It is at this point that the practicalities of such actions should be considered by the historian. The argument of this concluding chapter has been that, although the failure of potential revolution was not a foregone conclusion and although stability was usually maintained more by ideological than by physical force, ultimately the government of Britain never lost the will, power or the means of controlling by physical force those who wished to force change by violent action.

Britain *was* different. This is the easy explanation for the failure of revolution, but the challenge is to explain *why*. The distinctiveness of Britain was not ordained 'at heaven's command', but was the creation of men who, building on some historical differences in institutions and traditions, were determined that the course of British history should be different from that of Europe in the age of revolutions. A sense of pride in constitutional liberties and of the capacity of the political system to evolve without revolution assisted the maintenance of stability for most of the time and ensured a smoothness and continuity in political change which was not known in countries with more autocratic and less flexible institutions. In 1849, G. J. Holyoake told his audience of Chartists, 'We have a proverb that "they manage these things better in France." I trust the distinction will be ours of saying that "we manage these things better in England".'[147]

The complacency of Victorian liberalism was already setting in but it was a view which, like stability itself, was created not inborn. The phrase 'whig history' is used too liberally to denigrate all histories that depend on the idea of constitutional progress. During the period 1790–1850, those who wished to change the system learned from the failures of their predecessors and in that sense progressed. They saw that it was not possible for a nation to free itself purely by an act of will. Garibaldi was to learn that with the failure of Mazzini's dreams for Italy in 1849. So too did George Julian Harney. Despite his letter to Engels in 1846, in March 1848 his editorial in the *Northern Star* shows him still hoping for revolutionary change in England on the coat-tails of revolution in France. But, in November 1849, as he surveyed the wreck of the continental revolutions and the dark winter which had followed the 'springtime of the peoples', he wrote the obituary of serious revolutionary aspirations in Britain:

> Perhaps the events on the Continent, within the last year, are the strongest argument that could be adduced in favour of an unceasing, gradual, peaceable, and resolute aggressive popular movement. The revolutionary earthquake which shook thrones to the dust, and scattered kings, queens, royal dukes and duchesses, princes and nobles, like sea birds in a storm, has passed away. What are its present results? The old tyrannies restored in almost every country where Liberty achieved a brief and fleeting triumph. . . . The meteor has flashed, dazzled and disappeared, leaving profounder darkness behind it. That in the course of nature another convulsive upheaving of the forcibly repressed, but universal discontent which exists in these countries, will occur again, there can be no doubt – but is there any reason to believe with better results, if the conflicting parties are similarly composed? The old rulers of the world have been trained to the exercise of force and fraud. They understand thoroughly the full use of these weapons. The people have neither the education nor the means to contend with them on their own battle-field. They should be wise, therefore and choose one more favourable for the development of the powers they unquestionably possess. The strength of an unorganised majority is no match for that of a well-disciplined and well-armed minority. What then? ORGANISE THE MAJORITY. How? Popular progress in

Why was there no revolution?

England supplies an answer. Inch by inch the ground has been forced from the oligarchy; every advantage thus slowly won has been as sturdily retained, and with each successive advance the power of the people grows stronger – that of their adversaries less, Can there be any doubt as to the ultimate issue?

The spirit of gradual reform had of necessity triumphed over the will to revolution. Arguing against an extremist reform strategy in the 1860s, the Manchester Owenite and Chartist, Robert Cooper, reflected on the lessons he had learned in the 1840s: faced with 'extreme proceedings . . . the government would be instigated to put down our meetings, and, if need be, incarcerate our leaders, leaving the people once more a prey to disappointment and suffering'.[148] He was not the first to have reached this conclusion. If the threat of justified revolution constrained British governments to pay more than lip-service to constitutionalism and the rule of law, the realities of government force ultimately taught most reformers the practical as well as theoretical virtues of constitutionalism and peaceful agitation for reform within the law. By 1850, Britain had learned to be different through what the *Northern Star* called 'dear-bought past experience'.[149]

Notes

1 See above, p. 7.
2 S. Prickett, *England and the French Revolution* (London, Macmillan, 1989), pp. 2–5; Williams, *Keywords* – 'Revolution'.
3 *OED* – 'Revolution'
4 Quoted and translated by P. Wende, '1848: Reform or Revolution' pp. 152–3, in Blanning and Wende (eds), *Reform in Great Britain and Germany*, pp. 145–57.
5 E. Burke, *Reflection on the Revolution in France*. Everyman edition (London, Dent, 1964), p. 82. The same device of belittling was used in loyalist propaganda by persistent references to Thomas Paine as 'Tom'.
6 B. Brierley, *Home Memories, and Recollections of a Life* (Manchester, Heywood, 1886), p. 23.
7 D. Thompson, 'Who were "the People" in 1842?', in M. Chase and I. Dyck (eds), *Living and Learning* (Aldershot, Scolar Press, 1996), pp. 118–32; Vernon, *Politics and the People*, pp. 302–3.
8 *OED* – 'Mob'
9 *Hansard's Parliamentary Debates*, House of Commons, 12 July 1839, col. 245.
10 J. A. Epstein, '"Our real constitution": trial, defence and radical memory in the Age of Revolution' in Vernon, *Re-reading the Constitution*, pp. 22–51; also Epstein, *Radical Expression*, pp. 3–28.
11 Thale (ed.), *LCS*, pp. 322–7.

12 Deposition of William Stevens, *Cobbett's Weekly Political Register*, 33:18 (16 May 1818), col. 553.

13 *Northern Star*, 18 May 1839

14 See above, pp. 70–1.

15 Manchester Central Library, J B. Smith MSS, R. Cobden to J. B. Smith, 4 December 1841, as quoted in L. Brown, 'The Chartists and the Anti-Corn Law League', p. 348 in A. Briggs (ed.), *Chartist Studies* (London, Macmillan, 1959, reprinted 1965), pp. 342–71.

16 Fulcher, 'The English people and their constitution', p. 78.

17 McCord, *Anti-Corn Law League*, pp. 108–36.

18 G. J. Holyoake, 'Why have we had no revolution in England?', *Reasoner*, 7:1 (4 July 1849), p. 1.

19 B. R. Mitchell, *European Historical Statistics, 1750–1970* (London, Macmillan, 1978), Tables A1 and A2.

20 PRO, HO 40/1(8), fos 17–19, F. L. Wood to Earl Fitzwilliam, 17 June 1812.

21 'Prospects of our Cause', *Chartist*, 30 June 1839.

22 Bamford, *Passages*, p. 7.

23 *Hansard's Parliamentary Debates*, House of Commons, 12 July 1839, col. 246.

24 H. T. Dickinson, 'Popular Conservatism and Militant Loyalism, 1789–1815', p. 110 in H. T. Dickinson (ed.), *Britain and the French Revolution, 1789–1815* (London, Macmillan, 1989), pp. 103–25. For the intellectual defence of the conservative position, see also his *Liberty and Property*, pp. 270–318 and A. D. Harvey, *Britain in the Early Nineteenth Century*, pp. 106–14.

25 E. P. Thompson, 'The Moral Economy of the English Crowd in the Eighteenth Century' and 'The Moral Economy Reviewed' in *Customs in Common* (London, Penguin Books, 1993), pp. 185–258 and 259–351.

26 *Cobbett's Weekly Political Register*, 20:21, (23 November 1816), col. 672.

27 H. Cunningham, 'The Language of Patriotism, 1750–1914', *History Workshop Journal*, 12 (Autumn 1981), pp. 8–33, and the subsequent debate in 14 (Autumn 1982), p. 179, and 16 (Autumn 1983), pp. 189–90.

28 M. D. George, *English Political Caricature, 1793–1832: A Study in Opinion and Propaganda* (Oxford, Clarendon Press, 1959), pp. 2–3 and Plate 1.

29 *Brewer's Dictionary of Phrase and Fable*, 14th edition (London, Cassell, 1992), entries under 'Heart of Oak', 'National Anthem' and 'Rule Britannia'. See also Colley, *Britons*, pp. 43–4.

30 B. Brierley, *Old Radicals and Young Reformers: A Sketch for the Times* (Manchester, Heywood, 1860), pp. 8–9.

31 For a discussion of this changing concept, 'public opinion', as varied as the allied concept of 'the people', see D Wahrman, 'Public Opinion, violence and the limits of constitutional politics' in Vernon, *Re-reading the Constitution*, pp. 83–122.

32 D. Eastwood, 'Patriotism and the English state in the 1790s', pp. 154–7, in Philp (ed.), *French Revolution*, pp. 146–68.

33 R. R. Dozier, *For King, Constitution and Country. The English Loyalists and the French Revolution* (Lexington, University Press of Kentucky, 1983), pp. 55–75; Dickinson, 'Popular Conservatism', pp. 114–16. My thanks to Michael Phillips of the University of York for the information about Blake in Lambeth.

34 A. Booth, 'Popular loyalism and public violence in the north-west of England, 1790–1800', *Social History*, 8:3 (October 1983), pp. 295–313.

35 'Meeting of Delegates of the Loyal Associations of Manchester and Salford', *Manchester Mercury*, 10 February 1795.

36 Eastwood, 'Patriotism', pp. 158–61.

37 M. Taylor, 'John Bull and the iconography of public opinion in England, *c.* 1712–1929', p. 104, *Past & Present*, 134 (February 1992), pp. 93–128.

38 R. Wells, 'English society and revolutionary politics in the 1790s: the case for insurrection', pp. 215–26, in Philp (ed.), *French Revolution*, pp. 188–226.

39 PRO, HO 40/1(8), fos 7–9, Francis Lindley Wood to Earl Fitzwilliam, 11 June 1812.

40 *Leeds Intelligencer*, 3 May 1832; *Leeds Mercury*, 28 April, 5 May 1832.

41 Christie, *Stress and Stability*.

42 *Annual Register* (1831), Chronicle for 19 October 1831, cols. 165–6.

43 C. A. Hulbert, *Annals of the Church in Slaithwaite* (London, Longman, 1864), pp. 178, 181, 223; and *Annals of the Church and Parish of Almondbury, Yorkshire* (London, Longmans, 1882), p. 212.

44 R. Wells, *Wretched Faces: Famine in Wartime England, 1793–1801* (Gloucester, Sutton, 1988), p. 295.

45 Wells, *Wretched Faces*, p. 313.

46 Darvall, *Popular Disturbances*, pp. 19–20.

47 B. R. Mitchell, *Abstract of British Historical Statistics* (Cambridge, Cambridge University Press, 1962), p. 410.

48 T. Carlyle, 'Chartism' (1839), p. 198 in *Selected Essays* (London, Dent 1915, reprinted 1972), pp. 165–238.

49 Edsall, *The Anti-Poor Law Movement*, pp. 202–3.

50 Journal, 3 December 1839, printed in W. Napier, *The Life and Opinions of General Sir Charles James Napier*, 4 vols., second edition (London, John Murray, 1857), vol. 2, pp. 93–4 (hereafter *Napier*).

51 Report of John Layhe, 30 April 1843, to the Annual Meeting of the Manchester Ministry to the Poor, *Ninth Report to the Ministry of the Poor* (Manchester, Forrest, 1843), pp. 7–8.

52 E. C. Gaskell, *Mary Barton: A Tale of Manchester Life* (London, Chapman & Hall, 1848).

53 Christie, *Stress and Stability*, pp. 126–30.

54 Halévy, *England in 1815*, pp. 387, 425.

55 Thompson, *The Making*, pp. 385–440.

56 R. Hole, 'English Tracts and Sermons as media of debate on the French Revolution, 1789–99', pp. 19–29 in Philp (ed.), *French Revolution*, pp. 18–37.

57 R. Hole (ed.), *Selected Writings of Hannah More* (London, Pickering, 1996), pp. xii–xiii.

58 Wells, *Insurrection*, p. 200; Dinwiddy, *Radicalism and Reform*, p. 388.

59 Reay, *Last Rising of the Agricultural Labourers*, pp. 146–7.

60 Conference XLIX (1792), in *Minutes of the Methodist Conference*, 3 vols (London, Blanchard, 1813), vol. 1, p. 260.

61 D. Hempton, *Methodism and Politics in British Society, 1750–1850* (London, Hutchinson, 1984), pp. 98–104.

62 M. S. Edwards, *Purge this Realm. A Life of Joseph Rayner Stephens* (London, Epworth, 1994), p. 22.

63 S. Bamford, *Early Days* [1849], ed. W. H. Chaloner (London, Cass, 1967) pp. 42–3.

64 *A Brief Memoir of the late Revd William Richardson, Sub-Chanter of York Cathedral, &c*, second edition (York, Wolstenholme, 1822), p. 53.

65 West Yorkshire Archive Service, Wakefield, C 84/1, Records of the meetings of the Elland Clerical Society, 1795–1898, entries for 5/6 October 1797 and 26/27 April 1798. I am grateful to Mr R. L. Peach of Bootham School and Prof. A. H. Sommerstein of the University of Nottingham for helping me identify the Greek phrase taken from 2 Timothy 3:1, where the context is apocalyptic.

66 F. Peel, *Spen Valley: Past & Present* (Heckmondwike, Senior & Co., 1893), pp. 236, 396–9.

67 Emsley, *British Society*, p. 9.

68 Brewer, *The Sinews of Power* (London, Unwin Hyman, 1989), pp. xvii–xx.

69 Brewer and Styles (eds), *Ungovernable People*, pp. 13–20.

70 On popular constitutionalism, see the essays in Vernon, *Re-reading the Constitution*, by Epstein, Fulcher and Wahrman, pp. 3–122.

71 J. Cannon, *Aristocratic Century: The Peerage of Eighteenth-century England* (Cambridge, Cambridge University Press, 1984), pp. 34–59, 113.

72 Cannon, *Aristocratic Century*, pp. 118–23.

73 Cannon, *Aristocratic Century*, pp. 20–5.

74 These points can be substantiated by reference to any listing of county families, such as J. Foster, *Pedigrees of the County Families of Yorkshire*, 3 vols (London, Head, 1874).

75 I. R. Christie, *British 'Non-Élite' MPs, 1715–1820* (Oxford, Clarendon Press, 1995), p. 206; see also A. D. Harvey, *Britain in the Early Nineteenth Century*, pp. 6–37.

76 P. Harling and P. Mandler, 'From "Fiscal-Military" State to Laissez-faire State, 1760–1850', *Journal of British Studies*, 32:2 (April 1993), pp. 44–70.

77 *Reasoner*, 7:162 (4 July 1849), p. 1.

78 Emsley, *British Society*, p. 67.

79 Smith, *Whig Principles*, pp. 346–7.

80 Cannon, *Aristocratic Century*, p. 125.

81 C. Emsley, 'An aspect of Pitt's "Terror": prosecutions for sedition during the 1790s', pp. 155–163, *Social History*, 6:2 (May 1981), pp. 155–84.

82 Meikle, *Scotland and the French Revolution*, pp. 134–6, 144–5; Epstein, '"Our Real Constitution"', pp. 34–5.

83 Emsley, 'An aspect of Pitt's "Terror"', pp. 163–75.

84 Saville, *1848*, p. 133.

85 W. H. Wickwar, *The Struggle for the Freedom of the Press, 1819–1832* (London, Allen & Unwin, 1928), pp. 35–6.

86 Wickwar, *Struggle for the Freedom*, pp. 35–7.

87 Wickwar, *Struggle for the Freedom*, pp. 180–205; *Republican*, 11:26 (1 July 1825), pp. 818–20.

88 Devon CRO, Sidmouth Papers, 1794/OZ 43, Henry Addington to Hiley Addington, 8 November 1794, as quoted in Emsley, 'An aspect of Pitt's "Terror"', p. 175.

89 BIHR, Hickleton MSS, A4/7, Earl Fitzwilliam to F. L. Wood, 15 June 1812.

90 5 Victoria, cap 315, An Act to define the Jurisdiction of Justices in General and Quarter Sessions.

91 Vernon, *Politics and the People*, pp. 295–307; G. Stedman Jones, 'Rethinking

Chartism', in *Languages of Class: Studies in English Working Class History, 1832–1982* (Cambridge, Cambridge University Press, 1983), pp. 90–178.

92 Jenkins, *General Strike*, pp. 223, 229–32.

93 Jones, *Last Rising*, p. 197.

94 Mather, *Public Order*, pp. 47–8.

95 34 Edward III, cap. 1, quoted in R. Vogler, *Reading the Riot Act: The Magistracy, the Police and the Army in Civil Disorder* (Milton Keynes, Open University, 1991), p. 13.

96 1 George I, cap. 5, quoted in R. Vogler, *Reading the Riot Act*, p. 1.

97 Wellesley (ed), *Despatches*, vol. 8, p. 225.

98 PRO, HO 40/1(8), fos 17–19, F L. Wood to Earl Fitzwilliam, 17 June 1812.

99 C. J. Napier to Colonel Wemyss, 16 August 1839, printed in *Napier* vol. 2, p. 79.

100 Mather, *Public Order*, p. 47; J. W. Fortescue, *A History of the British Army*, 13 vols. (London, Macmillan, 1899–1930), vol. 7, pp. 205–7.

101 Darvall, *Popular Disturbances*, pp. 252–4.

102 J. R. Western, *The English Militia in the Eighteenth Century* (London, Routledge and Kegan Paul, 1965), pp. 127–45.

103 Fortescue, *British Army*, vol. 4, pp. 888–9; vol. 5, pp. 198–207; vol. 6, pp. 180–3; vol. 7, pp. 34–5; vol. 11, p. 43; Emsley, *British Society*, pp. 53–5.

104 Fortescue, *British Army*, vol. 7, pp. 199–222; vol. 11, p. 43; J. R. Western, 'The Volunteer Movement as an anti-revolutionary force, 1793–1801', *English Historical Review* 71 (1956), pp. 603–14.

105 BIHR, Hickleton MSS, A4/7, F. L. Wood to F. Lumley, 10 June 1812 [copy].

106 Western, *English Militia*, pp. 273–302.

107 PRO, HO 102/14, fo. 216, Rev J. Lapsie to Henry Dundas, 28 August 1797.

108 PRO, HO 102/15, fo. 78, Lord Melrose to Duke of Portland, 7 September 1797.

109 Logue, *Popular Disturbances in Scotland*, pp. 109–13.

110 J. Stevenson, 'Food Riots in England, 1792–1818', pp. 47–8 in R. Quinault and J. Stevenson (eds), *Popular Protest and Public Order*, pp. 33–74.

111 Wells, *Wretched Faces*, pp. 120–32.

112 Quoted in Wells, *Wretched Faces*, p. 154.

113 Darvall, *Popular Disturbances*, pp. 250–73.

114 Fortescue, *British Army*, vol. 11, pp. 46–64; Mather, *Public Order*, p. 143; J. Stevenson, 'Social Control and the Prevention of Riots in England, 1789–1829', pp. 37–8 in A. P. Donajgrodzki (ed.), *Social Control in Nineteenth Century Britain* (London, Croom Helm, 1977), pp. 27–50.

115 Journal, 15 August 1839, in *Napier* vol. 2, p. 73.

116 C. J. Napier to S. M. Phillipps, 25 April 1839 and C. J. Napier to the Under-Secretary, 11 May 1839, in *Napier* vol. 2, pp. 20, 32; Mather, *Public Order*, pp. 35, 146–7.

117 C. Emsley, *The English Police. A political and social history*, second edition (Harlow, Longman, 1991), p. 29.

118 Mather, *Public Order*, p. 97. In 1833, there were only 211 police in Marylebone compared with 256 under the old system – Emsley, *English Police,* p. 27.

119 PRO, HO 45/264, fos 288–9, Lord Wharncliffe to Sir James Graham, 3 October 1842; Mather, *Public Order*, pp. 130–1.

120 Mather, *Public Order*, pp. 153–6; Goodway, *London Chartism*, pp. 147–9.

121 See above, p. 26.
122 BIHR, Hickleton MSS, A4/7, F. L. Wood to F. Lumley, 10 June 1812 [copy]; Jones, *Last Rising*, pp. 97–8.
123 C. J. Napier to Colonel Wemyss, 22 April 1839, in *Napier* vol. 2, pp. 13–14.
124 C. J. Napier to the magistrates of the West Riding, 24 April 1839, in *Napier* vol. 2, p. 16.
125 PP (1844), 318, *Fifth Report from the Select Committee on Railways*, 24 May 1844: evidence of Sir J. W. Gordon, 1 March 1844, Q. 1995.
126 C. J. Napier to Sir Hew Ross, 7 December 1839, in *Napier* vol. 2, p. 94.
127 Journal, 30 March 1839, in *Napier* vol. 2, p. 7.
128 Journal, March 1839, in *Napier* vol. 2, p. 4.
129 Brierley, *Home Memories*, p. 24.
130 A. Somerville, *The Autobiography of a Working Man* [1848], new edition (London, Turnstile Press, 1951), p. 159.
131 C. J. Napier to W. Napier, July 1839, in *Napier* vol. 2, pp. 54–5. Lord John Russell forbade the experiment, for fear of what the papers might say.
132 Wilks, *South Wales*, pp. 151–2, quoting from Ap Id Anfryn [Gwilym Hughes], *The Late Dr Price (of Llantrisant). The Famous Arch-Druid* (Cardiff, 1890), p. 10.
133 *State Trials at Large: The Whole Proceedings on the Trials of Col Despard, and the other State Prisoners, before a Special Commission, at the New Sessions House, Horsemonger Lane, Southwark, Feb. 7 and 9, 1803* (London, R. Bent & John Mudie, [1803]), p. 27.
134 Journal, 18 April 1839, in *Napier* vol. 2, p. 11.
135 *Reasoner* 7:162, (4 July 1849), p. 1.
136 G. J. Harney to F. Engels, 30 March 1846, reprinted in F. G. Black and R. M. Black (eds), *The Harney Papers* (Assen, Van Gorcum & Comp., 1969), p. 240.
137 Western, *English Militia*, pp. 71–2.
138 PRO, HO 45/1(8), fo 7–9, F. L. Wood to Earl Fitzwilliam, 11 June 1812.
139 Dozier, *For King, Constitution and Country*, pp. 40–4, 186–7.
140 'Second Report of the Secret Committee of the House of Lords Respecting Seditious Practices, *Cobbett's Parliamentary History*, House of Lords, 7 June 1794, cols. 891–2.
141 Mather, *Public Order*, p. 19.
142 *Annual Register* (1795), History of Europe, p. 156. For a fuller version of this quotation, see Debate on Sheridan's motion for repeal of the Habeas Corpus Suspension Act, *Cobbett's Parliamentary History*, House of Commons, 5 January 1795, col. 1066.
143 Journal, 1 December 1839, in *Napier* vol. 2, p. 98.
144 Journal, 6 August 1839, in *Napier* vol. 2, p. 69.
145 H Butterfield, *The Whig Interpretation of History* [1931], reprinted (London, G. Bell, 1968), p. 19.
146 Bamford, *Passages*, pp. 105–8.
147 *Reasoner*, 7:162 (4 July 1849), p. 1.
148 Tyne and Wear Archives, Joseph Cowen Papers, TWAS 634/C1738, Robert Cooper to Joseph Cowen, 28 July 1862.
149 *Northern Star*, 17 November 1849.

Appendix: wheat and bread prices, 1790–1850

Year	Wheat s. d.	Bread d.	Year	Wheat s. d.	Bread d.	Year	Wheat s. d.	Bread d.
1790	54 9	7.0	1811	95 3	14.0	1832	58 8	10.0
1791	48 7	6.3	1812	126 6	17.0	1833	52 11	8.5
1792	43 0	5.9	1813	109 9	15.7	1834	46 2	8.0
1793	49 3	6.8	1814	74 4	11.4	1835	39 4	7.0
1794	52 3	7.0	1815	65 7	10.4	1836	48 6	8.0
1795	75 2	9.6	1816	78 6	16.8	1837	55 10	8.5
1796	78 7	9.7	1817	96 11	13.3	1838	64 7	10.0
1797	53 9	7.6	1818	86 3	11.6	1839	70 8	10.0
1798	51 10	7.7	1819	74 6	11.5	1840	66 4	10.0
1799	69 0	9.6	1820	67 10	10.1	1841	64 4	9.0
1800	113 10	15.3	1821	56 1	9.5	1842	57 3	9.5
1801	119 6	15.5	1822	44 7	9.5	1843	50 1	7.5
1802	69 10	9.5	1823	53 4	10.3	1844	51 3	8.5
1803	58 10	8.7	1824	63 11	10.5	1845	50 10	7.5
1804	62 3	9.7	1825	68 6	10.5	1846	54 8	8.5
1805	89 9	13.1	1826	58 8	9.5	1847	69 9	11.5
1806	79 1	11.7	1827	58 6	9.5	1848	50 6	7.5
1807	75 4	10.8	1828	52 11	9.5	1849	44 3	7.0
1808	81 4	11.6	1829	46 2	10.5	1850	40 3	6.75
1809	97 4	13.7	1830	64 3	10.5			
1810	106 5	14.7	1831	66 4	10.0			

Source: B. R. Mitchell, *Abstract of British Historical Statistics* (Cambridge, Cambridge University Press, 1962), pp. 488–9 and 498. Wheat prices are per Imperial Quarter (448 pounds weight or 203.4 kg) taken from statistical returns from a large number of towns throughout Britain (and Ireland after 1800). Bread prices are for a 4 pound (1.8 kg) wheaten loaf in London (see Mitchell for details). Prices are expressed in pre-decimal currency: conversion: 1 shilling (s) = 12 pennies (d) = 5 pence.

Select bibliography

Ashton, O., Fyson, R. and Roberts, S. (eds), *The Chartist Legacy* (Rendlesham, Merlin, 1999).

Belchem, J., *'Orator' Hunt: Henry Hunt and English Working-class Radicalism* (Oxford, Clarendon Press, 1985).

Belchem, J., 'Nationalism, republicanism and exile: Irish emigrants and the revolutions of 1848', *Past & Present*, 146 (February 1995), pp. 103–35.

Booth, A., 'Popular loyalism and public violence in the north-west of England, 1790–1800', *Social History*, 8:3 (October 1983), pp. 295–313.

Christie, I. R., *Stress and Stability in Late-Eighteenth Century Britain* (Oxford, Oxford University Press, 1984).

Church, R. A. and Chapman, S. D., 'Gravener Henson and the making of the English working class', in E. L. Jones and G. E. Mingay (eds), *Land, Labour and Population in the Industrial Revolution* (London, Arnold, 1967), pp. 131–61.

Cole, G. D. H., *British Working Class Movements: Select Documents, 1789–1875* (London, Macmillan, 1965).

Colley, L., *Britons: Forging the Nation, 1707–1837* (London and New Haven, Yale University Press, 1992).

Darvall, F. O., *Popular Disturbances and Public Order in Regency England, being an Account of the Luddite and other Disorders in England during the Years 1811–1817 and of the Attitude and Activity of the Authorities* (London, Oxford University Press, 1934).

Dickinson, H. T., *Liberty and Property: Political Ideology in Eighteenth-century Britain* (London, Weidenfeld & Nicholson, 1977), paperback edition (London, Methuen, 1979).

Dickinson, H. T., *British Radicalism and the French Revolution, 1789–1815* (Oxford, Blackwell, 1985).

Dickinson, H. T. (ed.), *Britain and the French Revolution, 1789–1815* (London, Macmillan, 1989).

Dinwiddy, J. R., 'The "Black Lamp" in Yorkshire, 1801–1802', *Past & Present*, 64 (August 1974), pp. 113–23.

Dinwiddy, J. R., *Radicalism and Reform in Britain, 1780–1850* (London, Hambledon Press, 1992).

Dozier, R. R., *For King, Constitution and Country: The English Loyalists and the French Revolution* (Lexington, University Press of Kentucky, 1983).

Edsall, N. C., *The Anti-Poor Law Movement, 1834–1844* (Manchester, Manchester University Press, 1971).

Elliott, M., 'The "Despard Conspiracy" reconsidered', *Past & Present*, 75 (May 1977), pp. 46–61.

Elliott, M., *Partners in Revolution: The United Irishmen and France* (London and New Haven, Yale University Press, 1982).

Ellis, P. B. and Mac a' Ghobhainn, S., *The Scottish Insurrection of 1820* (London, Gollancz, 1970), re-issued (London, Pluto Press, 1989).

Emsley, C., 'The London "Insurrection" of December 1792: fact, fiction, or fantasy?', *Journal of British Studies*, 17:2 (Spring 1978), pp. 66–86.

Emsley, C., *British Society and the French Wars, 1793–1815* (London, Macmillan, 1979).

Emsley, C., 'The Home Office and its sources of information and investigation, 1791–1801', *English Historical Review*, 94 (1979), pp. 532–61.

Emsley, C., 'An aspect of Pitt's "Terror": prosecutions for sedition during the 1790s', *Social History*, 6:2 (May 1981), pp. 155–84.

Emsley, C., 'Repression, "terror" and the rule of law in England during the decade of the French Revolution', *English Historical Review* 100 (1985), pp. 801–25.

Emsley, C., *The English Police: A Political and Social History*, second edition (Harlow, Longman, 1991).

Epstein, J., *The Lion of Freedom: Feargus O'Connor and the Chartist Movement, 1832–1842* (London, Croom Helm, 1982).

Epstein, J., *Radical Expression: Political Language, Ritual, and Symbol in England, 1790–1850* (New York and Oxford, Oxford University Press, 1994).

Gammage, R. G., *History of the Chartist Movement, 1837–1854*, second edition [1894], reprinted (New York, Kelley, 1969).

Goodway, D., *London Chartism* (Cambridge, Cambridge University Press, 1982).

Goodwin, A., *The Friends of Liberty: The English Democratic Movement in the Age of the French Revolution* (London, Hutchinson, 1979).

Hobsbawm, E. J. and Rudé, G., *Captain Swing* (London, Lawrence & Wishart, 1969).

Hone, J. A., *For the Cause of Truth: Radicalism in London, 1796–1821* (Oxford, Oxford University Press, 1982).

Jenkins, M., *The General Strike of 1842* (London, Lawrence & Wishart, 1980).

Jones, C. (ed.), *Britain and Revolutionary France: Conflict, Subversion and Propaganda*, Exeter Studies in History No. 5 (Exeter, University of Exeter, 1983).

Jones, D. V. J., *Before Rebecca* (London, Allen Lane, 1973).

Jones, D. V. J., *Chartism and the Chartists* (London, Allen Lane, 1975).

Jones, D. V. J., *The Last Rising: The Newport Insurrection of 1839* (Oxford, Clarendon Press, 1985).

Logue, K. J., *Popular Disturbances in Scotland, 1780–1815* (Edinburgh, Donald, 1979).

McCalman, I., *Radical Underworld: Prophets, Revolutionaries and Pornographers in London, 1795–1840* (Cambridge, Cambridge University Press, 1988).

Mather, F. C., *Public Order in the Age of the Chartists* (Manchester, Manchester University Press, 1959).

Meikle, H. W., *Scotland and the French Revolution* (Edinburgh, Maclehose, 1912), reprinted (New York, Augustus Kelley, 1969).

O'Gorman, F., *The Whig Party and the French Revolution* (London, Macmillan, 1967).

Parssinen, T. M., 'The Revolutionary Party in London, 1816–20'. *Bulletin of the Institute of Historical Research*, 45:111 (May 1972), pp. 266–82.

Select bibliography

Peacock, A. J., *Bread or Blood: A Study of the Agrarian Riots in East Anglia in 1816* (London, Gollancz, 1965).

Peacock, A. J., *Bradford Chartism, 1838–1840* (York, St Anthony's Press, 1969).

Philp, M. (ed.), *The French Revolution and British Popular Politics* (Cambridge, Cambridge University Press, 1991).

Pickering, P. A., *Chartism and the Chartists in Manchester and Salford* (London, Macmillan, 1995).

Pollard, S. and Holmes, C. (eds), *Essays in the Economic and Social History of South Yorkshire* (Sheffield, South Yorkshire County Council, 1976).

Prothero, I., *Artisans and Politics in Early Nineteenth-Century London: John Gast and his Times* (Folkestone, Dawson, 1979), republished (London, Methuen, 1981).

Read, D., *Peterloo. The 'Massacre' and its Background* (Manchester, Manchester University Press, 1958).

Reay, B., *The Last Rising of the Agricultural Labourers: Rural Life and Protest in Nineteenth-Century England* (Oxford, Clarendon Press, 1990).

Reid, R., *Land of Lost Content. The Luddite Revolt, 1812* (London, Heinemann, 1986).

Rowe, D. J. (ed.), *London Radicalism, 1830–1843* (London, London Record Society, 1970).

Rudé, G., 'English Rural and Urban Disturbances 1830–1831', *Past & Present*, 37 (July 1967), pp. 87–102.

Rudé, G., 'Why was there no revolution in England in 1830 or 1848?', in Kossok, M. (ed.), *Studien über die Revolution* (Berlin, 1969), reprinted in H. J. Kaye (ed.), *The Face of the Crowd* (Atlantic Highlands, Humanities Press International, 1988), pp. 148–63.

Saville, J., *1848* (Cambridge, Cambridge University Press, 1987).

Schoyen, A. R., *The Chartist Challenge* (London, Heinemann, 1958).

Smith, A. W., 'Irish Rebels and English radicals, 1798–1820'. *Past & Present*, 7 (April 1955), pp. 78–85.

Smith, E. A., *Whig Principles and Party Politics: Earl Fitzwilliam and the Whig Party, 1748–1833* (Manchester, Manchester University Press, 1975).

Stevens, J., *England's Last Revolution: Pentrich, 1817* (Buxton, Moorland Publishing Company, 1977).

Stevenson, J., *Popular Disturbances in England, 1700–1870* (London, Longman, 1979).

Stevenson, J. (ed.), *London in the Age of Reform* (Oxford, Blackwell, 1977).

Stevenson, J. and Quinault, R. (eds), *Popular Protest and Public Order* (London, Allen & Unwin, 1974), pp. 115–40.

Thale, M. (ed.), *Selections from the Papers of the London Corresponding Society, 1792–1799* (Cambridge, Cambridge University Press, 1983).

Thomis, M. I., *The Luddites: Machine-Breaking in Regency England* (Newton Abbot, David & Charles, 1970).

Thomis, M. I and Holt, P., *Threats of Revolution, 1789–1848* (London, Macmillan, 1977).

Thompson, D., *The Chartists* (London, Temple Smith, 1984).

Thompson, D. and Epstein, J. (eds), *The Chartist Experience* (London, Macmillan, 1982).

Thompson, E. P., *The Making of the English Working Class* (London, Gollancz, 1963), Penguin edition (Harmondsworth, 1968).

Thompson, E. P., *Customs in Common* (London, Penguin, 1993).

Select bibliography

Vernon, J., *Politics and the People: A Study in English Political Culture*, c. *1815–1867* (Cambridge, Cambridge University Press, 1993).

Vernon, J. (ed.), *Re-reading the Constitution: New Narratives in the Political History of England's Long Nineteenth Century* (Cambridge, Cambridge University Press, 1996).

Wells, R., 'Rural Rebels in Southern England in the 1830s', in C. Emsley and J. Walvin (eds), *Artisans, Peasants and Proletarians, 1760–1860* (London, Croom Helm, 1985), pp. 124–65.

Wells, R., *Insurrection: The British Experience, 1795–1803* (Gloucester, Sutton, 1986).

Wells, R., *Wretched Faces: Famine in Wartime England, 1793–1801* (Gloucester, Sutton, 1988).

Western, J. R., 'The Volunteer Movement as an anti-revolutionary force, 1793–1801', *English Historical Review*, 71 (1956), pp. 603–14.

Wilks, I., *South Wales and the Rising of 1839: Class Struggle as Armed Struggle* (London, Croom Helm, 1984).

Williams, G. A., *The Merthyr Rising* (London, Croom Helm, 1978).

Worrall, D., *Radical Culture: Discourse, Resistance and Surveillance, 1790–1820* (Hemel Hempstead, Harvester Wheatsheaf, 1992).

Wright, D. G., *The Chartist Risings in Bradford* (Bradford, Bradford Libraries, 1977).

Index

Note: 'n.' after a page reference indicates the number of a note on that page.

Index

Index

Index

Index